TEXTS AND VERSIONS OF THE HEBREW BIBLE

1

Editor
James K. Aitken, University of Cambridge, UK

Published Under

LIBRARY OF HEBREW BIBLE
OLD TESTAMENT STUDIES

682

Formerly Journal for the Study of the Old Testament Supplement Series

Editors
Claudia V. Camp, Texas Christian University
Andrew Mein, University of Durham, UK

Founding Editors
David J. A. Clines, Philip R. Davies and David M. Gunn

Editorial Board
Alan Cooper, Susan Gillingham, John Goldingay,
Norman K. Gottwald, James E. Harding, John Jarick, Carol Meyers,
Daniel L. Smith-Christopher, Francesca Stavrakopoulou,
James W. Watts

LONDON • NEW YORK • OXFORD • NEW DELHI • SYDNEY

HEBREW WORDPLAY AND SEPTUAGINT TRANSLATION TECHNIQUE IN THE FOURTH BOOK OF THE PSALTER

Elizabeth H. P. Backfish

t&tclark
LONDON • NEW YORK • OXFORD • NEW DELHI • SYDNEY

T&T CLARK
Bloomsbury Publishing Plc
50 Bedford Square, London, WC1B 3DP, UK
1385 Broadway, New York, NY 10018, USA
29 Earlsfort Terrace, Dublin 2, Ireland

BLOOMSBURY, T&T CLARK and the T&T Clark logo
are trademarks of Bloomsbury Publishing Plc

First published in Great Britain in 2019 by the Continuum International Publishing Group Ltd
This paperback edition published in 2021

Copyright © Elizabeth H. P. Backfish, 2019

Elizabeth H. P. Backfish has asserted her right under the Copyright,
Designs and Patents Act, 1988, to be identified as Author of this work.

For legal purposes the Acknowledgements on p. xiii constitute
an extension of this copyright page.

All rights reserved. No part of this publication may be reproduced or
transmitted in any form or by any means, electronic or mechanical,
including photocopying, recording, or any information storage or retrieval
system, without prior permission in writing from the publishers.

Bloomsbury Publishing Plc does not have any control over, or responsibility for,
any third-party websites referred to or in this book. All internet addresses given
in this book were correct at the time of going to press. The author and publisher
regret any inconvenience caused if addresses have changed or sites have
ceased to exist, but can accept no responsibility for any such changes.

A catalogue record for this book is available from the British Library.

Library of Congress Cataloging-in-Publication Data:

Names: Backfish, Elizabeth H. P., author.
Title: Hebrew wordplay and Septuagint translation technique in the fourth
book of the Psalter / by Elizabeth H. P. Backfish.
Description: 1 [edition]. | New York: T&T Clark, 2019. | Series: Library of
Hebrew Bible/Old Testament studies, ISSN 2513-8758; volume 682 |
Includes bibliographical references and index.
Identifiers: LCCN 2019016122 | ISBN 9780567687104 (hardback) |
ISBN 9780567689467 (epub)
Subjects: LCSH: Bible. Psalms, XC-CVI. Hebrew–Criticism, Textual. | Bible.
Psalms, XC-CVI. Hebrew–Versions–Masoretic text–Translating. | Plays on
words–Translating. | Bible. Psalms, XC-CVI. Greek–Criticism, Textual. |
Bible. Psalms, XC-CVI. Greek. Versions–Septuagint–Translating.
Classification: LCC BS1430.52 .B33 2019 | DDC 223/.2044–dc23
LC record available at https://lccn.loc.gov/2019016122

ISBN: HB: 978-0-5676-8710-4
PB: 978-0-5677-0035-3
ePDF: 978-0-5676-8711-1
eBook: 978-0-5676-8946-7

Series: Library of Hebrew Bible/Old Testament Studies, volume 682

Typeset by Forthcoming Publications Ltd

To find out more about our authors and books visit
www.bloomsbury.com and sign up for our newsletters.

To Michael

Contents

List of Tables	ix
List of Symbols	xi
Acknowledgments	xiii

Chapter 1
INTRODUCTION — 1
  Research on Wordplay within the Hebrew Bible — 2
  Research on the Septuagint, Translation Technique,
      and Its Use of Wordplay — 6
    Contexts of LXX Psalms — 6
    Characterizing the Translation Technique of the LXX
      in General and Psalms in Particular — 10
    LXX Translation of Rhetorical and Literary Devices — 16
  The Study of Wordplay in Literary Theory — 20
    Historical Review — 20
    The Linguistic Nature of Wordplay in Modern Theory — 25
  Definitions — 31
    Defining Wordplay — 31
    A Typology of Wordplay — 34
  Research Methodology — 39
    General Methodological Concerns — 39
    Methodology for Identifying Wordplay in the MT and the LXX — 42

Chapter 2
WRITING THE RIGHT WORDS:
WORDPLAY WITHIN BOOK IV OF THE HEBREW PSALTER — 50
  Wordplay in Psalm 90 — 50
  Wordplay in Psalm 91 — 60
  Wordplay in Psalm 92 — 65
  Wordplay in Psalm 93 — 67
  Wordplay in Psalm 94 — 69
  Wordplay in Psalm 95 — 74
  Wordplay in Psalm 96 — 76
  Wordplay in Psalm 97 — 77

Wordplay in Psalms 98–100	80
Wordplay in Psalm 101	81
Wordplay in Psalm 102	82
Wordplay in Psalm 103	89
Wordplay in Psalm 104	91
Wordplay in Psalm 105	94
Wordplay in Psalm 106	96
Summary of Findings	104
Conclusion	113

Chapter 3
LXX TRANSLATION OF WORDPLAY IN BOOK IV OF THE PSALMS:
WRITING THE RIGHT WORDS FROM LEFT TO RIGHT   115
   Analysis of the LXX's Translation Technique of Hebrew Wordplay   117
   Wordplays Represented in the LXX   117
      LXX Replicates the Same Wordplay   118
      LXX Represents a Similar Wordplay   122
   Wordplays Not Represented in the LXX   144
      LXX Renders the Sense of the Wordplay   144
      Textual Variations in the LXX Translation of Wordplay   148
   Conclusions   151

Chapter 4
CONCLUSION   162
   Empirical Findings   162
   Contributions of this Study   165
      Contribution to Wordplay Studies   166
      Contribution to Hebrew Exegesis   166
      Contribution to Septuagint Studies   167
      Contribution to the Theological Interpretation of Psalms   168
      Contribution to Communication Theory   169
   Recommendations for Further Study   170

Bibliography	172
Index of References	181
Index of Authors	185

List of Tables

Table 1.	LXX Wordplay Translation Compared with LXX Overall Wordplay Use	47
Table 2.	Rating of Confidence in the MT Wordplay	106
Table 3.	Distribution of Categories and Subcategories of Wordplay	108
Table 4.	Distribution of Wordplay Subcategories in Each Psalm of Book IV	109
Table 5.	Distribution of Wordplay Categories in Each Psalm of Book IV	110
Table 6.	Distribution of Wordplay in Book IV by Genre	112
Table 7.	Summary Distribution of Wordplay in Book IV by Genre	112
Table 8.	Translation Tendencies in Individual Psalms	152
Table 9.	Summary of LXX Translation of Hebrew Wordplay According to Category	153
Table 10.	Types of Transformations in the LXX Made in Order to Render Hebrew Wordplay	155
Table 11.	Distribution of LXX Transformations in Individual Psalms	156
Table 12.	Rating of Confidence in the LXX Wordplay Translation	158

LIST OF SYMBOLS

[...]   Omission of one or more lines in a psalm

XXX XXX [XXX]   Three means of highlighting and connecting key words involved in wordplays

ACKNOWLEDGMENTS

This book was borne out of a personal love for Hebrew poetics and LXX studies, but it was made possible by the help of many people for whom I am very grateful. Since this is a revised version of my PhD dissertation, I am first grateful for the academic community at Trinity Evangelical Divinity School (TEDS) who taught, shaped, and encouraged me during my time there. Most notably, I am grateful for my dissertation supervisor, Dennis Magary, whose wisdom and attention to detail guided this project, and whose friendship continues to guide my career in biblical studies. Thanks also to my examiners and their valuable feedback, Willem VanGemeren and Richard Averbeck. I am also grateful for the friends and colleagues with whom I studied, and who are now scholars in various venues of kingdom work: Jillian Ross, Ingrid Faro, May Young, Andy Abernethy, Yacouba Sanon, Ron Hayden, Neal Huddleston, Todd Patterson, and Scott Booth.

A special thanks goes to those at my current academic context at William Jessup University, especially the dean of my department, David Timms, who consistently encourages and makes space for my scholarship. I am also grateful for my colleague and friend, Cynthia Shafer-Elliott, who has proven to be an invaluable traveling companion on the path of wisdom (Prov 13:20a). Finally, thanks go to all of my students, but especially those who have braved my Hebrew classes and endured my excitement over every case of wordplay we come across.

I am also grateful to the TVHB series editor, Jim Aitken, who saw the potential in this project and offered critical feedback. Thanks too to Duncan Burns, for his attention to detail and swift communication in the typesetting phase of this book's production.

Finally, and most importantly, I wish to acknowledge my family: my parents, Dana and Steve Pruitt, who instilled in me the love of reading and research; my children, Dana and Drew, whose curiosity sharpens my own; and to my husband, Michael, who loves me when I don't deserve it, makes me laugh when I need it, and is stuck with me regardless.

Chapter 1

INTRODUCTION

Just as each musical instrument holds a unique place and purpose within the orchestral consort, so also wordplay serves the poet as a unique literary tool for creatively and effectively communicating a message. It is, therefore, not surprising that the psalmists used this trope to entertain, challenge, and inspire their readers. The Greek translators of the Hebrew psalms had a formidable responsibility to render Hebrew wordplay to the best of their ability. However, even the most able translators would have struggled to render poetry into a receptor language, much less a component of poetry that is so dependent on the relationship between the sound and meaning of the original. This book seeks to understand better the Septuagint (LXX) translators' approach to Hebrew wordplay by exploring the linguistic nature of wordplay, identifying its presence in Book IV of the Hebrew Psalter, and analyzing the LXX's rendering of these occurrences.

The use of wordplay in biblical poetry and prose has long been recognized by biblical scholars, and yet a full-scale study of wordplay in the Psalter awaits exploration. Likewise, the translation techniques employed to convey various poetic devices in the LXX have shed light on the translators' understanding of Hebrew poetry, as well as their role as translators, and yet a study of the rendering of wordplay in the LXX also awaits further research. Since the renewed focus on modern linguistics and literary theory in the field of biblical studies, the opportunity to analyze wordplay in Book IV of the Hebrew Psalter and to explore that multi-faceted poetic device in Greek translation is particularly ripe for an extended study.

The following introduction will review the history of research on wordplay within biblical scholarship and LXX studies. A separate discussion on wordplay within literary theory, including its history, linguistic nature, typology, and function, will follow, offering a more nuanced and emic understanding of the trope. Several important methodological guideposts will then conclude this chapter.

Research on Wordplay within the Hebrew Bible

Wordplay is prevalent in all known languages worldwide, so it is not surprising that every book of the Old Testament contains this trope.[1] Readers of the Old Testament have long recognized and appreciated this literary phenomenon. The manifold interpretations to which wordplay lends itself were happily exploited within rabbinic Judaism.[2] According to Roberta Frank, medieval Europe generally believed that "the world of the divine was imagined to require a separate, more sacred language than that used by men," so biblical wordplay was expected.[3] According to Chaucer, "goddes speken in amphibologies" ("God spoke in ambiguities"), and Old English scriptural verse tried to replicate wordplays, exegete them, and even create additional wordplays.[4] Biblical scholarship, however, sustained a relative lack of interest in wordplay until the late nineteenth century, when the first monograph-length work on the subject was written by Immanuel Moses Casanowicz. His 1892 dissertation entitled *Paronomasia in the Old Testament* was later published in 1894.

Casanowicz's methodology reflected that of his era and served as a model for later studies on biblical wordplay. In *Paronomasia in the Old Testament*, he describes the nature and use of paronomasia in classical, modern, and Semitic languages. He then discusses various types of paronomasia in the Old Testament, offering examples. The entire last

---

1. J. J. Glück, "Paronomasia in Biblical Literature," *Semitics* 1 (1970): 51; cf., Isaac Kalimi, "Paronomasia in the Book of Chronicles," *JSOT* 67 (1995): 27–8. Immanuel Moses Casanowicz identified wordplays in every Old Testament book save Obadiah (*Paronomasia in the Old Testament* [Boston: Norwood, 1984]), while Ehud Ben Zvi identifies several of Obadiah's wordplays in his work, *A Historical-Critical Study of the Book of Obadiah*, BZAW 242 (Berlin: de Gruyter, 1996).

2. Shubet Spero explains this phenomenon and goes on to ground the rabbinic interpretation in actual biblical use of the trope, "Multiplicity of Meaning as a Device in Biblical Narrative," *Judaism* 34 (1985): 462–73; cf. Anthony J. Petrotta, *Lexis Ludens: Wordplay and the Book of Micah* (New York: Lang, 1991), 21.

By "rabbinic" I do not refer to the scribal exegesis prior to 70 CE, but to the more homogenized rabbinic hermeneutics that followed. For an excellent discussion of Jewish interpretation prior to and following 70 CE, see David Instone Brewer's *Techniques and Assumptions in Jewish Exegesis before 70 CE*, TSAJ (Tübingen: Mohr, 1992).

3. Roberta Frank, "Some Uses of Paronomasia in Old English Scriptural Verse," *Speculum* 47 (1972): 222.

4. Ibid., 222–3.

half (over 40 pages) of the study is an appended, near-exhaustive list of wordplays in the Old Testament, arranged alphabetically, with neither explanation nor conclusions. Casanowicz's work advanced the study of biblical wordplay by offering definitions and classifications of different types of wordplay, as well as collating these wordplays in an easily accessible format. Casanowicz was undeniably a pioneer in the study of wordplay, but pioneers forge the way for others to follow and build. Three aspects of Casanowicz's ground-breaking work yield room for advance: (1) Casanowicz defines wordplay as a subcategory of paronomasia, which is comprised of sound-paronomasia and sense-paronomasia. Because he considers sense-paronomasia to be "an artificial offspring" of sound-paronomasia,[5] he focuses almost exclusively on the latter, thereby passing over many semantic wordplays. (2) Casanowicz simply lists the biblical paronomasia he has found. There is no development or analysis of different types of paronomasia and their patterns, or the identification of tendencies within certain corpora. (3) Casanowicz's study predates the many advances in literary scholarship on poetic rhetoric.[6]

Until the 1970s, biblical scholars followed Casanowicz's lead in method and perspective, largely in isolation from literary scholarship.[7] Anthony J. Petrotta insightfully summarizes this divide between biblical and literary scholars:

> In contradistinction to biblical studies, the characteristics of literary-critical studies of wordplay are not sound but meaning, not listing examples but discourse about the passage or line where the wordplay occurs, and not "embellishment" but various functions from structuring to pathos.[8]

---

5. Casanowicz, *Paronomasia*, 12.
6. Some of the most important twentieth-century works on wordplay by literary scholars include William Empson, *Seven Types of Ambiguity* (Edinburgh: T. & A. Constable, 1947 [first published in 1930]); James Brown, "Eight Types of Puns" *Publications of the Modern Language Association of America* 71 (1956): 14–26; Stephen Ullmann, *Semantics: An Introduction to the Science of Meaning* (New York: Harper & Row, 1979); Walter Redfern, *Puns* (Oxford: Blackwell, 1984); and Jonathan D. Culler, ed., *On Puns: The Foundation of Letters* (Oxford: Blackwell, 1988).
7. Even as late as 1964, A. Guillaume's oft-cited article, "Paronomasia in the Old Testament," *JSS* (1964): 282–90, fails to define paronomasia, limits the trope's usefulness to lexicography, and offers no summary or concluding implications.
8. Petrotta, *Lexis Ludens*, 9. Petrotta places "embellishment" in quotation marks because this was the attitude and exact descriptor of G. R. Driver in "Playing on Words," in *Proceedings of the 4th World Congress of Jewish Studies* (Jerusalem: World Union of Jewish Studies, 1967), 121–29.

Clearly, biblical scholarship needed to join hands with literary scholarship, not least of all in the study of wordplay.

The past four decades have seen nothing short of a literary revolution in biblical studies. By applying the tools of modern linguistics and literary theory to Hebrew poetry, scholars such as Terence Collins, Stephen Geller, Adele Berlin and Robert Alter have advanced our understanding of biblical poetry and given us a richer and more accurate understanding of poetic devices and rhetorical functions.[9]

Although not yet fully utilizing these modern literary insights, J. J. Glück offered in 1970 one of the first substantial works on biblical wordplay since Casanowicz. In his "Paronomasia in Biblical Literature," Glück uses paronomasia, wordplay, and pun interchangeably, but he classifies wordplay into six linguistic categories: equivocal (*double entendre*), metaphonic, parosonantic, farraginous (similar to onomatopoeia), associative (using syntax), and assonantic.[10] He does not offer much by way of summary analysis, but he concludes with a positive note echoed throughout his article, namely that wordplay is no crass pun, but "an inseparable part of the word-magic, the subtle eloquence of the Bible."[11] Thus, Glück offers helpful classification (if not definitions) based on a solid relationship between literary and biblical studies, as well as a shift in perspective concerning the positive and rhetorically-rich nature of wordplay.

Another important work from 1970 is William Holladay's "Form and Word-Play in David's Lament over Saul and Jonathan."[12] Written just two years after James Muilenburg's influential Presidential address to the Society of Biblical Literature, "Form Criticism and Beyond," Holladay attempts to exercise rhetorical criticism on 2 Sam 1:18-27 by showing how an intricate system of interlocking wordplays affects the structure of the pericope.[13] The following two decades saw other important works

---

9. See, e.g., Terence Collins, *Line-forms in Hebrew Poetry: A Grammatical Approach to the Stylistic Study of the Hebrew Prophets* (Rome: Biblical Institute, 1978); Stephen Geller, *Parallelism in Early Biblical Poetry* (Missoula, MT: Scholars Press, 1979); Robert Alter, *The Art of Biblical Poetry* (New York: Basic, 1985); and Adele Berlin, *The Dynamics of Biblical Parallelism* (Indianapolis: Indiana University Press, 1985).

10. Glück, "Paronomasia in Biblical Literature," 53–75.

11. Ibid., 78.

12. William Holladay, "Form and Word-Play in David's Lament over Saul and Jonathan," *VT* (1970): 153–89.

13. Ibid., 153, 156.

on wordplay, each offering new insights into the phenomenon of Hebrew wordplay.[14]

Although the study of biblical wordplay had come a long way since Casanowicz, it was not until 1991 that another monograph-length study appeared. In his revised dissertation, *Lexis Ludens: Wordplay and the Book of Micah*, Anthony Petrotta spends nearly half of his study contextualizing, defining, classifying, and explaining the function and significance of wordplay. Although at times overly harsh about older studies on wordplay,[15] his study is monumental in his application of linguistics, his understanding of the relationship between wordplay and ambiguity, and the centrality of humor in the trope. The second half of Petrotta's work applies this nuanced understanding of wordplay to the book of Micah. In the 25 years since Petrotta's publication, no other monograph on biblical wordplay in a single corpus has been published.

Several other important studies since Petrotta have contributed to our understanding of wordplay. The 1990s saw E. L. Greenstein's dictionary article in *Anchor Bible Dictionary*, which carefully classified the various types and functions of wordplays,[16] and Isaac Kalimi's article, "Paronomasia in the Book of Chronicles," which identifies wordplays within Chronicles not mentioned in Casanowicz's work.[17] The beginning of the millennium then saw the landmark collection of essays edited by Scott Noegel in *Puns and Pundits: Word Play in the Hebrew Bible and Ancient Near Eastern Literature*, which incorporates not only recent insights from modern literary theory, but also those from ancient Near East research.[18] Finally, Knut Heim has written the most recent dictionary article for *Dictionary of the Old Testament: Wisdom, Poetry and Writings*,

---

14. Jack Sasson, "Word Play in the O.T.," in *IDBSup*, ed. George A. Buttrick (Nashville: Abingdon, 1976), 968–70; Bruce Halpern and Richard Elliot Friedman, "Composition and Paronomasia in the Book of Jonah," *HAR* 4 (1980): 79–92; Wilfred Watson, *Classical Hebrew Poetry: A Guide to Its Techniques* (Sheffield: JSOT, 1984); Robert Chisholm, "Wordplay in the Eight-Century Prophets," *BSac* 144 (1987): 44–52.

15. For example, Petrotta accuses Casanowicz of describing paronomasia as "primitive" (*Lexis Ludens*, 23) when, in actuality, Casanowicz is referring only to alliteration and is using "primitive" to describe a stage in language without any negative connotation. See Casanowicz, *Paronomasia*, 8.

16. E. L. Greenstein, "Wordplay, Hebrew," *ABD* 6:968–71.

17. I. Kalimi, "Paronomasia in the Book of Chronicles," *JSOT* 67 (1995): 27–41.

18. Scott Noegel, ed., *Puns and Pundits: Word Play in the Hebrew Bible and Ancient Near Eastern Literature* (Bethesda, MD: CDL, 2000).

"Wordplay," which shows an insightful understanding of semantics, as well as a helpful classification.[19]

There are currently no studies devoted exclusively to wordplay within the Psalms. Several articles highlight a single wordplay.[20] Other contributions discuss wordplay in a given psalm.[21] Some commentaries and works on translation include examples from the Psalter,[22] but no single work offers both a detailed methodology and exhaustive analysis of the book of Psalms or of any of its five books.

Research on the Septuagint, Translation Technique, and Its Use of Wordplay

Contexts of LXX Psalms

There exists no consensus regarding the origin and nature of the LXX translation. Scholars disagree, for example, on whether the extant translations should be treated as reflections of the original translation or as recensions and revisions of an older, lost translation. Jannes Smith offers

---

19. Knut Heim, "Wordplay," in *Dictionary of the Old Testament: Wisdom, Poetry and Writings*, ed. Tremper Longman III and Peter Enns (Downers Grove: InterVarsity, 2008), 925–9.

20. E.g., see John S. Kselman, "Double Entendre in Psalm 59," in *Book of Psalms: Composition and Reception*, ed. Peter W. Flint and Patrick D. Miller, Jr. (Leiden: Brill, 2005), and "Janus Parallelism in Psalm 75:2," *JBL* 121 (2002): 531–2; Paul R. Raabe, "Deliberate Ambiguity in the Psalter," *JBL* 110 (1991): 213–27. Significant works on wordplay outside of the Psalms include Oliver Shaw Rankin, "Alliteration in Hebrew Poetry," *JTS* 31 (1930): 285–91; Jack M. Sasson, "Word-Play in Gen 6:8-9," *CBQ* 37 (1975): 165–6; and Al Wolters, "*Ṣôpiyyâ* (Prov 31:27) as Hymnic Participle and Play on *Sophia*," *JBL* 104 (1985): 577–87; Valérie Kabergs, "Lovely Wordplay in Canticles 8,6a," *ZAW* 126 (2014): 261–4.

21. For example, Lowell K. Handy offers a detailed discussion of all phonetic and semantic poetic devices in Ps. 82, "Sounds, Words and Meanings in Psalm 82," *JSOT* 47 (1990): 51–66. See also Bénédicte Lemmelijn, Marieke Dhont, and Valérie Kabergs, "'The Medium is the Message': On the 'Meaningfulness' of Stylistic Features in Psalm 145," *Indian Theological Studies* 50 (2013): 133–52.

22. E.g., Mitchell Dahood discusses several wordplays and lists all of those within lament psalms in his commentary, *Psalms: Introduction, Translation, and Notes*, 3 vols., AB 16, 17, 17A (Garden City, NY: Doubleday, 1996). One helpful dissertation discusses the difficulty in rendering Hebrew wordplays into English, and especially Chinese: Guek-Eng Violet Lee Lim, "Cognitive Process and Linguistic Forms in Old Testament Hebrew and Chinese Cultures: Implications for Translation (Oriental, Occidental Language)" (PhD diss., Fuller Theological Seminary, School of World Mission, 1986).

1. Introduction

the most convincing arguments for treating the LXX as a reflection of the original translation: (1) the translators at times used various Greek words for the same Hebrew words; (2) at other times they used the same Greek word for various Hebrew words; and (3) they seemed to struggle occasionally with the meaning of the Hebrew original.[23]

Most scholars agree that the LXX Psalter was translated as early as the second century BCE,[24] or as late as the first century CE.[25] Sometime during the second century BCE is the current preference among scholars;[26] however, as Jennifer Dines explains, "Nearly all these attempts at dating are very tentative and there is seldom a consensus."[27] Because koine Greek remained fairly stable during this window of time, and because there is little external evidence, it is impossible at this time to pinpoint the date of composition further than that.[28]

---

23. Jannes Smith, *Translated Hallelujahs: A Linguistic and Exegetical Commentary on Select Septuagint Psalms* (Leuven: Peeters, 2011), 3–5. Smith also refutes the suggestion that the LXX translation of the psalms should be associated with the *kaige* group (5-6).

24. See, e.g., Tyler F. Williams's "Towards a Date for the Old Greek Psalter," in *The Old Greek Psalter: Studies in Honour of Albert Pietersma*, ed. Robert J. V. Hiebert, Claude E. Cox, and Peter J. Gentry, JSOTSup 332 (Sheffield: Sheffield Academic, 2001), 248–76. Some scholars, such as N. Collins and S. Honigman (to a lesser extent), believe the Book of Aristeas to be historical and written in the early third century BCE, thus holding an even earlier view of the translation of the LXX, Johann Cook, "The Translation of a Translation: Some Methodological Considerations on the Translation of the Septuagint," in *Translating a Translation: The LXX and Its Modern Translations in the Context of Early Judaism*, ed. H. Ausloos, J. Cook, F. García Martínez, B. Lemmelijn, and M. Vervenne (Leuven: Uitgeverij Peters, 2008), 11–12.

25. Qumran evidence suggests that the Psalter went through several editorial editions, changing in content and canonical order. For arguments in favor of a later date for a solidified Psalter (and thus a later date for the LXX translation), see Peter W. Flint, "The Book of Psalms in Light of the Dead Sea Scrolls," *VT* 48 (1998): 453–72; idem, *The Dead Sea Psalms Scrolls and the Book of Psalms*, STDJ 17 (Leiden: Brill, 1997); S. Sanders, *The Dead Sea Psalms Scroll* (Ithaca, NY: Cornell University Press, 1967); Dwight D. Swanson, "Qumran and the Psalms," in *Interpreting the Psalms: Issues and Approaches*, ed. David Firth and Philip S. Johnston (Downers Grove, IL: IVP Academic, 2005), 247–62.

26. James K. Aitken, "Psalms," in *The T&T Clark Companion to the Septuagint*, ed. James K. Aitken (London: Bloomsbury T&T Clark, 2015), 320.

27. Jennifer M. Dines, *The Septuagint*, ed. Michael A. Knibb (London/New York: T&T Clark, 2004), 46.

28. See, e.g., James Aitken's comparative studies with external Greek sources of the time, "Phonological Phenomena in Greek Papyri and Inscriptions and Their Significance for the Septuagint," in *Studies in The Greek Bible: Essays in Honor*

As for location, scholars still disagree whether LXX Psalms was translated in Egypt or Palestine; however, the affinity of the LXX translation technique with Egyptian translation practice and the disassociation of the LXX with the *kaige* tradition, make an Egyptian provenance much more likely.²⁹ Textual evidence from Egyptian petition documents and religious texts (hymns to Isis and Osiris, for example) may also favor an Egyptian provenance, as it is likely that the LXX translator borrowed certain lexemes in the semantic field of salvation, praise, and mercy.³⁰

As for the question of whether the translation of LXX Psalms was made by one translator (or unified group of translators) or by many distinct translators, most scholars affirm the unity of their translation, that the book was either translated by a single individual or a group working closely together.³¹

The translator's cultural context might have influenced his or her translation of wordplay in particular. The translator was torn between two cultures and two languages, and between the need to communicate

---

of Francis T. Gignac, S.J., ed. Jeremy Corley and Vincent Skemp, CBQMS 44 (Washington, D.C.: The Catholic Biblical Association of America, 2008), 256–77.

29. Albert Pietersma, "Septuagint Research: A Plea for a Return to Basic Issues," *VT* 35 (1985): esp. 304–11; also, by the same author, "On the Place of Origin of the Old Greek Psalter," in *The World of the Aramaeans*. Vol. 1, *Biblical Studies in Honour of Paul-Eugene Dion*, ed. P. M. M. Daviau, JSOTSup 324 (Sheffield: Sheffield Academic, 2001), 252–74; and Smith, *Translated Hallelujahs*, 12–13.

James Aitken has shown that the translations from Egyptian Demotic to koine Greek during the same time period (during the Ptolemaic Dynasty) evidence a similar translation technique to that of the LXX, namely a similar balance between formal equivalence and freedom: "The Septuagint and Egyptian Translation Methods," in *XV Congress of the IOSCS, Munich 2013*, ed. Wolfgang Kraus, Michaël N. van der Meer, and Martin Meiser, Septuagint and Cognate Studies (Atlanta: SBL, 2016), 269–94.

30. While the direction of borrowing is inconclusive, Aitken's analysis of the evidence favors LXX borrowing of common religious terms. Even regardless of lexical priority, Aitken's analysis shows that the LXX translation of the Psalms was influenced by Egyptian cultic texts, which were in circulation in Palestine, but whose influence would have been far more likely to affect the text if the translator lived in Egypt. See James K. Aitken, "Jewish Worship Amid Greeks: The Lexical Context of the Old Greek Psalter," in *The Temple in Text and Tradition: A Festschrift in Honour of Robert Hayward*, ed. R. Timothy McLay, LSTS (London: Bloomsbury, 2015), 48–70.

31. Francis Woodgate Mozley, *The Psalter of the Church: The Septuagint Psalms Compared with the Hebrew, with Various Notes* (Cambridge: Cambridge University Press), xii. See also Smith's excellent and more recent discussion in *Translated Hallelujahs*, 31.

clearly and accurately and the responsibility to uphold the holiness of the text. Presuming an Alexandrian provenance, John Lee argues that the LXX translators was quite capable in both Hebrew and Greek. Their aptitude for Hebrew is attributable to their Jewish identity and their understanding of the *Vorlage*, while his skill in the devices of Greek language and rhetoric can be gleaned from their "secure place in a cosmopolitan Hellenistic city."[32] Aitken posits that the LXX translator was likely from or associated with the scribal class in Ptolemaic Egypt, thus more highly educated and integrated into Egyptian society that previously proposed.[33]

During the period of LXX translation there were various views on the nature of the Hebrew Scriptures. In the first century C.E., Philo of Alexandria argued that translation must be literal in order to prevent interpretation supplanting the original text and in order for the LXX to maintain equal status with the Hebrew text. However, Tessa Rajak argues that other Jews were much more flexible. Even the Essenes, who were strict in so many other ways, made adjustments to the Hebrew text and did not consider its holiness devalued when altered.[34] Similarly, Theo A. W. van der Louw notes that the ancient Jewish perception of translation ranged widely from those who held to a "particularist notion of the holy tongue" with skepticism of translation to those who held to a "universalist" notion that meaning can be fully translated throughout languages.[35] Thus, much like today, there were a variety of opinions regarding what made the Hebrew Bible sacred and how that holiness could be preserved in translation.

---

32. John A. L. Lee, "Translations of the Old Testament: Greek," in *Handbook of Classical Rhetoric in the Hellenistic Period: 330 B.C.–A.D. 400*, ed. Stanley E. Porter (Boston: Brill, 2001), 776.

33. Aitken bases his theory on a thorough linguistic, comparative, and historical analysis of the LXX, "The Language of the Septuagint," in *The Jewish-Greek Tradition in Antiquity and the Byzantine Empire*, ed. James Aitken and James Carleton Paget (New York: Cambridge University Press, 2014), 132–3. Olofsson, on the other hand, argues that the Alexandrian Jews lived in ghettos and were usually not as well-instructed in advanced Greek grammar and rhetoric, Staffan Olofsson, *The LXX Version: A Guide to the Translation Technique of the Septuagint*, ConBOT 30 (Stockholm: Almqvist & Wiksell International. 1990), 30–3.

34. Tessa Rajak, *Translation and Survival: The Greek Bible of the Ancient Jewish Diaspora* (Oxford: Oxford University Press, 2009), 139–42.

35. Theo A. W. Van der Louw, *Transformations in the Septuagint: Towards an Interaction of Septuagint Studies and Translation Studies* (Leuven: Peeters, 2007), 54.

Rajak notes how surprising it would have been that the scriptures were rendered into common koine Greek, rather than classical Greek. Choosing the common language, however, was a necessary means to the dual-end of the translator. As Rajak argues, "Septuagint language, I suggest, encapsulates the paradox of its successive communities, poised between two worlds. It represents a resolution of two powerful drives, the pull of acculturation and the anxiety of cultural annihilation."[36] Redfern's insights also shed light on how this dual perspective and dual purpose are actually an asset for identifying and appreciating wordplay:

> Punning appeals particularly to exiles (whether external or inner) for, having two homes and languages, the exile has a binary, split perspective (or strabismus) on his adopted culture... [Y]ou see the second language from the outside, and its mechanisms, its automatisms, are that much more apparent to you.[37]

Thus, the etic perspective of the translators may not only have helped them recognize the poet's use of wordplay, but also to appreciate it. It should therefore not be surprising that we find their efforts at transferring wordplay across language boundaries to be so exemplary, as the analysis in Chapter 3 of the present study will show.

Characterizing the Translation Technique of the LXX in General and Psalms in Particular

Translation technique refers to the general style or way that a translator renders a source text into his/her target language. In the case of the LXX, this technique was likely not a self-conscious practice. According to Jennifer Dines, "their method is likely to have been ad hoc, experimental, not always consistent, as they grappled with the challenges and difficulties of a task for which there were at first no models."[38] What we are looking for, then, are patterns and tendencies in the translational work of the LXX Psalter, particularly with regard to the representation of wordplay.

The task of characterizing translation technique includes quantitative and qualitative aspects. Quantitative factors would include whether or not a text was translated in a word-for-word fashion, contains pluses and minuses, and follows the original syntax. Qualitative features would be evidenced by the choice of and consistency with semantic equivalents and the level of interpretation. These factors are vital to consider before

---

36. Rajak, *Translation and Survival*, 126.
37. Redfern, *Puns*, 164.
38. Dines, *The Septuagint*, 118.

making any kind of statement on translation technique because it is only when we establish the translational norms of a given book that we can comment on when those norms are abandoned, for example, for the sake of rendering wordplay. A discussion on the LXX translational norms will introduce the analysis in Chapter 3.

An understanding of semantics is necessary in order to evaluate the qualitative translation technique of the LXX, and the past five or so decades have seen significant contributions to that end. James Barr argued in *The Semantics of Biblical Language* for the identification of meaning in sentences rather than isolated words.[39] Later, in 1979, Barr wrote *The Typology of Literalism in Ancient Biblical Tradition*, which asserts that literalism is not always an ignorant or inferior translation technique, but is, in fact, variegated and often purposeful and appropriate.[40]

Given this nuanced understanding of literalism, more recent scholarship has suggested that the LXX translation of the book of Psalms is towards the literal end of the spectrum.[41] This tendency is consistent with Cicero's distinction between literary and non-literary documents, the former being translated more freely and the latter being translated more literally. As a sacred text, the Psalter is best classified as a non-literary document. Also, the Writings were probably the last group of books to be translated, and books translated later are generally characterized by a

---

39. James Barr, *The Semantics of Biblical Language* (London: Oxford University Press, 1961).

40. James Barr, *The Typology of Literalism in Ancient Biblical Tradition* (Göttingen: Vandenhoeck & Ruprecht, 1979). Albert Pietersma suggests that "word-based" is a better designator than "literal" or "word-for-word" because it highlights that the translator's primary concern was that each word be communicated and that the translation remain as transparent as possible. See his "Exegesis in the Septuagint: Possibilities and Limits (The Psalter as a Case in Point)," in *Septuagint Research: Issues and Challenges in the Study of the Greek Jewish Scriptures*, ed. Wolfgang Kraus and R. Glenn Wooden, SBLSCS 53 (Leiden: Brill, 2006), 38.

41. Staffan Olofsson, who finds himself in good company with scholars such as Baetgen, Berg, Thackeray, Flasher, Mozley, Barr, and Sailhamer, *The LXX Version*, 77. Another indicator of literalness in the Psalms is the unusual use of the pronoun. In Greek, the possessive pronoun would normally come before its noun, whereas in the LXX Psalms, it follows its noun 2250 out of 2270 times, which resembles the use of the suffixed possessive pronoun in the Hebrew. Ibid., 15. Olofsson also notes that the translation of the LXX was possibly modeled after the "court dragoman oral tradition," which was characterized by strict precision in rendering theological words and less consistency in translating words that were not essential to the message. Ibid., 5–6.

greater degree of literalness.⁴² James Barr also suggests that a more literal translation enabled the translators to suggest or exploit multiple meanings in the text, or at least enabled them to preserve some of the ambiguity in the Hebrew.⁴³ This motive is particularly helpful in assessing the LXX translator's understanding of the Hebrew wordplay, of which ambiguity is a key ingredient.

The Psalms translation should not, however, be characterized as overly rigid or simplistically interlinear⁴⁴ as it exhibits a sense of controlled freedom in rendering the source text with consideration of lexical variety and style, as this study will show. In his analysis of the pluses of the LXX Psalter, Randall X. Gauthier exposes how lexical comparisons between the Masoretic text and LXX have misconstrued the character of the Psalms translation, which has a similar vocabulary count as the MT, but often uses that vocabulary in ways that deviate from the MT, a feature overlooked by sheer statistical analysis, and a feature that requires a close reading of the text and a descriptive analysis.⁴⁵

Albert Pietersma also helped to advance the conversation beyond the simplification of literal versus free by characterizing the translators' role on a spectrum between "medium," whose primary agenda was to represent each element of the source text, even at the expense of making the translation dependent on the source for right understanding, and "author," whose primary agenda was to produce a text that could be understood on its own.⁴⁶

---

42. Olofsson, *The LXX Version*, 8–9. Aejmelaeus contends that the translator of the book of Psalms was more concerned with qualitative aspects, which is one explanation for why it is closer to the literal end of the spectrum and why its poetic quality seems inferior to contemporary Greek poetry; see Anneli Aejmelaeus, "Characterizing Criteria for the Characterization of the Septuagint Translators: Experimenting on the Greek Psalter," in Hiebert et al., eds., *Old Greek Psalter*, 71.

43. Barr, *Typology*, 324–5; Olofsson, *The LXX Version*, 7.

44. It is not my intention to critique the interlinear model of the LXX, but I wish to guard against a simplistic view of the LXX that sees it as a "crutch" for Hellenistic Hebrew students with little value on its own.

45. Randall X. Gauthier, "Examining the 'Pluses' in the Greek Psalter: A Study of the Septuagint Translation Qua Communication," in *Septuagint and Reception: Essays Prepared for the Association for the Study of the Septuagint in South Africa*, ed. Johann Cook (Leiden: Brill NV, 2009), 45–76.

46. Pietersma, "Exegesis in the Septuagint," 36; cf. Cameron Boyd-Taylor, ed., *A Question of Methodology: Albert Pietersma, Collected Essays on the Septuagint*, Biblical Tools and Studies 14 (Leuven: Peeters, 2013).

Staffan Olafsson's published dissertation, *The LXX Version: A Guide to the Translation Technique of the Septuagint*, builds on the best of LXX scholarship and offers an excellent background of the LXX and methodology for its interpretation vis-à-vis the MT. He informs his readers that the literalness of the LXX translators often had more to do with their methodology than with a deficit in their knowledge of Hebrew and Greek and that the LXX translators were quite apt in both Hebrew and Greek.[47] His sentiments echo those of Henry J. Thackeray, who wrote the following a century prior:

> The distinction between the earlier and the later books is a real one; the reason for the change is to be sought, it appears, rather in a growing reverence for the letter of the Hebrew than in ignorance of Greek.[48]

Thomas J. Kraus likewise attributes many LXX variants to the translator's methodology, arguing, "I am convinced that a knee-jerk reference to an unknown and/or lost '*Vorlage*' is not more than *argumentum ex silentio*, and it does not adequately account for the various and varied differences between the Hebrew MT and the Greek LXX."[49]

The dominating concern over the *Vorlage* of the LXX and whether the translation technique was literal or free, has given way in the past few decades to other concerns: (1) widening criteria for characterizing translation technique from lexical, grammatical, and syntactical choices of the translators to include rhetorical elements and poetic features,

---

47. Olofsson admits that the translators had several deficiencies. Deficiencies in their understanding of the Hebrew, however, are often explained by their misunderstanding of the unpointed Hebrew *Vorlage* and their overreliance on Aramaic; see Olofsson, *The LXX Version*, 30–3. Aejmelaeus ("Characterizing Criteria for the Characterization of the Septuagint Translators," 72) agrees that the LXX translation of the Psalms is fine, particularly considering the translators' constraints. John Sailhamer's excellent study on the LXX's translation technique for the Hebrew verbs argues that the LXX translator exhibits "a reasonably well-informed knowledge of the Hebrew verb" (*The Translational Technique of the Greek Septuagint for the Hebrew Verbs and Participles in Psalms 3–41*, Studies in Biblical Greek 2 [New York: Lang, 1991], 209).

48. Henry John Thackeray, *A Grammar of the Old Testament in Greek According to the Septuagint* (Cambridge: Cambridge University Press, 1909), 30.

49. Kraus, "Translating the Septuagint Psalms—Some 'Lesefrüchte', and their Value for an Analysis of the Rhetoric (and Style) of the Septuagint (Psalms)," in *Et Sapienter et Eloquenter: Studies on Rhetorical and Stylistic Features of the Septuagint*, ed. Eberhard Bons and Thomas J. Kraus (Göttingen: Vandenhoeck & Ruprecht, 2011), 68.

such as wordplay, and (2) shifting analytical motives from normative to descriptive. The first concern is outlined in Anneli Aejmelaeus's essay entitled "Characterizing Criteria for the Characterization of the Septuagint Translators: Experimenting on the Greek Psalter" in the Festschrift for Professor Albert Pietersma.[50] Aejmelaeus advises:

> What one needs in order to gain a more reliable and complete picture of this translator, as well as others of his kind, is new and other criteria for the characterization of "translation technique."[51]

In addition to widening the criteria for characterizing translation technique, LXX translation studies have also shifted from a normative to a descriptive approach. This approach focuses on the target text's "adequacy," which is determined by comparison.[52] The word "adequacy," however, seems a bit misleading since, according to Jacobus A. Naudé, the descriptive approach departs from the normative approach, which dominated prior to 1980 and which was most interested in the quality of the translation; instead, Naudé explains, "The focus [of the descriptive analysis] is rather on a description and explanation of the translation in the light of the translators' ideology, strategies, cultural norms, etc."[53] Gauthier's study of the pluses in the LXX Psalter exposes the need for descriptive analysis and models, showing that what may first appear from the data like a rigid translation is in fact much more complex.[54]

Theo A. W. van der Louw has written a significant study on the translation technique of the LXX, particularly his study of "transformations," which he defines as "shifts or changes (linguistic or other) with respect to an invariant core that occur in translation from source text to target text."[55]

---

50. Aejmelaeus, "Characterizing Criteria for the Characterization of the Septuagint Translators."

51. Ibid., 55–6.

52. Van der Louw, *Transformations in the Septuagint*, 20–1.

53. Jacobus A. Naudé, "It's All Greek: The Septuagint and Recent Developments in Translation Studies," in Ausloos et al., eds., *Translating a Translation*, 243.

Aejmelaeus also argues for a descriptive approach for characterizing translation technique: "Translation technique cannot be anything more than a collective name for all the different renderings used by a translator. Study of translation technique aims at describing the end-product of a translator's work" ("Translation Technique and Intention of the Translator," in *On the Trail of the Septuagint Translators: Collected Essays*, ed. Anneli Aejmelaeus [Kampen: Kok Pharos, 1993], 69).

54. Gauthier, "Examining the 'Pluses' in the Greek Psalter."

55. Van der Louw, *Transformations in the Septuagint*, 383.

1. Introduction

If the target text differs significantly from the assumed source text (MT in this case), interpreters too often conclude that the target text differed from the MT, scribal error was involved, or the translator had theological or ideological motives for changing the text. Van der Louw proposes a more nuanced approach in assessing these variances, arguing that transformations were made because a literal translation would not be feasible or adequate. In other words, the translator's motive in rendering the source text as he did was more often a matter of translational preference. He offers the following classification system of these transformations:[56]

Graphological translation
Phonological translation
Transcription / borrowing (loanword)
Loan translation (calque)
Literal Translation
Modulations or lexical changes
    a. Antonymic translation
    b. Converse translation
    c. Reversal of cause and effect
    d. Specification
    e. Generalization
    f. Modification
    g. Cultural "equivalent"
Transposition or grammatical changes
    a. Change of accidence
    b. Change of word class
    c. Change of syntactic function
    d. Change in word and clause order
"Addition"
"Omission"
Redistribution of semantic features
Situational translation
Idiomatic translation of idiom
Non-idiomatic translation
Explicitation
Implicitation
Anaphoric translation Stylistic translation and compensation
Morphematic translation

---

56. Ibid., 61–2. For detailed descriptions of each category, see his elaboration in 62–92. The categories employed by the LXX translators will be discussed in the conclusion of this chapter; Van der Louw's full list is included for thoroughness and so that readers can determine for themselves which transformations best describe the translation technique in each analyzed case of wordplay.

These categories of transformations can be combined in various ways, and some are more common than others, as will become apparent in Chapter 3.

Van der Louw categorizes even word-for-word translations as a type of transformation, and he explains that literal syntax translations are best suited for short sentences such as in the cola of Hebrew poetry.[57] This may explain, in part, why the LXX version of the Psalter is generally characterized as "literal." He also notes that stylistic translation and compensation is common in poetry because the form is more important than the semantic equivalence.[58] Thus, when the LXX translator is attempting to represent the same wordplay or a similar wordplay into his target language, it should not be surprising when he uses semantic, grammatical, or syntactical variations.[59]

LXX Translation of Rhetorical and Literary Devices

With these contributions to LXX translation technique have also come a greater recognition of the rhetorical and literary features of the LXX. Jan Joosten's methodology for analyzing LXX translation technique with regard to the LXX translation of Hebrew idiom is particularly pertinent to this present work because of his focus on one particular literary device that is difficult to communicate across languages. In order to characterize the philosophy and translation technique of the LXX translator, Joosten posits, "The way forward is to analyze single features of the Septuagint's translation technique in depth and to try to relate the results to larger issues."[60] Joosten does just that by analyzing the various renderings of Hebrew idiom throughout the LXX. He identifies three categories of idiom translation method: literal renderings, sense renderings, and a hybrid rendering that he refers to as "Type C." Within this latter category, the translator would retain some element of the idiom, but render it in a way that would be understandable in the source language. For example, the Hebrew text of 1 Sam 4:20 reads וְלֹא־שָׁתָה לִבָּהּ (literally, "and she did not set her heart"), which has the sense of "she did not understand."

---

57. Ibid., 64.

58. Ibid., 84.

59. Jan de Waard ("'Homophony' in the Septuagint," *Bib* 62 [1981]: 551–61) takes a similar approach to the LXX translation of Isaiah, showing how various phonological translations create semantic and grammatical variants.

60. Jan Joosten, "Translating the Untranslatable: Septuagint Renderings of Hebrew Idioms," in *"Translation is Required": The Septuagint in Retrospect and Prospect*, ed. Robert J. V. Hiebert, Septuagint and Cognate Studies 56 (Atlanta: Society of Biblical Literature, 2010), 60.

The LXX translator used creativity to retain both the sense and the color of the idiom by translating it, καὶ οὐκ ἐνόησεν ἡ καρδία αὐτῆς ("her heart did not understand").[61] From his analysis, Joosten concludes that the translator shows great understanding of the source text, but his use of various rendering methods exhibits a flexibility and even inconsistency that reflects his inexperience as a translator.[62]

Joosten's work is a complementary study to this present volume, as both seek to understand the nature of the LXX by focusing on how one type of literary feature is rendered from the Hebrew. It is also instructive because the same variety of renderings is also found with regards to wordplay rendering. The translator used both literal and free renderings of the Hebrew wordplays, but he also employed creative hybrids or accommodations, similar to Joosten's "Type C" idioms. In such cases, the translator used a different category of wordplay, or he made a wordplay on adjacent lines to the original wordplay, showing the same kind of dexterity observed with idiom translation technique. Joosten's summary of the translation technique of idiom mirrors the characterization that this present study supports:

> Although the translational process sometimes demands that one should abandon either the wording of the source text or its global meaning, the Seventy were not at ease with this alternative. More often than not, they refused this basic dilemma and tried to compose in Greek an expression that paid tribute to both the wording and the sense.[63]

As we will see, this attention to both sense and style was paid to wordplay as well.

Mirjam Vorm-Croughs's work on plusses and minuses in the LXX translation of Isaiah shows that the translator (of Isaiah, at least) had such an aptitude for and interest in rhetorical devices that he would make addition or omission transformations independent of the Hebrew text. For example, a plus that might otherwise be written off as dittography is better identified as creating an *inclusio* around a key literary unit.[64] Vorm-Crough explains that this acute interest in literary devices is understandable given the shift in Hellenistic culture around the first century BCE from interests in oral communication and persuasion to the literary

---

61. Ibid., 68.
62. Ibid., 69.
63. Ibid.
64. Mirjam Vorm-Croughs, *The Old Greek of Isaiah: An Analysis of Its Pluses and Minuses*, SBLSCS 61 (Atlanta: Society of Biblical Literature, 2014), 217–98.

realm.⁶⁵ This move in rhetoric from oral to written, and from persuasion to style, means that the LXX translators lived in a world that placed great value on literary devices such as repetition, parallelism, ellipsis, and (of course) wordplay.

Eberhard Bons and Thomas Kraus's edited volume, *Et Sapienter et Eloquenter: Studies on Rhetorical and Stylistic Features of the Septuagint*, offers various important essays, the most relevant to this study being the editors' own contributions.⁶⁶ Looking specifically at the LXX Psalter, Eberhard Bons identifies examples of hyperbaton, alliteration, and paronomasia, illustrating "the existence and diffusion of rhetorical devices in the Greek Psalter that cannot be explained by a slavish translation of a Hebrew *Vorlage*."⁶⁷ Kraus's essay looks at several cases of either probable or improbable stylistic flourish or rhetoric in the LXX Psalms. He offers several important warnings that guide his analysis, showing how tighter methodology can help distinguish a phenomenon that is really in the text from something contrived from the "wishful thinking" or "tunnel vision" of the reader. First, one must guard against seeing what one wants to see in the text. This is why there must be criteria, guidelines, and an honest rating system of the strength of the potential phenomena in the text. Second, one must keep in mind the historical distance between the LXX and the MT, and between the Hebrew text that we have before us today and the *Vorlage* of the LXX thousands of years.⁶⁸

Hans Ausloos, Bénédicte Lemmelign, and Valérie Kabergs have outlined new criteria for characterizing the LXX translational technique of wordplay in their essay, "The Study of Aetiological Wordplay as a Content-Related Criterion in the Characterization of LXX Translation Technique."⁶⁹ They argue for a third means of characterizing translation

---

65. Ibid., 218.
66. Bons and Kraus, ed., *Et Sapienter et Eloquenter*.
67. Bons, "Rhetorical Devices in the Septuagint Psalter," in Bons and Kraus, ed., *Et Sapienter et Eloquenter*, 79. See also Bon's essay, "Die Rede von Gott in den Psalmen^LXX," in *Im Brennpunkt: Die Septuaginta. Band 3: Studien zur Theologie, Anthropologie, Ekklesiolgoie, Eschatologie, und Liturgie der Griechischen Bibel*, ed. H. H. Fabry and D. Böhler, BWANT 174 (Stuttgart: Kohlhammer, 2007), 182–202.
68. Kraus, "Translating the Septuagint Psalms," 54.
69. Hans Ausloos, Bénédicte Lemmelign, and Valérie Kabergs, "The Study of Aetiological Wordplay as a Content-Related Criterion in the Characterization of LXX Translation Technique," in *Die Septuaginta: Entstehung, Sprache, Geschichte: 3. Internationale Fachtagung Veranstaltet von Septuaginta Deutsch (LXX.D), Wuppertal 22.–25. Juli 2010*, ed. Siegfried Kreuzer, Martin Meiser, and Marcus Sigismund, WUNT 286 (Tübingen: Mohr Siebeck, 2012), 273–94. See also Bénédicte Lemmelign,

technique, intended to be the complement of the quantitative research represented by James Barr and Emanuel Tov and the qualitative research of the Finnish school. The third method they propose employs "content-related" criteria, which, in their own words, looks at "the way that the LXX translator has dealt with very specific questions related to the content of the Hebrew/Greek text."[70] Jargon, *hapax legomena*, and aetiological wordplays are exemplar criteria.[71] Ausloos, Lemmelign, and Kabergs' 2012 essay "The Study of Aetiological Wordplay as a Content-Related Criterion in the Characterization of LXX Translation Technique" represents some of the fruit of this widening criteria for characterizing translation technique.[72]

It can be seen that in recent years greater attention has been given to the playfulness of LXX translations. Even where the translators are following closely their Hebrew *Vorlage*,[73] they are able to produce effects that conform to literary style in Greek. It is therefore feasible in this

---

"Two Methodological Trails in Recent Studies on the Translation Technique of the Septuagint," in *Helsinki Perspectives on the Translation Technique of the Septuagint: Proceedings of the IOSCS Congress in Helsinki 1999*, ed. Raija Sollamo and Seppo Sipilä, Publications of the Finnish Exegetical Society 82 (Göttingen: Vandenhoeck & Ruprecht, 2001).

70. Ausloos, Lemmelign, and Kabergs, "The Study of Aetiological Wordplay," 275.

71. To be fair, scholars did not altogether ignore such criteria, as the following articles represent: Emanuel Tov, "Loan-Words, Homophony, and Transliteration in the Septuagint," *Bib* 60 (1979): 216–36; de Waard, "'Homophony' in the Septuagint."

Aetiological wordplays are those involving the names of people, places, and events and their origins. As with other types of wordplay, the translators have a very difficult task given that the Hebrew wordplays are based on sounds and meanings specific to that language and the aetiologies are lacking in the target language if either the similarity in sound is lost or the meaning is lost (through transliteration). The researcher's task, however, is relatively easy because the aetiological wordplays are explicit and would have been obvious to the LXX translator. As such, there is no question as to whether or not the wordplay was genuine or whether or not the translators recognized the presence of wordplay. With other types of wordplay, it is sometimes difficult to discern whether the Hebrew wordplay itself would have been understood by the original readers, whether the translators recognized the presence of wordplay in the Hebrew, and finally whether the translators' attempt to render the wordplay was intentional, unless he was able to render a similar one.

72. Ausloos, Lemmelign, and Kabergs, "The Study of Aetiological Wordplay."

73. See, e.g., James K. Aitken, "Rhetoric and Poetry in Greek Ecclesiastes," *BIOSCS* 38 (2006): 55–78.

book to ask how far the translators adapted word-play in the Hebrew and managed to reflect it in their Greek translation. The effect may not always be the same in Hebrew as in Greek, but the translators were sensitive to the sound and sense of their Greek.

The Study of Wordplay in Literary Theory

Wordplay is a by-product of the necessity of language to use a manageable number of words (or signs) to refer to a virtually infinite number of referents. And if words have multiple meanings that are distinguished only by their contexts, then authors and speakers of any language can enlist these multiple meanings through wordplay. Thus, wordplay has been a global reality and a subject for scholarly reflection for as long as written history can attest.

Historical Review

The history of wordplay and its study reveals an oscillating perception of its value and function. The following section will review that history in order to understand the contexts of the original Hebrew authors, the LXX translators, and the literary and biblical critics of wordplay who have since contributed to the conversation.

Fundamental to the ancients' understanding of wordplay was their understanding of the relationship between sound and meaning, and between word and referent. According to Frederick Ahl, ancient Egyptians would use a picture of a word in place of another word that had a similar sound, with the implication that sound and meaning were somehow related.[74] In the earliest Egyptian texts, the Pyramid Texts, wordplay was used less for aesthetics than for practical purposes of signaling a shared realm of meaning by virtue of a shared etymology.[75] The Epic of Gilgamesh is replete with puns, including a clever play between the words for corn (*kibtu*) and the sound that corn makes being ground (*kuku*), and

---

74. Frederick Ahl, *Metaformations: Soundplay and Wordplay in Ovid and Other Classical Poets* (Ithaca: Cornell University Press, 1885), 19. According to the Egyptologist Richard Parkinson, wordplays were "deeply interwoven into the language, life and religion of the ancient Egyptians," and are extant as far back as the Pyramid Texts of the Old Kingdom (third millennium BCE). See John Pollack, *The Pun Also Rises: How the Humble Pun Revolutionized Language, Changed History, and Made Wordplay More Than Some Antics* (New York: Gotham, 2011), 129.

75. Antonio Lopriendo, "Puns and Word Play in Ancient Egypt," in Noegel, ed., *Puns and Pundits*, 8–9.

their secondary meanings of grief and misfortune,[76] as well as examples of puns on proper names and Janus parallelism.[77] According to John Pollack, wordplay was often used in very serious matters of discourse, even deadly serious matters.[78] During the Old Babylonian Period, princes challenged each other to punning duels, which would often end in deadly conflicts.[79] The Assyrians and other ancient Near Eastern peoples also used wordplay for humor, as structural devices, in omens, and for numerous other purposes similar to those found in the Old Testament.[80]

In the fifth century BCE, Plato's *Cratylus* offers the first written work on linguistics, and specifically on the relationship between words and meaning. In the dialogue, Socrates has two interlocutors, Hermogenes and Cratylus. Hermogenes represents what modern linguists call "conventionalism" and argues that convention alone dictates the relationship between words and their referents; the same words could just as easily be used to designate other objects, if that were the convention. Cratylus represents modern "naturalists," arguing that words naturally correspond to their referents. Socrates, whom scholars agree represented Plato's views, criticizes Hermogenes' extreme conventionalism, but then, after a long explanation of etymological connections between Greek words and their referents (which would seem very weak, if not ridiculous, by modern standards), he likewise criticizes Cratylus' extreme naturalism. It seems most likely that he landed somewhere in the middle, advocating naturalism as the ideal linguistic model, but conceding that language, being imperfect, was often based merely on convention.[81] This view is

---

76. Pollack, *The Pun Also Rises*, 3. According to Pollack, the first evidence of a pun was a visual pun in the form of a statue from around 35,000 BCE. On one side is the figure of a woman, and on the other side is a figure of a male genitalia, which evinces visual wordplay from before the advent of written language (ibid., 124).

77. For examples of more possible word and sound plays in Sumerian literature, see Jacob Klein and Yitschak Sefati, "Word Play in Sumerian Literature," in Noegel, ed., *Puns and Pundits*, 23–61.

78. Pollack, *The Pun Also Rises*, xxii.

79. Ibid., 2.

80. For examples of Akkadian word and sound play in religious, legal, and popular texts, see Victor (Avigdor) Hurowitz, "Alliterative Allusions, Rebus Writing, and Paronomastic Punishment: Some Aspects of Word Play in Akkadian Literature" (63–88); Anne Draffkorn Kilmer, "More Word Play in Akkadian Poetic Texts" (89–101); and Sheldon W. Greaves, "Ominous Homophony and Portentous Puns in Akkadian Omens" (103–15), all in Noegel, ed., *Puns and Pundits*.

81. David Sedley, "Plato's *Cratylus*," in *The Stanford Encyclopedia of Philosophy (Fall 2008 Edition)*, ed. Edward N. Zalta. Online: http://plato.stanford.edu/archives/fall2008/ entries/plato-cratylus/ (accessed 10/3/2012).

supported by his use of wordplays throughout the dialogue, showing that even if words are "naturally" paired with certain referents, they contain other senses that are not.[82]

If one discounts the (at least moderate) naturalism in Plato's *Cratylus* because Socrates was potentially deriding wordplay through his use of it, it is more difficult to discount the advocacy of wordplay in other ancient writers, such as Marcus Terentius Varro, Vergil, Cicero, and Titus Lucretius Carus.[83] Varro was a Roman scholar and member of the Old Platonic Academy in the first century BCE who believed that words of similar sound had a similar origin.[84] In fact, his view of etymology probably led to his unique and complex use of wordplay at the syllable level, rather than at the word level.[85] Four centuries later, in *The City of God* (6.2), Augustine refuted Varro as the prime authority of linguistics, showing that Varro's views were widely held in the ancient world.[86] Other ancient works that displayed a love for wordplay include Vergil's *Aeneid*, Statius' *Thebaid*, Ovid's poetry, and even Emperor Nero's biographical material, according to the historian Suetonius.[87] According to Ahl, "Such use of language calls into question our assumption that simplicity, earnestness, and stability lie at the heart of 'serious' ancient literature."[88]

The methodology of Plato, Varro, and other Greek ancients in employing wordplay is particularly helpful in understanding the intellectual milieu of the LXX translators. For example, etymological wordplays focused on the syllable, rather than the word, but the length of vowels, the doubling or lack of doubling of a consonant, and the exchange of certain consonants for others did not preclude an etymological wordplay.[89] Latin wordplays on Greek words, as well as other languages, were also common

---

82. This ancient debate over the natural or conventional function of language has been taken up in recent times, with respect to the Hebrew Bible specifically, by Leo I. Weinstock, who concludes that there exists some, albeit limited, connection between sound and meaning; see his "Sound and Meaning in Biblical Hebrew," *JSS* 28 (1983): 49–61.

83. Lucrecius, for example, argued that fire and firewood shared a similar atomic structure, just as their Latin names are similar (*ignis* and *ligna*). He considered this connection a necessary result of "purposeful chance" because words reflect reality; see Redfern, *Puns*, 41–2.

84. Ahl, *Metaformations*, 24.

85. Ibid., 35.

86. Ibid., 22.

87. Ibid., 43, 55. Suetonius recorded the lives of twelve Caesars in *De Vita Caesarum*.

88. Ibid., 22.

89. Ibid., 56–9.

in the ancient world.⁹⁰ Such bilingual wordplay also manifests itself in the MT, which uses the unusual form צוֹפִיָּה to describe the virtuous woman in Prov. 31:27 and also to allude to the Greek word for wisdom, σοφία.⁹¹

However, some ancient rhetoricians did not approve of polysemantic wordplays in particular. Writing in the first century C.E., Quintilian insulted the trope by saying, "There are other ways in which words are used with different meanings, either as they are, or altered merely by lengthening or shortening a vowel. This is a feeble device even as a joke, and I am surprised to see that instructions are given for it."⁹² Driven by a desire for precision and effectiveness, Quintilian believed that punning merely obfuscated the message. He did, however, praise the careful and judicious use of paronomasia, of which the LXX translator made excellent use, as we will see Chapter 3.⁹³

Medieval Hebrew poets and Jewish scholars utilized wordplay frequently in their own writings, and they were particularly sensitive to wordplay in Scripture. Moses ibn Ezra (c. 1055–c. 1140), for example, attributed the use of medieval Hebrew wordplay to its precedent in Scripture.⁹⁴ Wordplay, as well as allegory, was also widely embraced by the Roman Catholic church from the earliest centuries through most of the Middle Ages. Throughout the Middle Ages and into the sixteenth century, Europeans found warrant for wordplay in Scripture, particularly in Jesus' own wordplay to Peter in Matt. 16:18 ("You are Peter [Πέτρος], and on this rock [πέτρα] I will build my church…").⁹⁵ The love for wordplay in sixteenth-century England is attested by William Shakespeare's profuse use of the trope in his work. M. M. Mahood counts an average of 78 wordplays in each of his plays.⁹⁶

90. Ibid., 60.

91. Wolters, "*Ṣôpiyyâ*," 577.

92. Quintilian, *The Orator's Education*, Books 9-10, Loeb Classical Library (Cambridge, MA: Harvard University Press, 2001), 9.3.70. Quintilian qualifies this statement several paragraphs later, adding that punning repetition was acceptable if the change of meaning was absolutely unambiguous (9.3.86).

93. Quintilian, *The Orator's Education* 9.73, 76.

94. David S. Segal, "Pun and Structure in Medieval Hebrew Poetry: The Case of Shmuel Hanagid," in Noegel, ed., *Puns and Pundits*, 308–9.

95. M. M. Mahood, *Shakespeare's Wordplay* (London: Methuen, 1957), 9.

96. Ibid., 164. Mahood's observation of the importance of wordplay in Shakekspeare's works could be applied universally to poetry: "A poet makes his discovery of poetic truth only through an exploration of the meanings of words. Because of this, the study of Shakespeare's wordplay can take us to the central experience of each play as surely as can our interest in its imagery, its way of re-telling an old tale, and its explicit statements" (55).

However, wordplay began to fall out of favor sometime in the seventeenth century. According to Catherine Bates, the Enlightenment agenda of stabilizing language is largely to blame for the device's downfall.[97] The rejection of the supernatural for the natural may also be a factor, as Maureen Quilligan explains, "In the Middle Ages wordplay was a sign of God's harmonious design; in the seventeenth century it had become a sign of that design's failure."[98] Pollack traces the demise of wordplay in eighteenth-century England to class snobbery. By this time, upper and lower classes found themselves together more often, such as in the newly instituted coffee houses, in which all classes sat together at a long common table. Prior to this desegregation, the upper class enjoyed wordplay, but in an effort to distinguish themselves from the lower classes with whom they now mingled, they adopted new rules of etiquette and decorum, which disallowed wordplay. Hence, the expressions "pardon the pun" and later "no pun intended" came into use.[99] In the mid-nineteenth century, according to Redfern, puns were even forbidden in sermons and literature.[100] Wordplay remained popular in America, however, with such notable punsters as Benjamin Franklin and Cotton Mather. Preachers even punned from their pulpits.[101]

By the nineteenth and early twentieth centuries, scholars were split as to their view of wordplay, both in England and America. British authors such as Samuel Taylor Coleridge and Lord Byron in the late eighteenth and early nineteenth centuries, and Lewis Carroll later in the nineteenth century tried to defend and re-popularize wordplay.[102] American proponents of wordplay included Abraham Lincoln, Henry David Thoreau, and Graham Bell,[103] and Austrian psychoanalyst Sigmund Freud found the trope very important, believing that the secondary meanings represented repressed feelings.[104] In his classic work, *A Dictionary of Modern English Usage*, published in 1926, Henry Fowler cleverly defended wordplay saying, "Puns are good, bad, and indifferent, and only those who lack the wit to make them are unaware of the fact."[105]

---

97. Catherine Bates, "The Point of Puns," *Modern Philology* 96 (1999): 426.
98. Maureen Quilligan, *The Language of Allegory: Defining the Genre* (Ithaca, NY: Cornell University Press, 1979), 182.
99. Pollack, *The Pun Also Rises*, 84.
100. Redfern, *Puns*, 51.
101. Pollack (*The Pun Also Rises*, 90) notes that Native Americans also punned.
102. Redfern, *Puns*, 65.
103. Pollack, *The Pun Also Rises*, 92.
104. Quilligan, *The Language of Allegory*, 35; Redfern, *Puns*, 80.
105. Pollack, *The Pun Also Rises*, 103.

Even into the twentieth century, many scholars sidelined wordplay as a "traitor" to language and meaning. Saussure distained wordplays, calling them "feeble puns based upon the ridiculous confusions which may result from homonymy pure and simple."[106] James Joyce tried resurrecting wordplay and portmanteau in his final work, published in 1938, *Finnegan's Wake*. G. K. Chesterton, too, defended punsters against those who criticized wordplay and yet, hypocritically, used words with negative sounds (such as dogma rather than doctrine) for their argumentation, calling their ailment "the disease of the suppressed pun."[107] Distinguishing explicit, unapologetic wordplay from such sly use of "ugly" sounding words, he argued, "Now I for one greatly prefer the sort of frivolity that is thrown to the surface like froth to the sort of frivolity that festers under the surface like slime."[108] However, it was not until the early and mid-twentieth century that wordplay really began its revival, and its importance in literary scholarship has only increased to date.[109] This increased appreciation has resulted in a diversity of analyses and research topics on the subject. One of the greatest modern contributions to the field of wordplay has been in the area of linguistics, to which we will now turn.

The Linguistic Nature of Wordplay in Modern Theory
Having reviewed the philosophical, social, and semantic issues that caused wordplay to be interpreted and appreciated (or depreciated) in various ways throughout history, we turn now to the nature of wordplay itself. The following discussion will address several important linguistic issues in an attempt to approach the phenomenon of wordplay from an emic perspective.

Central to any discussion on wordplay is the concept of ambiguity. In Stephen Ullmann's important work, *Semantics*, he discusses ambiguity at length. He claims, "By far the most important type of ambiguity…is that due to *lexical* factors."[110] Because most words out of practical necessity have multiple meanings, ambiguity is a potential feature of communication. However, ambiguity is usually avoided because communication happens at the utterance level, wherein authorial intent is generally discernable through the context. Even if the surface structure of an utterance is

---

106. In *Course in General Linguistics* (1916), cited in Bates, "The Point of Puns," 424.
107. G. K. Chesterton, *The Well and the Shallows* (London: Sheed & Ward, 1935), 10.
108. Ibid., 11.
109. Redfern (*Puns*, 76) attributes this revival to the influence of surrealism.
110. Ullmann, *Semantics*, 158.

ambiguous, the deep structure, including the context, usually reveals the intended meaning.[111] Ullmann's opinion of the potential ambiguity that stems from polyvalency is rightfully optimistic: "What is astonishing is not that the machine [of communication] occasionally breaks down, but that it breaks down so rarely."[112] Aristotle used the potential semantic confusion as an analogy for critiquing argumentation. Just as lexical ambiguity can be resolved through a thorough understanding of the context and the word's range of meaning, so also can confusing arguments be understood through a thorough understanding of sound argumentation and the marks of fallacious reasoning.[113] Thus, ambiguity is not something to be carelessly shunned, but rather carefully studied.

As we have noted, the literary context of an ambiguous word (or a wordplay in particular) is usually the interpretative key to understanding the sense(s) of the word and the intent of the author. However, according to Derek Attridge, information theory holds that the stronger the contextual clues as to a word's meaning, the less power that word has in itself. He explains, "[T]he more predictable a given item in a message, the less information it carries; the totally predictable word conveys, in itself, absolutely nothing."[114] This is because the word's own sense becomes redundant, having already been determined by its context.

Ambiguity can happen by accident, either on the part of the author or the reader. In the case of wordplay, however, ambiguity is purposeful, and the author controls when, how, and if the ambiguity is clarified.[115] Attridge explains this deliberate use of ambiguity saying

> The pun, however, is not just an ambiguity that has crept into an utterance unawares, to embarrass or amuse before being dismissed; it is ambiguity *unashamed of itself*, and this is what makes it a scandal and not just an inconvenience. In place of a context designed to suppress latent ambiguity,

---

111. Derek Attridge, "Unpacking the Portmanteau, or Who's Afraid of *Finnegans Wake?*," in Culler, ed., *On Puns*, 141. Ullmann (*Semantics*, 169) notes other safeguards in determining a polysemous word: gender, inflexion, syntax, and the use of additional words.

112. Ullmann, *Semantics*, 168.

113. Aristotle, *On Sophistical Refutations* (E. S. Forster, LCL), 13.

114. Attridge, "Unpacking the Portmanteau," 142.

115. Redfern (*Puns*, 123) describes the intentional and accidental phenomena of ambiguity thus: "Puns remind us both of our mastery and of our lack of control over language: this is their primordial ambiguity. We are always in danger of punning." Attridge, who overall views puns positively, comments that puns "expose the fallen nature of language and thus the world" ("Unpacking the Portmanteau," 140).

the pun is the product of a context deliberately constructed to *enforce* an ambiguity, to render impossible the choice between meanings, to leave the reader or hearer endlessly oscillating in semantic space.[116]

L. G. Heller uses ambiguity as a guiding principle in her typology of wordplay, in that some wordplays begin with two possible meanings and then clarify the intended meaning (disambiguational), whereas other wordplays begin with one probable meaning and then introduce another possible meaning (ambiguational).[117] Most wordplays eventually disambiguate, at least at the deep level. In fact, Catherine Bates describes this disambiguation as being crucial to the integrity of language and communication:

> To understand a pun is necessarily to disambiguate it, for one has not got the joke otherwise. It is to put the linguistic house back in order and to restore the everyday, sober method of expression.[118]

Because the disambiguation of wordplay is essential for effective communication, it is essential for the ideal reader and exegete to be able to interpret wordplay, not least of all in Scripture.

The polyvalency responsible for this lexical ambiguity manifests itself in two forms: polysemy and homonymy.[119] Polysemy is when the same word has multiple meanings, whereas homonymy is when different words (with different meanings) are identical (or similar) in sound or form. Because homonymous words can have the same form, it is often difficult to distinguish them from a polysemous word.[120] One means of distinction is through the word's etymology. If a word with multiple senses at one time had a single, common sense previously, then polysemy is at work; if the multiple senses cannot be traced to a common origin, then the identical forms are actually two different words, and homonymy is at work.[121] This criterion can be highly speculative, however, particularly in

---

116. Attridge, "Unpacking the Portmanteau," 141 (emphasis original).

117. Heller refers to this second category as "nondisambiguational," "Toward a General Typology of the Pun," in *Linguistic Perspectives on Literature*, ed. Marvin K. L. Ching, Michael C. Haley, and Ronald F. Lunsford (London: Routledge & Kegan Paul, 1980), 308.

118. Bates, "The Point of Puns," 428.

119. These linguistic categories are also two of the main categories of wordplay and will be discussed further below as they pertain to a typology of wordplay.

120. Ullmann, *Semantics*, 159.

121. Ibid., 169.

ancient languages such as Hebrew in which the etymological backgrounds of words are clouded by years of unrecorded history or limited manuscript evidence. Another means of distinction is the degree to which the multiple senses are related. The more similar the senses, the more likely that the word is polysemous; the more divergent the senses, the more likely that multiple words are homonymous.[122] Again, this criterion is highly subjective and not always effectual.[123]

Semiotics, or the linguistic study of signs, offers important contributions for the study of wordplay. Ferdinand de Saussure, the father of semiotics, believed that words could only be defined negatively, by what they are not, rather than positively, by what they are.[124] Many modern linguists, and scholars of wordplay in particular, believe that the nature of wordplay disproves Saussure's theory.[125] That a sign can change referents within the same context also challenges Saussure's theory that each signifier (sign) has an "inseparable" signified (referent).[126] Catherine Bates's critique is persuasive:

---

122. Ibid.

123. Ullmann (ibid., 159) himself explains that polysemy can arise from the use of metaphor, foreign influence, and specialization, all of which would produce widely divergent senses.

Although the etymology of words (and thus the identification of polysemy versus homonymy) is often difficult to determine, it is sometimes the basis for a wordplay. Jonathan Culler defines etymological wordplay as a "diachronic version of punning… motivating the meaning of words through punning derivatives" ("The Call of the Phoneme: Introduction," in Culler, ed., *On Puns*, 2). Culler offers this definition within a discussion of the irony that the *Oxford English Dictionary* considers the word "pun" to be of "uncertain origin" (ibid., 1). Linguists distinguish real etymologies from folk etymologies, which assume a common origin to all words sharing any similar phonemes or syllables, and which are far less respected. They also distinguish between puns, which play between synchronic senses, and etymologies, which play between diachronic senses (ibid., 3; Attridge, for example, ridicules folk etymologies as ridiculous, "Unpacking the Portmanteau," 142–3).

124. Saussure believed that words were not signs until the signifier and signified were combined, thus creating meaning (semantics) from otherwise arbitrary symbols or sounds; see *Course in General Linguistics*, trans. Roy Harris (LaSalle, IL: Open Court, 1986). Throughout this project, however, "word" may be used interchangeably with "sign," and "meaning" or "sense" may be used interchangeably with "referent" or "signified."

125. Culler, "The Call of the Phoneme: Introduction," 12.

126. Attridge, "Unpacking the Portmanteau," 140.

> It is not that puns expose the arbitrariness of signification (every sign does that) but that puns reveal the discrimination of meaning to be a haphazard, approximate, and error-prone affair. A pun...fractures the sign and disturbs those neat relations which, in Saussure's diagrams, tie signified and signifier together in tidily serried ranks.[127]

Because wordplay seems to subvert some of Saussure's most important theories of linguistics, some modern linguists treat wordplay with contempt, as a "traitor" of language.[128] But is wordplay really such a renegade? Bates argues that "a sign is no less a sign for pointing in several directions at once," especially when rightly interpreted by the attentive reader.[129]

This right interpretation involves an interplay between author, text, and reader. A genuine wordplay reflects the intentions of the author. Even in Shakespeare's *Macbeth*, for example, Lady Macbeth's brilliant punning reflects the creative genius of the author, and certainly not the humorless character herself.[130] Wordplay also requires readers to take a particularly active role in understanding the meaning intended by the author. The ideal reader's right interpretation determines the efficacy of the wordplay, and thus the successful communication of meaning.

But the right interpretation of wordplay requires more than a close reading of the text and a word's literary context. Authors write within certain cultural and social contexts, and only when readers share those contexts, or at least understand them in an emic way, can they rightly interpret a word's intended meaning(s). Pollack distinguishes between syntagmatic puns and paradigmatic puns. Syntagmatic puns provide the reader with all of the necessary information, or context, to interpret the wordplay. Paradigmatic puns require the reader to understand the author's social and cultural contexts in order to understand the wordplay.[131] This presumed shared context between the author and reader is obviously more difficult to discern the farther removed the reader is from the provenance of the text.

---

127. Bates, "The Point of Puns," 424.
128. Ibid.
129. Ibid., 428. Bates continues, "Whether the pun is cursed as a traitor to language or blessed as the welcomed guest who brings two meanings for the price of one, its tendency to distort or to extend meaning is dealt with by the interpretive process which, however playfully, ultimately restores priority to the serious business of making sense, to showing what a pun finally means" (428–9).
130. Culler, "The Call of the Phoneme: Introduction," 8.
131. Pollack, *The Pun Also Rises*, 11–12.

Proponents of linguistic relativity argued that language and cultural contexts (including worldviews) were so inextricably embedded that communication across languages was impossible. In other words, there existed no universals or insufficient shared conceptual space for adequate translation.[132] While the cultural context and non-verbal aspects of a source language create a challenge for communicating the more implicit aspects of a message into a target language, such a task is not insurmountable because language groups do in fact have a great deal of shared experiences, not least of all by virtue of their shared physical world. This is the response of relevance theory, which has largely stepped in to fill the void left by linguistic relativity. Promoted by scholars such as Deidre Wilson and Dan Sperber,[133] relevance theory promises a nuanced, balanced approach to translation theory that takes seriously the complexity of the human mind and the task of communicating across language and culture, while at the same time affirming the human brain's remarkable way of accommodating for these synapses and limitations.[134]

Postmodern interpreters tend to believe that the reader, rather than the author, creates meaning.[135] What we are advocating here, however, is the importance of the reader to complete the speech-act of communication, to actualize or receive the meaning, not to create it. Another interest in postmodern circles is the paradigm shift from the "concept" to the "puncept." According to Gregory Ulmer, "The puncept, we may now understand, is not a gathering or collecting of properties at all, as in the concept, but a scattering, a dissemination, a throwing of the dice."[136] As with many postmodern approaches, however, the "puncept" organizational principle (or disorganizational principle!) seems not only to play with ambiguity, but also to turn all communication into ambiguity and meaninglessness, without restraints.

Another facet of linguistics that is important for our understanding of wordplay is the difference between the surface and deep structures of a text. The surface structure of a wordplay involves the initial sense of

---

132. See, e.g., John B. Carroll, ed., *Language, Thought, and Reality: Selected Writings of Benjamin Lee Whorf* (Cambridge, MA: MIT, 1956).

133. Deidre Wilson and Dan Sperber, *Meaning and Relevance* (Cambridge: Cambridge University Press, 2012).

134. For an excellent discussion of the implications of relevance theory for biblical translation feasibility and considerations, see Karen H. Jobes, "Relevance Theory and the Translation of Scripture," *JETS* 50 (2007): 773–98.

135. E.g., Quilligan, *The Language of Allegory*, 21.

136. Gregory Ulmer, "The Puncept in Grammatology," in Culler, ed., *On Puns*, 188.

a word, or the sense that best fits the context. The deep structure goes beyond the sense first assumed by the reader to a secondary sense that gets at the heart of the author's purpose in using the wordplay. In its deep structure, wordplay is similar to other figures, such as allegory and metaphor, and even functions like a microcosm of these figures.[137] Stefan Kjerkegaard compares metaphor and wordplay thus:

> [M]etaphor creates a convergence between several semantic fields by covering up the differences between them and in so doing often makes poetry happen. Wordplay, on the other hand, fixes the difference in the mind, thus maintaining the convergence in its very expression.[138]

According to Redfern, "wordplay often seeks to mime reality in some way,"[139] and understanding wordplay can help us understand analogical relationships: "And analogy, like punning, senses likeness at the core of difference."[140] Just as analogies attempt to show similarities between different things, so also wordplay juxtaposes different words and/or different meanings in order to highlight connections between them. In fact, although allegorical interpretations predated the church, Christian theologians were the first to extend their understanding of wordplay into an actual genre on a large scale, namely the genre of allegory.[141]

Definitions

Scholars define and categorize wordplay in various ways, so it is vital to define and delineate the boundaries of wordplay for this study, as well as the numerous types of wordplay.

Defining Wordplay

Stefan Kjerkegaard describes wordplay as "an interaction between a semiotic deficit and a semantic surplus,"[142] which is to say that the economy of language requires more meanings than signs. Knut Heim,

---

137. Heller, "Toward a General Typology of the Pun," 306.
138. Stefan Kjerkegaard, "Seven Days without a Pun Makes One Weak: Two Functions of Wordplay in Literature and Literary Theory," *Journal of Literature, Language and Linguistics* 3 (2011): 4.
139. Redfern, *Puns*, 41.
140. Ibid., 45.
141. Quilligan, *The Language of Allegory*, 19. Quilligan adds, "allegorical narrative unfolds as a series of punning commentaries, related to one another on the most literal of verbal levels—the sounds of words" (22).
142. Kjerkegaard, "Seven Days without a Pun Makes One Weak," 1.

in *The Dictionary of Wisdom and Poetry*, writes "Wordplays are playful but significant uses of one and the same word or phrase with different meanings or of different words or phrases with the same 'meanings'."[143] Wilfred Watson posits, "Wordplay is based on *lexical ambiguity* which is simply a way of saying that words can be polyvalent."[144] Watson's more general definition is fleshed out with examples and categories, but as it stands, the definition is simultaneously too broad and too limited. It is too broad because polyvalency in itself is not wordplay; rather, the author's exploitation of a word's polyvalency for a particular purpose is wordplay. Moreover, lexical ambiguity exists only when the context does not demarcate a word's intended sense; wordplay exists only when such ambiguity is intentionally not immediately disambiguated or when secondary meanings are potentially suggested. Watson's definition is too limited because it excludes all wordplays that play on sound rather than meaning, which excludes many forms of paronomasia. Redfern describes wordplays as "turns on words," explaining that the second meaning "pivots" around the first.[145] As for a formal definition, however, Redfern prefers to remain as general as possible: "Perhaps all we really need, in terms of rhetorical nomenclature, is the idea of trope: a pun is a figurative use of a word or phrase."[146] Luis Alonso Schökel defines word-play succinctly and well thus: "Play on words exploits the polyvalence of meaning of one word, or the similarity of sound of various words."[147] This definition aptly includes both the semantic and phonetic dimensions of wordplay.

Valérie Kabergs and Hans Ausloos offer a thorough discussion of the definition of wordplay, helpfully distinguishing it from the word "paronomasia." In Casanowicz's wake, the two words have often been confused or used interchangeably.[148] However, Kabergs and Ausloos

---

143. Heim, "Wordplay," 925. Derek Attridge ("Unpacking the Portmanteau," 144) defines wordplay (or puns, specifically) in a similar way, as either one word with two meanings or as two homophones "in a particular context made to coalesce."

144. Watson, *Classical Hebrew Poetry*, 237.

145. Redfern, *Puns*, 23.

146. Ibid., 82. Despite this broad definition, when Redfern discusses wordplay, he has in mind a particular type of figure of speech, perhaps allowing his readers to deduce their own particular definitions of wordplay.

147. Luis Alonso Schökel, *A Manual of Hebrew Poetics*, SubBi 11 (Rome: Pontificio Istituto Biblico, 1988), 29.

148. Casanowicz (*Paronomasia*, 12) used paronomasia as the broader term and wordplay as specifically playing on meaning, i.e., pun. Subsequent scholars, including Glück, A. Guillaume, and Halpern and Friedman, either followed Casanowicz's lead

argue that wordplay is the broader category, while paronomasia is a type of wordplay wherein the poet uses "the proximity of two words with a different meaning but a similar sound pattern."[149] This study maintains that same distinction.

For this project, wordplay will be defined as a literary device based on the exploitation of phonetic similarity and/or semantic ambiguity that has a structural or rhetorical function.[150] The functional aspect is integral to the definition of wordplay: wordplay is employed for a purpose, and without purpose, it is incidental. Conversely, if it is not incidental, it has a purpose and the reader has a responsibility to discern that purpose. This definition also includes the play on both phonetic similarity and semantic ambiguity, meaning that some wordplays involve only a play on sound or only a play on meaning, while others involve both.

Herein lies the only difference between Kabergs and Ausloos's definition of wordplay and that of this study: while Kabergs and Ausloos limit wordplay to only those figures that play on both meaning and sound, this study includes plays that are, or appear to be, only playing on sound. The reason for this broader definition in this study is two-fold. First, it includes figures that many other scholars have dubbed wordplay; in other words, many scholars use this broader definition. Second, and more critical, it is often very difficult to discern whether a play on meaning is intentional. Many words used in paronomasia, for example, are clearly juxtaposed for their similarity in sound (and thus a wordplay by our

---

or interpreted the Greek components of "paronomasia," παρα and ονομασια, meaning "by the side of" and "naming," respectively, to denote wordplay in general. However, according to Petrotta, "In classical usage, paronomasia usually refers to words in proximity that differ only slightly in form and have a different meaning" (*Lexis Ludens*, 6; see also Valérie Kabergs and Hans Ausloos, "Paronomasia or Wordplay? A Babel-Like Confusion Towards a Definition of Hebrew Wordplay," *Bib* 93 [2012]: 7), and this book will assume this specialized definition. Schökel (*A Manual of Hebrew Poetics*, 30) uses the words in the most unique way, defining paronomasia as wordplays involving proper names, reasoning that in such wordplays meaning is irrelevant.

149. Kabergs and Ausloos, "Paronomasia or Wordplay?," 7.

150. Geoffrey Hartman ("The Voice of the Shuttle: Language from the Point of View of Literature," in *Beyond Formalism: Literary Essays, 1958–1970* [New Haven: Yale University Press, 1970], 347) offers a memorable definition of wordplay in relation to homonymic (and homophonic) plays and polysemantic plays: "You can define a pun as two meanings competing for the same phonemic space or as one sound bringing forth semantic twins, but however you look at it, it's a crowded situation."

definition) but the function or purpose of the play is not always clear; it could be merely aesthetics, or to maintain the readers' interest, or it could be a play on meaning, but sometimes the latter function is not obvious and thus inconclusive.[151]

A Typology of Wordplay

Having reviewed history and linguistic features of wordplay, and having established a working definition, we may now attempt to classify different types of wordplay. The following taxonomy of wordplay will serve as the classification system for this project. The three, primary types of wordplay are homophonic plays, paronomastic plays, and polysemantic plays.

Homophonic plays are primarily plays on sound in which two words sound, but are not spelled, exactly the same. While such plays are common in English and other languages, they are less common in Hebrew and are in fact altogether absent in Psalms 90–106. Therefore, although this category is important to mention for the sake of completeness and methodology, this study will henceforth refer to the two primary categories of wordplay that are employed in the psalms under consideration.

Paronomastic wordplays involve similar-sounding words and include a wide variety of subcategories, including alliteration, assonance, rhyme, metaphony, parasonancy, root letter transposition, and root play. For this study, alliteration will refer generally to all repetition of consonants and even consonant-vowel combinations. Consonance, which is the repetition of consonants irrespective of their placement in tone or non-stressed syllables, is usually distinguished from alliteration, which typically refers to consonant repetition on tone syllables. In this study, however, alliteration refers to all phonetic repetition that involves consonants (and possibly vowels in addition). Assonance refers specifically to vowel repetition, and rhyme refers to repetition of consonant-vowel combination at the end of words (end rhyme). In the subcategory of metaphony, vowels are changed but the consonants are not, and in parasonancy only one of the root letters is changed. Root letter transpositions are plays in which only the order of the root letters differs, and root plays involve the same root used in different ways, usually in different word classes. In order to distinguish wordplay from "lighter" forms of phonetic correspondence, cases of alliteration and assonance that involve only one phoneme will not be considered wordplay for the purpose of this study. While such cases of phonetic similarity are often deliberate poetic devices and will occasionally warrant mention in the analysis, we will distinguish between such

---

151. Kabergs and Ausloos, "Paronomasia or Wordplay," 14.

cases of "light" alliteration and assonance and those involving multiple phonemes.[152]

Polysemantic wordplays are plays on words involving multiple meanings and include three subcategories: *double entendre*, implicit paronomasia, and punning repetition.[153] These plays usually involve only one word, either used alone or repeated to make the wordplay explicit. If the word is used alone, it alludes to another meaning or another similar-sounding word with another meaning. The former is *double entendre* (also called equivoque or syllepsis), such as in the poetic device of Janus parallelism. The latter is implicit paronomasia; it is still within the category of polysemy because the one word plays with alternate meanings, but it borrows sound-play from paronomasia in order to activate such wordplay. If the word is repeated in punning repetition, or antanaclasis, the second use has a different referent. Although many scholars use "pun" and "wordplay" interchangeably, a pun is more technically a polysemantic or homophonic play on two different words or meanings.

It was noted above that scholars distinguish between polysemy and homonymy; thus, polysemantic wordplays, which play on multiple meanings of the same word, and homonymic wordplays, which play on two different words that look and sound exactly alike, could also be distinguished. While such a distinction is sometimes possible to make in modern languages, wherein the etymology of each word is more accessible, it is often difficult to distinguish between homonyms with different origins and one word with multiple meanings. Some parameters include classifying those words with similar meanings and polysemantic while more disparate meanings reflect disparate etymologies and thus different

---

152. This distinction may seem arbitrary, but it is easier to demarcate than those based on function, i.e., those cases wherein the play on meaning is uncertain.

153. Some scholars consider polysemantic wordplays to be more sophisticated or powerful. Ullmann (*Semantics*, 188) explains, "Puns based on polysemy are on the whole more interesting than the homonymic [or paronomastic] type since there is more subtlety in playing on meanings than on chance similarities of sounds." Paul Hammond and Patrick Hughes (*Upon the Pun: Dual Meanings in Words and Pictures* [London: W. H. Allen, 1978], 1) refer to polysemantic plays as having a "rational, erudite quality," while homophonic plays (and paronomastic, by extension) have a "capricious and irrational quality." It is interesting to note that the opposite opinion held sway two millennia ago, as represented by Quintilian's preference for paronomasia and cautious or even critical evaluation of polysemy; see his *The Orator's Education* 9.3.70.

Some scholars, such as Hammond and Hughes, use "play on words" more specifically to refer to polysemantic plays (*Upon the Pun*, 1), but this study will be using "wordplay" to refer to all three categories of "play."

origins. Such distinctions are too difficult to make for many Hebrew words, whose etymologies are now lost. Moreover, such distinctions may not have been known to the poet, so classifying wordplay on such dubious grounds is unhelpful and even confusing for such a study as this. Therefore, homonymic wordplay will be considered within polysemantic wordplay in this study.

We have already noted the historical trend to confuse the words "paronomasia" and "wordplay," but another error was made when "paronomasia" was seen as strictly a play on sound, while polysemantic wordplay was a play on meaning. Such a hard distinction is unfortunate because some paronomastic and polysemantic wordplays involve both meaning and sound. For example, some paronomastic plays also play on meaning by making connections between words that are similar, different, causally related, or ironically connected in order to make a point that might not otherwise be obvious on the surface level of the text. Similarly, implicit paronomasia is a polysemantic wordplay that uses sound to allude to another word. A better construal of the relationship between sound and meaning is to consider that phonetic play is a definitive aspect of paronomasia, while semantic play is a possible function or purpose of the play. Likewise, semantic play is a definitive aspect of polysemy, but sound play is also a potential element.

In addition to these primary categories of paronomastic and polysemantic wordplays, this study will address, although to a lesser extent, several others. Complex wordplays, for example, involve multiple wordplays working together in proximity. Sometimes they are working together on a rhetorical level, making a similar point or drawing the same contrast between the same things. Most often complex wordplays work together on a structural level as well, with interlocking, chiastic, or patterned wordplays. Some wordplays in this study are close in proximity, but they do not function together as a complex wordplay; they are best understood as independent wordplays (e.g. Ps. 90:10 contains three independent wordplays that are not complex). Plays on proper nouns, such as names and places, are very common in the Pentateuch and historical books, but not in the psalms, particularly in Book IV where names are very sparse. Visual wordplays, including gematria and notrikon, are more cryptic, and sometimes speculative, forms of wordplay.[154] Associative wordplays

---

154. In addition to visual wordplays that are dependent on the written word, Hammond and Hughes (*Upon the Pun*) juxtapose puns in language with puns in art, using the two to elucidate each other. Kabergs and Ausloos ("Paronomasia or Wordplay," 18) exclude all forms of visual wordplay from their definition because they do not employ sound.

are based on syntax and involve exchanging an expected word within a phrase for one that is not expected and thus surprising.[155] Intralinguistic wordplays play on consecutive words that have a different meaning when combined.[156] Interlinguistic wordplays involve a word that sounds like another from a different language.[157] Of these additional wordplay categories, the only ones found in Psalms 90–106 are complex wordplays, all of which involve paronomastic and/or polysemantic wordplays.

The following is a summary of the categorization employed in this study:[158]

Paronomastic	Polysemantic	Others
Alliteration	*Double entendre*	Complex
Assonance	Implicit Paronomasia	[Proper Nouns]
Rhyme	Punning Repetition	[Aeteoliological]
Metaphony		[Visual]
Parasonancy		[Associative/Syntax]
Root Play/Root Letter		[Intralinguistic]
Transposition		[Interlinguistic]

Another categorical division of wordplays is whether or not they are made explicit by the author. Wordplays are made explicit by repeating the word, or a similar word, to make the secondary reference clear,[159] whereas implicit wordplays only allude to the secondary sense.[160] These categories

---

155. Glück ("Paronomasia in Biblical Literature," 72) gives the example of the phrase "circumcise your heart," in which "heart" is the unexpected word. Similarly, Pollack (*The Pun Also Rises*, 16) discusses "chiasmus," which transposes adjacent words in order to create another meaning.

156. Heller ("Toward a General Typology of the Pun," 313) gives the example of "and Doyle" in a play implying the phrase "and oil."

157. Ibid., 312. See also Wolters, "Ṣôpiyyâ," and Gary A. Rendsburg, "Bilingual Wordplay in the Bible," *VT* 38 (1988): 354–57.

158. Homophonic wordplay is purposefully excluded because none are represented in Pss. 90–106.

159. Mahood refers to these plays as "unspoken puns," in Petrotta, *Lexis Ludens*, 16.

160. These are the primary categories in Heller's typology of wordplay, which is divided into "retentional nondisambiguational" wordplays (those whose meanings are immediately obvious) and "nonretentional disambiguational" wordplays (those whose double meanings are not initially obvious); see Heller, "Toward a General Typology of the Pun," 305. Heller offers many other criteria by which to classify

pertain primarily to polysemantic wordplay, where *double entendre* and implicit paronomasia are implicit wordplays, and punning repetition is explicit.

Wordplay can also be classified by function, which is an essential part of rightly understanding the trope.[161] Authors employ wordplay for various stylistic and rhetorical reasons. Stylistically, wordplay can be used as a structural device, linking lines, strophes, or entire poems. Rhetorically, it can also be used as a means of emphasis or irony.[162] The author who employs wordplay can also express multiple ideas at once, which explains why wordplay is so at home in the terseness of poetry. Paronomasia, more specifically, can draw connections between apparently disparate words and concepts, or show connections that highlight similarities, differences, or casual relationships.[163] Polysemy can reveal complexity in something that appears simple by calling to mind another idea. Wordplay can serve to amuse and surprise readers, or to maintain the readers' active participation.[164] In order to understand the text, the reader must think critically about the author's message. Maureen Quilligan explains

> The pun, by alerting the reader to the magic density of the text's language, will force the reader to become self-conscious of his own reading. The presence of the pun makes it not only easier for the reader to see connections across the surface of the text, but necessary.[165]

wordplay, which are helpful in understanding the trope, but which would be too confusing and cumbersome for use in this project. I have tried to strike a middle ground between Heller's thorough classification and Redfern's lack of classification.

161. Kjerkegaard ("Seven Days without a Pun Makes One Weak," 6) argues that the use of wordplay is vital for a "comprehensive means of dealing with wordplay and puns in literary theory."

162. Paul P. Saydon helpfully explains how repetition of sound, in all Semitic languages, serves to emphasize those words. This is especially clear in the repetition of the same word to create the superlative and in the use of two, synonymous words to create a hendiadys. Naturally, therefore, the repetition of sounds—be they consonants, vowels, or syllables—serves to underscore those words and the central idea to which they refer; see Saydon's "Assonance in Hebrew as a Means of Expressing Emphasis," *Bib* 36 (1955): 37–8.

163. Pollack's description (*The Pun Also Rises*, 143) of this function is noteworthy: "Punning was and remains a way to sling a verbal rope, in an instant, across vast conceptual canyons."

164. Heim, "Wordplay," 928–9.

165. Quilligan, *The Language of Allegory*, 41.

According to Heim, this active reading can "stir readers out of complacency," demanding their attention.[166]

Research Methodology

Several points of methodology will guide this analysis. This section will first cover general methodological concerns and then address the criteria for identifying wordplay in the MT and LXX.

General Methodological Concerns

In order to home in on what *will* be studied, it will be helpful to note what will *not* be studied. Two poetic devices, which some scholars classify as wordplay, will not be discussed: turns and sequencing plays. A turn is a literary device that involves the repetition of a root but, unlike root play or explicit polysemy, the repeated words bear the same basic meaning.[167] A sequencing play is a syntactical category defined by Petrotta that includes such literary devices as chiasm, parallelism, and acrostics. Although all literary devices in some way "play" with words, inclusion of Petrotta's category of sequencing wordplays would broaden the scope of this study too greatly.

Having noted what is outside of the scope of this study, it should be emphasized that no poetic analysis can be done in isolation, irrespective of other phenomena in the text. Each wordplay will be analyzed within its larger context, not just of the Hebrew source text or presumed *Vorlage*, but also of the Greek. Aejmelaeus reminds her readers that the LXX translators often made lexical decisions based on the Hebrew parallelism, which they were trying to reflect.[168] Therefore, wordplays cannot be analyzed in isolation from their larger contexts, their strophes, stanzas, and the psalm as a whole.

As for the Hebrew and Greek texts, the *Biblia Hebraica Stuttgartensia* edition of the MT will be used for the Hebrew, and the Göttingen edition of the LXX (Psalmi Cum Odis) will be used for the Greek.[169] Because

---

166. Heim, "Wordplay," 928.
167. Watson, *Classical Hebrew Poetry*, 239. Kabergs and Ausloos ("Paronomasia or Wordplay," 15) refer to these as *figura etymologica*.
168. Aejmelaeus, "Characterizing Criteria for the characterization of the Septuagint Translators," 70.
169. In his analysis of the LXX's rendering of the Hebrew verb, Sailhamer chooses to exclude any form that contains a variant in the apparatus of Psalmi Cum Odis. He does this so that "the results will not be based on a critically reconstructed text but on the most original text of the LXX so far as it is represented in all of the

neither the Leningrad Codex nor the Göttingen LXX perfectly represent the Old Greek text or its actual *Vorlage* we cannot assume that even the best texts that we have before us today represent the originals at every turn. Staffan Olofsson describes his confidence in both texts saying, "the *Vorlage* of the LXX Psalms is in fact close to the Massoretic text, and the deviations are easy to recognize."[170] It should be noted that variants listed in the apparatuses of both texts will be carefully analyzed, but only mentioned if they directly impact the wordplay under question. Text-critical issues that impinge on the exegesis of the text will be given careful consideration and discussed in relation to the wordplay in context.

It has been shown, especially with the comparative studies with the Dead Sea Scrolls (in particular) that the consonantal text of the MT had been accurately preserved since at least the Second Temple period. According to Geoffrey Khan, "The extant proto-Masoretic manuscripts show that the text had been fixed not only in content, but also in orthography by the 3rd century B.C.E."[171] Also, it is well-known that the original, preliterary vocalization of the Hebrew text is uncertain, and although most Hebrew wordplays involve only the consonantal text, some, such as assonance and metaphony, do involve vocalic pronunciation. Khan argues that the Masoretes did not introduce any new phonetic or linguistic phenomena, but preserved a reading system and vocalization that was already in use: "There is no evidence that the Masoretes reformed the reading tradition and felt free to introduce linguistic innovations of their own."[172] Indeed, using comparative orthography, the various reading traditions of the Hebrew text can be traced back to the Second Temple period, and even to the period before the exile and before the transition from paleo-Hebrew alphabet was replaced by the square Aramaic script. This historical picture provides a necessary degree of confidence in the correspondence between the pronunciation of the MT and the pronunciation of the text behind the LXX.

---

manuscripts" (*The Translational Technique of the Greek Septuagint*, 20). This study will make no such exclusions, though it will exercise caution when analyzing variant renderings.

170. Olofsson, "Law and Lawbreaking in the LXX Psalms," in *Der Septuagint-Psalter: Sprachliche und Theologische Aspekte*, ed. Erich Zenger, Herders Biblische Studien (Freiburg: Herder, 2001), 293.

171. Geoffrey Khan, "Biblical Hebrew, Linguistic Background of the Masoretic Text," in *Encyclopedia of Hebrew Language and Linguistics,* ed. Geoffrey Khan (Leiden/Boston: Brill, 2013), 304–15.

172. Ibid., 307.

In an effort to make this study as objective as possible, and its findings as useful as possible, this study will include a detailed tabulation of each wordplay in the MT and the LXX translation. Prior to computer-assisted Bible study that enables scholars to collect, analyze, and sort all necessary data, analysis of LXX translation technique was unavoidably more impressionistic—and intuitive.[173] With the assistance of technology to help access, manage, and manipulate textual data, this project can provide more comprehensive and assured results.

In addition to the use of computer software, an essential facet of this study is a detailed database, by which we have catalogued and sorted over 20 linguistic features of each wordplay and tagged the various strategies of translation employed by the LXX. The first step in creating this database was to compile the citations of all Hebrew wordplays in Psalms 90–106. We then identified features of each Hebrew wordplay, characteristics of the LXX rendering of the wordplay, and other aspects of the context of the passage. A few of the most important fields pertaining to the Hebrew wordplay included the category and subcategory of the wordplay, its function, and a rating of its strength or certainty. The most important fields pertaining to the LXX translation included noting whether the translators were able to represent the wordplay and to what degree, if a variant was involved, and if the translator made a change in order to render the wordplay. Attention was paid to thematic elements of the passage, whether the wordplay was within divine discourse, and the genre of the passage or psalm. The database created for this research made it possible to analyze wordplay in Book IV of the Psalter for both the MT and LXX, comprehensively and from a variety of perspectives, contributing to the thoroughness and reliability of the analysis.

This book is intended for an admittedly limited readership who is interested in Hebrew poetry, LXX studies, or both. However, I have to tried to broaden the readership as much as possible by providing ample translations and explaining field-specific terms. I also want to acknowledge what is sometimes a great divide in literary studies, between readers who seek meaning from authorial intention, and those who are more text or reader-focused. Some readers might be unconcerned or skeptical about justifying the author's intent in creating a wordplay or the translator's

---

173. For a critique of modern research that relies on intuition more than careful analysis, see Olofsson, *The LXX Version*, 25. A notable exception is Raija Sollamo's published dissertation, *Renderings of Hebrew Semiprepositions in the Septuagint* (Helsinki: Suomalainen Tiedeakatemia, 1979), which carefully analyzes and tabulates each rendering of the Hebrew semipreposition.

intent on rendering or not rendering the Hebrew wordplay in the LXX. For example, Thomas Kraus argues,

> Besides, it is often hard to tell whether an author has made a deliberate choice while writing or, in relation to the Septuagint, a translator while translating. Thus, it seems more appropriate to avoid 'style and rhetoric' when researching the 'language' or 'the Greek' of the Septuagint. Terms as 'language', 'the Greek (of the Septuagint)' or the like are less controversial and more useful for a pragmatic approach.[174]

While Kraus' cautious methodology is admirable, it does not seem consistent with his claim that the LXX translator made "deliberate interpretations" of the Hebrew text[175] or that some of the differences between the Hebrew and Greek texts are "plausibly attributed to a translator's creative and theological will."[176] Style and rhetoric are in both the MT and the LXX, and our inability to talk about them with certainty does not preclude our pursuit of them through the best means possible: the text. As much as I have tried to avoid psycho-analyzing the thoughts and intentions of ancient people who did not explicitly reveal their intentions, and as much as I have attempted to discuss neutrally the effect of text alone, such language about intentionality invariably crops up, especially with regard to the LXX translator, since one of our objectives is to discern the translation technique of the LXX, which is really just another way of saying the philosophy and method of the translator. Since that translator was a person who made decisions and had skills and limitations, we can hardly say anything about his work without creeping close to the precipice of the intentional fallacy. Of course, the view from the precipice is the most illuminating and exhilarating and, in our case, necessary.

Methodology for Identifying Wordplay in the MT and the LXX
This project requires methodological guidelines for distinguishing true wordplay from misconceptions or fancifully contrived illusions of wordplay. Although this analysis requires an element of subjectivity, there are certain guidelines that will prove helpful.[177] It will be helpful to divide the discussion between criteria for identifying wordplay and marks of wordplay.

---

174. Kraus, "Translating the Septuagint Psalms," 53.
175. Ibid., 62.
176. Ibid., 68.
177. It is important to emphasize that a completely objective system of identifying true wordplay is impossible and that, as with many hermeneutical endeavors, such an

Criteria for identifying wordplay are objective standards that must be met for a trope to qualify as wordplay. These criteria differ between polysemy and paronomasia. The identification of punning repetition (explicit wordplay) is fairly straight forward: the same word is used two or more times with different meanings within the same context (stanza, for the purpose of this study). Identifying *double entendre* and implicit paronomasia, however, is more interpretive and subjective than identifying punning repetition because it is implicit, partially hidden for the reader to disambiguate or discover. Indeed, that is part of the appeal of *double entendre* and, yet, it challenges the identification of the trope. For this study, the main criterion is function: Does the *double entendre* (or implicit paronomasia) serve an identifiable function? What effect is achieved through the allusion to another meaning (irony, contrast, connections with other parts of the poem)?

The most important criterion for identifying paronomasia is naturally the quality and strength of the sound repetition; the second word being played upon in paronomastic plays should contain at least two of the consonants of the first, and if those two consonants do not constitute half of the words, supplementary evidence of wordplay is required.[178] Different letters that are similar or identical in sound can constitute shared sound, since sound play is key, but there needs to be collaborative support, such as being completely adjacent and having a clear function (e.g., Ps. 105:22) or combining other wordplay categories and patterning with another wordplay (e.g., Ps. 102:17a, 18a).

A second important criterion for paronomasia is that the involved words should be close in proximity unless there is a clear structural or rhetorical reason for the separation. Wordplays with several intervening lines are called macro wordplays and a valid type of wordplay.[179] They are particularly effective in complex wordplays and when used as an *inclusio* around a strophe or stanza or to connect two disparate ideas in challenging ways, but additional support is needed in order to qualify these as genuine wordplays. For example, the wordplay between אֲדֹנָי מָעוֹן in Ps. 90:1b and

---

exercise necessarily requires an artful and imaginative close reading of the text. In explaining his own safeguards in interpreting deliberate ambiguity in the Psalms, Raabe ("Deliberate Ambiguity in the Psalter," 227) summarizes well this subjective nature saying, "I doubt, however, that we will ever be able to formulate such scientifically precise rules so as to remove all scholarly disagreement. There will always be some, well, ambiguity."

178. Greenstein, "Wordplay, Hebrew," 969.

179. Heim ("Wordplay," 928–9) discusses the "macrolevel" and "microlevel" functions of wordplay.

נֹעַם אֲדֹנָי in Ps. 90:17a is separated by 34 cola, but the strong, chiastic repetition of the sounds and the wordplay's function of forming an *inclusio* around the psalm support its identification as a wordplay.

Quite often, wordplays have contextual markers that further help to identify them. A clear function and very close proximity are two such markers noted above. Additionally, the use of *hapax legomena* when more common words would fit the context could also support the identification of a wordplay. Other contextual indicators of wordplay include irregular syntax, gender, meter, or inflection.[180] If a word pair in a potential wordplay is related structurally (e.g. in an *inclusio*, chiastic pattern, or parallelism), this relationship could also support its identification as a wordplay.

Of course, some features may seem like markers of wordplay when they are actually incidental. For example, Hebrew morphology often produces end rhyme and other forms of phonemic similarity that are not always a product of wordplay, but grammatical necessity.[181] Sound repetitions created by grammatical inflection do not by themselves constitute wordplay, but they might supplement other sound repetitions. Additionally, if the author could not have said the same thing another way, or if it would have been a strain to do so, any sound repetition or potential polysemy is very likely accidental, and not a wordplay.

According to these criteria, there are 74 wordplays in Book IV of the Hebrew Psalter, and they will be examined in the following chapter. However, they are not all equally persuasive; some are much more certain than others. In an effort to analyze their strength, each wordplay will be assigned a rating of strength where 1 = sure or strong; 2 = moderate; and 3 = weak (but still within the qualifying criteria discussed above). These ratings do not reflect the quality or strength of the wordplays themselves, but rather are a measure of the confidence we have in identifying them as legitimate wordplays. In other words, these ratings are a matter of method, not critique. These findings will be factored into the analysis at the end of the next chapter.

Methodologically, as with so many aspects of biblical interpretation, our approach to the LXX must be somewhat of a hermeneutical spiral, beginning with the source language, moving to the target language and translation technique, which will then help us to understand and possibly

---

180. Ibid., 927; Ullmann, *Semantics*, 168–9; Raabe, "Deliberate Ambiguity in the Psalter," 227.

181. Schökel believes that end rhyme produced through morphology is "poor," but can be effective if amassed, *A Manual of Hebrew Poetics*, 23. See also one of Casanowicz's more lasting contributions on "intentional and accidental congruence of sound," in *Paronomasia*, 27–8.

reinterpret the source language, continually spiraling forward towards the most precise interpretation possible.¹⁸² Within that hermeneutical spiral, this study is based on our current understanding of the translation technique of LXX Psalms and it seeks to use that characterization (the standard norms of the translator) to identify and evaluate rendering of wordplay into Greek. That analysis will then contribute to our growing understanding of the translation technique of the LXX Psalter.¹⁸³

The criteria for identifying Greek wordplay in the LXX is similar but also has its own set of parameters. Because the LXX translator had the challenge of trying to represent a wordplay in another language, and because we are primarily concerned with his recognition of that wordplay and attempt to render it with any type of similar poetic artistry, the criteria used for identifying wordplay will differ slightly when evaluating a potential wordplay attempt in the translation. First, while single-letter alliteration did not constitute as wordplay for the analysis of the Hebrew text, it will be considered as potential recognition or rendering of wordplay in the LXX, particularly when used with other markers of wordplay. Second, the criteria of proximity of words in play applies also to wordplay in the LXX, with the added guideline that the wordplay represented in the LXX needs to be close in proximity to the wordplay in the Hebrew. Often, the LXX translator could not represent the MT wordplay using the exact same words, so he would make a similar wordplay with adjacent words or even lines. In order to distinguish rendered wordplay from independent wordplay, the source wordplay and target wordplay must be no farther away than an adjacent line. The contextual marks for identifying Hebrew wordplays (e.g., irregular syntax or vocabulary, multiple wordplays working together, structural connections, and a discernable function of the wordplay) will also help to guide the identification of wordplay in the LXX.

Perhaps the most important methodological principle when factoring the LXX translator's rendering of Hebrew wordplay is the distinction between standard translation technique and deviations from that norm. Standard translation technique refers to what the translator of a given book typically did. These patterns include whether or not he was

---

182. Olofsson, *The LXX Version*, 65. Olofsson argues that complete reconstruction of any LXX book's *Vorlage* is still out of reach because too many unknown factors remain (67).

183. Similarly, Pietersma ("Septuagint Research: A Plea for a Return to Basic Issues," 299) argues that a thorough understanding of translation technique is an essential precursor to questions of origin and provenance, an insight that he credits to Soisalon-Soininen.

consistent in using the same Greek words to render the same Hebrew words, and whether or not he typically followed the syntax of the Hebrew when possible. Standard translation equivalents that appear to be creating a wordplay might be sheer chance. However, if a translator typically used one Greek lexeme for a particular Hebrew term, straying from this pattern may be a mark of his acknowledgment of the wordplay and an attempt at his own. Also, did the translator employ literary devices in the target language independent from the source language or did he attempt rendering the literary devices extant in the source text?

Another key factor is the element of choice: Did the translator have another semantic or grammatical option that he could have chosen?[184] Another indicator of potential wordplay in the LXX includes the use of transformations, which shows that the translator had to make choices that resulted in alterations in order to represent the poetic device of wordplay. In each case, these factors will need to be evaluated and weighted.

Jan Joosten argues that the case for intentional use of a stylistic flourish must be confirmed by two things: (1) the text must deviate in some way from the Hebrew *Vorlage* (that is, it cannot be a literal rendering of the source language), and (2) deviations made in order to conform to the conventions of Greek do not constitute a non-literal translation.[185] Still, there are some strong examples of wordplay in the Greek that do not meet these criteria and should nonetheless be included in the analysis for the reader to evaluate and to display the full spectrum of the translation techniques of the LXX translator. Therefore, we will provide a rating system (similar to that given to the Hebrew wordplays) that will measure the strength of the LXX wordplay rendering. A rating of 1 denotes a strong or sure rendering of the Hebrew wordplay, a rating of 2 will be given to renderings with a moderate amount of certainty, and a rating of 3 is reserved for weak renderings or representations of wordplay that might otherwise be strong, but do not vary from the translation norms.

It is also important to safeguard against the creation of false positives in the LXX translation of MT wordplay. If the LXX is replete with wordplays throughout, and if the translator used wordplay in the Greek where it does not appear in the Hebrew, then the correlations argued for in this study might be merely coincidental. However, the translator seldom uses wordplay independently from where it is found in the MT, and a strong majority of the LXX overall use of wordplay is used to render the phenomenon in the MT.

184. Olofsson, *The LXX Version*, 14.
185. Jan Joosten, "Rhetorical Ornamentation in the Septuagint: The Case of Grammatical Variation," in Bons and Kraus, ed., *Et Sapienter et Eloquenter*, 16.

The following table shows the total distribution of LXX wordplay in comparison to the distribution of wordplay in the MT:

Table 1. LXX Wordplay Translation Compared with
LXX Overall Wordplay (WP) Use

Psalm	Total MT WP	Total LXX WP	LXX Rendering of MT WP	LXX WP Excluding MT WP	% of LXX WP Used to Render MT WP
90	14	5	5	0	100
91	8	2	2	0	100
92	2	2	2	0	100
93	2	0	0	0	N/A
94	4	2	1	1	50
95	3	2	1	1	50
96	3	2	2	0	100
97	4	3	3	0	100
98	0	0	0	0	N/A
99	0	0	0	0	N/A
100	0	0	0	0	N/A
101	1	1	1	0	100
102	10	2	1	1	50
103	3	0	0	0	N/A
104	5	3	2	1	66.6
105	4	4	0	4	0
106	11	4	4	0	100
Total Number of WPs	74	32	24	8	
Percentage			32.4	25.0	75.0
Total Number of WPs Excluding Ps. 105	70	28	24	4	
Percentage Excluding Ps. 105			34.3	14.3	85.7

Notice that 75 percent of wordplays in the LXX are used to render wordplay in the MT, leaving only 25 percent of the total LXX wordplays independent from the MT wordplays. Independent wordplays are not surprising, given the translator's aptitude for the poetic device, and their scarcity (eight total in the entire corpus) supports the thesis that the LXX translator was indeed attempting to represent the trope in his source text.

Of these eight independent wordplays, half (four) are found in Psalm 105, where, moreover, the translator did not represent any of the Hebrew wordplays. This makes Psalm 105 a bit of an anomaly for Book IV, which is why the final two rows in the table calculate the data without respect to Psalm 105. If Psalm 105 is considered an outlier, statistically speaking, the data is even more convincing: 85.7 percent of the LXX wordplays are used to render MT wordplay, and only 14.3 percent (four total) are unrelated to the Hebrew wordplay.

The proportion of Greek wordplays used to render Hebrew wordplays is even more striking considering that the 75 percent of the Greek wordplay used to render Hebrew wordplay is condensed in only 25 percent of Book IV, i.e., the number of verses utilizing wordplay in the Hebrew. This following graph illustrates this distribution:

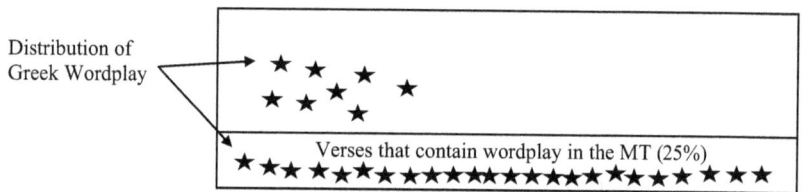

Taking Psalm 105 as a statistical outlier, the proportions are even more dramatic:

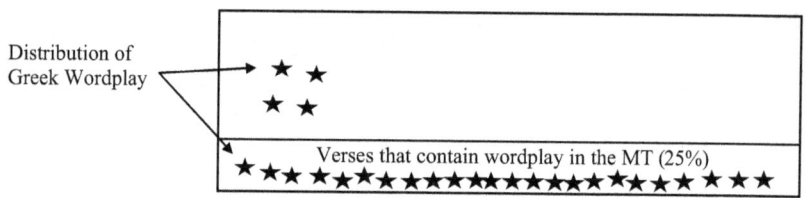

These data show a clear correlation between wordplay in the MT and the LXX, confirming that most wordplay in the LXX are used to render the phenomenon in the MT.

Even with these guidelines for identifying wordplays, both in the Hebrew and the Greek, it is important to remember that the line between true and contrived wordplay is not always clear. According to Catherine Bates, "the difference is one of degree but not of kind."[186] Of course, one must be careful not to create wordplays where none exist. Just as a cloud-gazer can see all sorts of fanciful figures in a cloudy sky, so too

---

186. Bates, "The Point of Puns," 432. Bates adds, "When it comes to deciding whether a pun is a pun or whether it is a good one or not, it seems to be less a matter of hard and fast rules than of how far a particular reader is prepared to go in giving scope to the suggestiveness of language—of the interpretive gamble he or she is willing to take" (432).

we must be cautious against seeing what is not there, and distinguishing constructions of our own imagination from the reality of the text. The recognition of wordplay is often dependent upon one's interpretative style; some readers are willing to be riskier and occasionally create their own "wordplays," whereas other readers may be safer and occasionally overlook or deny true wordplays. While ideal readers need to be careful not to say more than Scripture, they also must not say less than Scripture. Catherine Bates points out that a particularly important advantage of the "risky" interpreter is that he or she "knows the nature of the market better," and "may in the end be better at playing the game."[187] J. J. M. Roberts likewise encourages openness in his study on *double entendres* in First Isaiah, saying, "While one must remain aware of the danger of overreading, however, it is far more likely that our lack of familiarity with the wider connotations of classical Hebrew words and phrases will result in underreading, of missing intentional *double entendres*."[188]

Wordplay also requires the cooperation of imagination and reason, for both the author and the reader. John Pollack describes the fruitfulness of this combination, saying,

> It's about freeing our imagination to leap from one idea to the next to the next, even when those leaps seem illogical or impossible.... Puns reveal a mind free to roam frontiers of possibility, without shame or fear of being wrong.[189]

Imagination frees the mind to discover the possibilities of wordplay, and reason enables the mind to evaluate and distinguish between these possibilities. The approach in this study will be a balance of risk and safety, and of imagination and reason. We will approach each potential wordplay openly, assuming authenticity until proven guilty and, after a thorough analysis, we will hopefully be able to distinguish possible wordplays from certain ones.

---

187. Ibid., 435.
188. J. J. M. Roberts, "Double Entendre in First Isaiah," *CBQ* 54 (1992): 40.
189. Pollack, *The Pun Also Rises*, 143.

Chapter 2

WRITING THE RIGHT WORDS: WORDPLAY WITHIN BOOK IV OF THE HEBREW PSALTER

In this chapter, we will analyze the wordplays employed in Book IV of the MT's Psalter, moving canonically through Psalms 90–106. We will describe and classify each wordplay and its function. A brief conclusion will help to synthesize the results and draw some initial conclusions before turning to the LXX's translation in the next chapter.

Wordplay in Psalm 90

Psalm 90 revels in wordplays, containing in its 17 verses more wordplays than any other psalm in Book IV and 40 percent of all polysemantic wordplays. The psalm also exhibits diversity in wordplay subcategories and contains several macro-structural and complex wordplays.

Psalm 90 opens and closes with one such macro-structured wordplay within the category of paronomasia, specifically a chiastic root letter transposition. Verse 1b opens by attesting to the Lord that he is Israel's dwelling place and v. 17a concludes with a supplication for the Lord to let his pleasantness be upon Israel:

אֲדֹנָי¹ מָעוֹן אַתָּה לָּנוּ   1b   Lord, you have been our dwelling place

[...]

וִיהִי נֹעַם אֲדֹנָי אֱלֹהֵינוּ עָלֵינוּ   17a   And let the pleasantness of the Lord our God be upon us!

1. A few Hebrew manuscripts read מָעוֹז ("refuge"), which some scholars believe to be the *Vorlage* of the LXX (καταφυγή) as well; see Willem VanGemeren, *Psalms*, The Expositor's Bible Commentary (Grand Rapids, MI: Zondervan, 2008), 690. However, מָעוֹן is often used to refer to the dwelling place of God (e.g. Deut. 26:15;

The vocative אֲדֹנָי is repeated in reverse order (first and then second), and the consonants for מָעוֹן ("dwelling place") and נֹעַם ("pleasantness") are all in reversed, chiastic order.[2] Even the vowels are nearly identical, viz., a defective spelling of the holem waw replacing the plene spelling in v. 1, and a shift from a long "a" class vowel (qamats) to a short "a" class vowel (patach). This wordplay serves a structural function, creating a thematic frame for the psalm. It also draws attention to the pleasantness of the Lord as Israel's dwelling place, themes that will continue into Psalm 91.

In Ps. 90:3ab, the psalmist uses the verb שׁוּב twice in two different stems (Hiphil and Qal) and thus with two slightly different meanings:

תָּשֵׁב אֱנוֹשׁ עַד־דַּכָּא	3a	You return a mortal to dust,
וַתֹּאמֶר שׁוּבוּ בְנֵי־אָדָם	3b	And you say, "Return, O sons of humanity!"

These lines could be interpreted as being synonymously parallel, where the mortal described as being returning to the dust in his grave is also commanded to return to that death.[3] Some scholars, however, believe that these meanings are different enough to constitute antithetical parallelism between the lines, the first with the sense of returning to dust in death, and the second with the sense of returning to life. Hossfeld argues that the lines could be synonymous or synthetic, citing Eccl. 1:4 as a parallel:

Jer. 25:30; Ps. 68:6), which fits the context well; see Marvin E. Tate, *Psalms 51–100*, WBC 20 (Nashville: Thomas Nelson, 1990), 432; cf. Hans-Joachim Kraus, *Psalms 60–150: A Commentary*, 2 vols. (Minneapolis: Augsburg, 1989), 2:213. The *inclusio* wordplay explains the author's choice of words, which in turn marks the wordplay.

Some scholars also note paronomasia between מָעוֹן and עֲוֹנֹתֵינוּ ("our iniquities") in 90:8a, emphasizing that Israel's iniquities stood before God's dwelling place, or presence (John Goldingay, *Psalms: Psalms 90–150*, Baker Commentary on the Old Testament: Wisdom and Psalms [Grand Rapids, MI: Baker, 2008], 3:29; cf. S. D. Goitein, "'Ma'on'—A Reminder of Sin," *JSS* 10 [1965]: 52–3). Tate (*Psalms*, 432) also notes that a play on words here is possible. Although it is possible, it seems improbable and is not included in this study because the words are distant, share only one syllable, and the function is not convincing.

2. Dahood, *Psalms*, 322; Hossfeld and Zenger, *Psalms*, 2:419.

3. I use the term "synonymous" with some assumed nuance, as no two lines are truly synonymous anymore than any two lexemes are truly synonyms. However, the term is helpful insofar as it emphasizes the correspondence in similarity between the two lines. Kugel famously describes two parallel lines thus: "A is so, and *what's more*, B is so," arguing that the categories of synonymous and antithetical are misleadingly simplistic and limiting, and the category of synthetic parallelism became an imprecise catch-all,; see James Kugel, *The Idea of Biblical Poetry: Parallelism and Its History* (Baltimore: The Johns Hopkins University Press, 1981), see especially pp. 7–15.

> Der hebräische Text in V. 3 kann im synonymen Parallelismus als Ausdruck des Todesschicksals oder im synthetischen Parallelismus als Wechsel der Generationen im Stile von Koh 1,4 (eine Generation geht, eine andere kommt) interpretiert warden.[4]

If the lines are synonymously parallel and if both uses of שׁוב refer to man's passive or active return to non-life, there is still a shift in perspective. Whereas the first line describes the action, almost from a neutral or detached standpoint, the second stiche gives the reader a close-up view of God's active imperative, thus sharpening God's sovereign power over the lives of humanity and intensifying the perlocutionary effect. If so, this would be an example of what Robert Alter calls "anaphora," which is a type of "intensification" between two parallel lines.[5] However, this is a very mild intensification and arguably too redundant even for synonymous parallelism; it makes for no amplification or explication or further nuance in the second line, which is customary in parallelism.[6] This is more likely an example (albeit not the most convincing example) of a polysemantic punning repetition with the effect of heightening the contrast between God's ability to both end and restore life.

Two paronomastic wordplays in the macro-structure of Psalm 90 create a complex, chiastic wordplay in vv. 4 and 6:

כִּי אֶלֶף שָׁנִים בְּעֵינֶיךָ	4a	For a thousand years in your eyes
כְּיוֹם אֶתְמוֹל כִּי יַעֲבֹר	4b	[Are] like a day, yesterday, when it passes,
וְאַשְׁמוּרָה בַלָּיְלָה	4c	And like a watch in the night.
זְרַמְתָּם שֵׁנָה יִהְיוּ	5a	You swept them away [while] they were sleeping.
בַּבֹּקֶר כֶּחָצִיר יַחֲלֹף	5b	In the morning [they are] like grass being renewed.
בַּבֹּקֶר יָצִיץ וְחָלָף	6a	In the morning, it flourishes and is renewed
לָעֶרֶב יְמוֹלֵל וְיָבֵשׁ	6b	Until evening, it withers and dries up.

---

4. Frank-Lothar Hossfeld, "Akzentsetzungen der Septuagint aim vierten Psalmenbuch: Ps 90–106 (Ps 89–105 bzw. 106 LXX)," in Zenger, ed., *Der Septuaginta-Psalter*, 167. Hossfeld continues by explaining how the reader's interpretation of two different senses for שׁוב complement his interpretation of the entire psalm as a petition. Cf., Hossfeld and Zenger, *Psalms*, 2:417; Westermann, *The Living Psalms* (Edinburgh: T&T Clark, 1989), 160–1.
   5. Alter, *Art of Biblical Poetry*, 64.
   6. Kugel, *The Idea of Biblical Poetry*, 57.

The repetition of the letters מוֹל in the noun אֶתְמוֹל ("yesterday") in v. 4 and in the verb יְמוֹלֵל ("it withers") in v. 6 account for more than half of the words, and both words contain four consonants (plus the holem waw) and are relatively rare in the Old Testament (occurring eight and four times, respectively). The inclusion of אֶתְמוֹל is superfluous to the meter and even to the meaning of v. 4.[7] The wordplay between אֶתְמוֹל and יְמוֹלֵל has the effect of drawing a connection between the short-lived nature of a passing day (yesterday) and the withering of man's life, further highlighting man's transience in light of God's eternality. The word pair is separated by four intervening lines, and the three shared phonemes only constitute one closed syllable, which should caution us against identifying this wordplay with any certainty.

That said, there is structural and thematic significance to the separation, and two additional word pairs in chiastic arrangement, which draw attention to and support the wordplay between אֶתְמוֹל and יְמוֹלֵל. Structurally, vv. 3-6 comprise a stanza, and within that stanza vv. 4-6 expand on v. 3, which describes the Lord's sovereignty in returning man to dust, thus beginning the contrast between the Lord's eternality and man's transient existence.[8] Verse 4 begins with an asseverative, attesting to the certainty of what follows, namely a description of how fleeting are one's years from God's perspective, comparing humanity's life to grass that quickly flourishes and then withers just as quickly.[9] The placement of this word pair at the beginning and end (v. 4b and v. 6b) of this expansion draws attention to the sound correspondence and underscores the structure as well.

An additional wordplay between the verb יַעֲבֹר ("it passes") and the prepositional phrase לָעֶרֶב ("until evening"), works in tandem with the first, creating a chiasm. Aside from the verbal preformative in יַעֲבֹר and

---

7. In this study, meter is understood according to the stress theory of meter advocated by Watson, *Classical Hebrew Poetry*, 97–103.

8. VanGemeren interprets vv. 3-6 as a unified stanza concerned with "God's authority over people" (*Psalms*, 691). By contrast, see John Goldingay, *Psalms*, 3:20, who considers vv. 1-5 a stanza and vv. 6-12 a separate stanza, thus dividing vv. 5-6, which seems particularly odd considering the linking words and themes (בקר and חלף) and that the antecedent of the verbs in v. 6 is the grass in v. 5.

9. For the asseverative or emphatic use of כִּי, see Ronald J. Williams, *Hebrew Syntax: An Outline*, 2nd ed. (Toronto: University of Toronto Press, 1976), §449; Paul Joüon, *A Grammar of Biblical Hebrew*, trans. and rev. T. Muraoka (Rome: Pontificio Istituto Biblico, 2005), §164b-c; Ludwig Koehler and Walter Baumgartner, *HALOT*, Study Edition (Leiden: Brill, 2001), 470. A causal use of the particle is also possible (see most English translations) but the preceding line does not want for a reason; as such, the emphatic use should be preferred.

preposition in לָעֶרֶב, the roots of these words contain the same exact consonants, with the ultimate and penultimate consonants transposed, making this a striking example of root letter transposition. Again, this wordplay draws attention to things that pass quickly in vv. 4b and 6b. Both lines are metaphors for the passing of something. In v. 4b, it is the passing of time in God's eyes that is likened to a fleeting day. What seems like an eternity to us is a passing day to an eternal God. In v. 6b, the lifespan of man and woman (70 or 80 years, 90:10ab) is likened to the short life of grass, again using the figure of a day. These two metaphors, and the corresponding wordplays, emphasize that time and life pass differently for humanity, who are nothing in comparison to their immortal, eternal God.

The third word pair in this chiasm is between the contrasting words בַּלַּיְלָה ("in the night") and בַּבֹּקֶר ("in the morning"), which have identical prefixed prepositions and are linked through chiasm in the structure of the stanza.[10] This third word pair is not a wordplay, but it works within the complex wordplay to enhance its effectiveness and solidify its identification.

Another occurrence of wordplay in Psalm 90 is with the words וְחָלָף ("and is renewed") and וְיָבֵשׁ ("and dries up"), which each conclude the two lines of v. 6.

    בַּבֹּקֶר יָצִיץ וְחָלָף   6a   In the morning, it flourishes and is renewed

    לָעֶרֶב יְמוֹלֵל וְיָבֵשׁ   6b   Until evening, it withers and dries up.

This is a case of polysemantic *double entendre* followed by polysematic implicit paronomasia. The first lexeme חָלָף most clearly refers to the renewal of the grass in the morning, but it can also mean "to transgress."[11]

---

10. Because of the repetition of בַּבֹּקֶר in vv. 5b and 6a, some commentators claim that the word's use in v. 6a is due to dittography. Kraus (*Psalms*, 2:213) suggests that an additional mention of שָׁנָה ("year") in v. 5a was omitted due to haplography, and that the copulative יִהְיוּ should begin the second colon (despite the atnach marking its place as the final word in the colon) and that בַּבֹּקֶר is thus extraneous to the meter of the second line. Such emendation, however, would not alter the effectiveness of this wordplay since בַּלַּיְלָה would still correspond with בַּבֹּקֶר in v. 5b.

11. As noted above, some scholars identify a paronomastic wordplay here between עֹנוֹתֵינוּ and מָעוֹן in v. 1; see Goldingay, *Psalms*, 3:29; Goitein, "'Ma'on'—A Reminder of Sin," 52–3. However, because the similarity is only between the closed syllable עֹן, and because the words are greatly separated, it seems unlikely that this is an intentional wordplay. Goitein's argument that the purpose of such a wordplay is to identify God's dwelling place as a place for sin is also far-fetched, especially since that theme is absent in this psalm. Tate also rejects Goitein's interpretation, and

The primary sense of the second lexeme יָבֵשׁ is also its primary sense in this verse, describing how that same grass dries up by evening. However, the consonantal text can also mean "to be ashamed" (from בושׁ). If חָלַף is functioning as a *double entendre*, alluding to the transgression of humanity, its function in parallel with יָבֵשׁ suggests that just as the vibrant, renewed grass flourishes for a short time and then dries up and dies, so also it is not long before the transgressor is ashamed by his short-lived rebellion. The author is thus using implicit (metaphonic) paronomasia (between וְיָבֵשׁ and the alluded-to וַיֵּבֹשׁ) in addition to a polysemantic word play (between the two uses of חלף). The fact that this complex wordplay serves a clear theological function, along with the fact that these verbs occur in grammatical parallelism, supports the identification of this word pair as wordplay.

Verses 7-10 form the following stanza, and the poet uses several linking words to bind the stanza together. For example, the repetition of the verb כלה in vv. 7a and 9b forms an *inclusio* around that section. The nominal יוֹם is repeated in vv. 9a and 10a, linking v. 10 with the preceding lines. The poet also uses a paronomastic wordplay between פָּנֶיךָ ("your presence") and פָּנוּ ("turn") in vv. 8b and 9a to further bind together this central portion of the stanza:

שַׁתָּ עֲוֹנֹתֵינוּ לְנֶגְדֶּךָ [12]	8a	You set our iniquities before you,
עֲלֻמֵנוּ לִמְאוֹר פָּנֶיךָ	8b	Our hidden [sins] in the light of your presence.
כִּי כָל־יָמֵינוּ פָּנוּ בְעֶבְרָתֶךָ	9a	Indeed, all of our days turn in your rage.

The prepositional phrase פָּנֶיךָ is of course very common and expected in its context, but the verb פנה is not expected in the context of ending one's years, especially when the poet had at his disposal other, seemingly more appropriate words, such as תמם and חדל. This is supported by the fact that the LXX uses a common word for "finish" (ἐκλείπω) to translate פָּנוּ. Also, each of the four lines in vv. 8-9 contains three primary accents, except for v. 9a, which ends in בְעֶבְרָתֶךָ, immediately following פָּנוּ. It seems that the

---

agrees that the words are not etymologically derived, but he considers the wordplay possible (*Psalms*, 432). If any wordplay exists, it seems most likely that עֲוֹנֹתֵינוּ in v. 8 is alluding back to v. 1 (rather than the other way around), especially since it is parallel with the unique use of עֲלֻמֵנוּ ("our hidden [sins]"). The effect would be to suggest that our iniquities (v. 8a), like the sins that we try to hide (v. 8b), are a sorry "dwelling place" compared to the dwelling place (מָעוֹן) of the Lord (v. 1b).

12. *HALOT* (321) does not list this sense, but BDB (322) includes it, citing Isa. 24:5, where it is semantically parallel with רבע.

author may be attempting to use the alliteration of פָּנֶיךָ and פָּנוּ not only to link these verses, but also to highlight this additional word, and to show that God's wrath is the cause of man's transience.

Verses 9-11 present another interesting combination of key words in a three-fold case of parasonancy between בְעֶבְרָתֶךָ ("in your rage"), בִּגְבוּרֹת ("with strength"), and עֶבְרָתֶךָ ("your rage") in vv. 9a, 10b, and 11b, respectively:

כִּי כָל־יָמֵינוּ פָּנוּ בְעֶבְרָתֶךָ	9a	For all of our days turn in your rage.
כִּלִּינוּ שָׁנֵינוּ כְמוֹ־הֶגֶה	9b	We finish our years like a sigh.
יְמֵי־שְׁנוֹתֵינוּ בָהֶם שִׁבְעִים שָׁנָה	10a	The days of our years, in them are seventy years,
וְאִם בִּגְבוּרֹת שְׁמוֹנִים שָׁנָה	10b	Or, if with strength, eighty years.
וְרָהְבָּם עָמָל וָאָוֶן	10c	Yet their extent is toil and sorrow,
כִּי־גָז חִישׁ וַנָּעֻפָה	10d	For it quickly passes and we fly away.
מִי־יוֹדֵעַ עֹז אַפֶּךָ	11a	Who knows the strength of your anger?
וּכְיִרְאָתְךָ עֶבְרָתֶךָ	11b	And, according to the fear due to you, your rage?

Both lexemes and all three words share a ר, ב, and ת, and the first two share an additional initial ב, which supports the identification of the wordplay, along with the fact that בִּגְבוּרֹת is bracketed by two uses of the noun עֶבְרָה, both of which conclude their respective lines. This paronomastic parasonancy contrasts man's feeble strength in years and God's immense strength in his rage.

We mentioned above that vv. 9-10 are linked by the common use of יוֹם. The construct noun is unnecessary for clarity or meter in v. 10a, but links vv. 9-10 and creates a wordplay with the following line (10b):

יְמֵי־שְׁנוֹתֵינוּ בָהֶם שִׁבְעִים שָׁנָה	10a	The days of our years, in them are seventy years,
וְאִם בִּגְבוּרֹת שְׁמוֹנִים שָׁנָה	10b	Or, if with strength, eighty years.

The expression יְמֵי־שְׁנוֹתֵינוּ ("the days of our years") and the word שְׁמוֹנִים ("eighty") share the letters ו, נ, מ, שׁ, and י. This alliterative wordplay serves an aesthetic function of contributing poetic beauty and interest to the couplet, which is supported by the five-fold alliterative repetition of the שׁ, and also binds the two lines together, along with the common vocabulary.

The use שָׁנָה at the end of both lines, for example, is superfluous, but adds to the combination of šin plus a labial (mem and nun).

The next line offers an example of polysemy:

וְרָהְבָּם עָמָל וָאָוֶן   10c   Yet their extent is toil and sorrow,

The first word וְרָהְבָּם is a textual difficulty. The sense of "and their extent" fits the context, yet this meaning would be a *hapax* in the Old Testament for רהב. Many commentators and most of the English versions read with the emended וְרֻבָּם ("and their extent"), as the editors of *BHS* recommend, and as the translation above reflects.[13] The common meaning of the nominal רהב is "pride," and the verbal form of the root ranges in meaning from "acting arrogantly" to "storming against" in the Qal.[14] Given that the emended text best fits the context, the word וְרֻבָּם might be alluding to the similar form of רהב (which at some point made it into the textual tradition!) asserting that the arrogant are nothing but toil and short-lived.[15] There is no question that polysemy is at work. However, rather than *double entendre* (which plays between two meanings of the same word) this is an example of implicit paronomasia because the secondary meaning is associated with a word that sounds very much like the word explicitly stated in the text. Paronomastic wordplays are generally explicit, involving two or more words within the text that sound or look similar. In this case, the similar word is only alluded to by the poet.

Casanowicz identifies a wordplay between וָאָוֶן and עָמָל in this same verse (10c), identifying it as alliterative paronomasia, between the gutturals and qamats.[16] We will consider this an example of "light" alliteration, albeit not wordplay.

---

13. The NIV and ESV both read "their span," while the TNK has "best of them." Tate favors the versions describing the idea of the phrase as "the greater part of them" (*Psalms*, 435). The NAS and Kraus both maintain the MT's "pride," the latter rendering it "pageantry" (Kraus, *Psalms*, 2:213–14).

14. *HALOT* lists the interpretative possibilities, including "arrogant," "surging," and "the majority of them," though the latter is a result of emendation, 1193.

15. Even if the MT is retained, this would still be an example of wordplay between two different meanings of רהב, one primary meaning ("pageantry" or "extent"), and one implicit secondary meaning ("pride"), making it an example of *double entendre*. However, because I think that the evidence slightly favors the emended text, I will classify and tabulate it as polysemantic implicit parosonancy.

16. Casanowicz, *Paronomasia*, 30.

The next wordplay in Psalm 90 is in v. 12. The concluding words in each line, הוֹדַע ("teach" or "declare") and חָכְמָה ("wisdom"), create assonance:

לִמְנוֹת יָמֵינוּ כֵּן הוֹדַע   12a Therefore, teach [us] to number our days,

וְנָבִא לְבַב חָכְמָה   12b So that we may bring you a heart of wisdom.

The odd syntax in the first line supports the identification of this wordplay. First, the conjunction כֵּן ("therefore") most often precedes the clause it modifies.[17] Second, the imperative usually precedes the object.[18] Third, when the infinitive construct is used as a verbal complement, it typically follows that verb.[19] Moreover, the lines are not grammatically parallel, suggesting that the poet deliberately chose these words and arranged the syntax so as to alert the reader (or listener) to the wordplay.

The author also draws attention to the wordplay by using alliteration in both lines, first with the repetition of the letters מ and נ in יָמֵינוּ לִמְנוֹת ("to number our days"), and next with the letter ב in וְנָבִא לְבַב ("so that we may bring a heart"). The assonantal wordplay between הוֹדַע and חָכְמָה shows how the Lord alone teaches true wisdom and that without God's wisdom imparted to human hearts, their own endeavors are merely fleeting toils and sorrows (cf., v. 10). Thus, the phonetic connection between these lines underscores their causal relationship.

Scholars disagree, however, over the theological meaning of these lines, specifically what the psalmist means by "days" in v. 12a. The context of the psalm as a whole suggests that the expression "number our days" might refer to the brevity of life, contrasted with God's infinitude (these themes are central in vv. 2c, 4-6, 10).[20] However, according to Robert Clifford, the expression יָמֵינוּ לִמְנוֹת is used in Akkadian and Ugaritic not to denote the entirely of one's life, but to describe a distinct amount of time. Clifford therefore argues that the worshipping community is asking to know not

---

17. Bruce K. Waltke and M. O'Connor, *Introduction to Biblical Hebrew Syntax* (Winona Lake, IN: Eisenbrauns, 1990), §39.3.4c; Christo H. J. van der Merwe, Jackie A. Naudé, and Jan H. Kroeze, *A Biblical Hebrew Reference Grammar* (London: Sheffield Academic/Continuum, 2002), 338.

18. Although Biblical Hebrew typically uses a verb-object word order, deviation from this norm is not uncommon, especially in poetry, Adina M. Moshavi, *Word Order in the Biblical Hebrew Finite Clause: A Syntactic and Pragmatic Analysis of Preposing*, Linguistic Studies in Ancient West Semitic 4 (Winona Lake, IN: Eisenbrauns, 2010), 65.

19. Waltke and O'Connor, *Introduction*, §36.2.3b; §36.3.1.

20. E.g., VanGemeren, *Psalms*, 694.

how long they will live, but how long they will experience God's wrath.[21] The worshippers can only gain understanding if the Lord first teaches them how to count, or understand, their days (of life, or of affliction).

The following stanza is composed of vv. 13-16 and is linked by its use of initiating imperatives and sibilants in vv. 13-15 and result clauses in v. 14b and 16ab.[22] These verses are also connected by a complex wordplay, involving three wordplays, in vv. 14-16, the beginning of which marks the first result clause, and the end of which marks the second result clause. Two of the wordplays are cases of polysemantic punning repetition and the third wordplay is an example of paronomasia that serves to emphasize the final lines of this complex wordplay:

שׁוּבָה יְהוָה עַד־מָתָי	13a	Return, O Lord! How long?
וְהִנָּחֵם עַל־עֲבָדֶיךָ	13b	And have compassion upon your servants!
שַׂבְּעֵנוּ בַבֹּקֶר חַסְדֶּךָ	14a	Satisfy us in the morning with your lovingkindness,
וּנְרַנְּנָה [וְנִשְׂמְחָה] בְּכָל־יָמֵינוּ	14b	So that we may cry out and rejoice in all of our days!
[שַׂמְּחֵנוּ] כִּימוֹת עִנִּיתָנוּ	15a	Make us glad according to the days you afflicted us,
שְׁנוֹת רָאִינוּ רָעָה	15b	[The] years we saw evil,
יֵרָאֶה אֶל־עֲבָדֶיךָ פָעֳלֶךָ	16a	So that your deeds may be shown to your servants,
וַהֲדָרְךָ עַל־בְּנֵיהֶם	16b	And your splendor to their children!

The poet uses the same root for both word pairs, albeit in different stems and conjugations, and the word pairs are grammatically parallel. The first word pair, from the root שׂמח, shifts from a Qal cohortative ("that we may rejoice") to a Piel imperative ("make us glad!"), and from simple, intransitive action to transitive, fientive action. The second word pair, from the

---

21. Robert J. Clifford, "What Does the Psalmist Ask for in Psalms 39:5 and 90:12?," *JBL* 119 (2000): 65–6; cf. deClaissé-Walford et al., *Psalms*, 695–6.

22. VanGemeren, *Psalms*, 694. Verses 13-15 are also linked by their repeated emphasis on time, only instead of describing one's "days" as a "sigh," finished by God's rage (v. 9), the psalmist asks the Lord to return to him (rather than returning man to the dust [v. 3]) in pity, satisfying the psalmist in the morning (cf. vv. 5-6) so that the Lord may be worshiped throughout the psalmist's days. In the third couplet, the psalmist asks the Lord to make Israel glad "according to the days you afflicted us," redeeming the past for the future of worship.

root ראה, shifts from a Qal perfect ("we have seen") to a Niphal jussive ("let [your deeds] be shown"), and from the active voice to the passive. Both pairs shift to a volitional mode and both pairs link subsequent verses, occupying the penultimate word of the previous verse with the first word of the following verse. Because the author uses different stems with different senses, these word pairs qualify as polysemantic word play of punning repetition, specifically antanaclasis, or the repetition of the same root with different meanings.

The third wordplay between רָאִינוּ ("we saw"), רָעָה ("evil"), and יֵרָאֶה ("will be shown") is a case of paronomasia and further secures this wordplay as complex. The first two terms share a ר and qamats, the first and third (from the same root but in different modes) share a ר, qamats, and א, and the second and third share a ר, qamats, and ה. The function of this complex wordplay is primarily structural, to bind these verses and stanzas together, and aesthetic, much like the repeated sibilants in vv. 13-15 were used both structurally and aesthetically.

Wordplay in Psalm 91

Psalm 91 answers the laments and questions of Psalm 90 by offering reassurance of the Lord's protection against the many dangers that threaten humanity's brief existence. The usage of wordplay in Psalm 91 is similar to that of Psalm 90. Psalm 91 exhibits some of the features that also marked wordplay in Psalm 90, such as untypical syntax and the use of rare and unexpected words. Psalm 91 likewise uses patterning in complex wordplays (vv. 1-6, 11-13).

The psalm begins in v. 1 with a paronomastic wordplay:

יֹשֵׁב בְּסֵתֶר עֶלְיוֹן	1a	The one who dwells in the shelter of the Most High
בְּצֵל שַׁדַּי יִתְלוֹנָן	1b	Will abide in the shadow of the Almighty.

This play of alliteration and assonance is aesthetically appealing and reinforces the lineation, as both words complete the lines of the couplet. Their phonetic similarity and parallel structure also emphasize that the Most High (עֶלְיוֹן) is where the ideal reader and worshipper is to abide (יִתְלוֹנָן). The repetition of the ל, וֹ, and נ in the second syllable of each word, as well as the parallelism of the two words, supports the identification of this wordplay. The untypical syntax of the second line also suggests that the final word (יִתְלוֹנָן) is placed at the end of the line to create a parallel wordplay with עֶלְיוֹן. The syntax of the first line is subject (substantival participle) → preposition + absolute → construct. The syntax of the second line could more closely parallel the syntax of the preceding line and conform to typical verb-object syntax if it read יִתְלוֹנָן בְּצֵל שַׁדַּי ([subject] + verb → preposition + absolute → construct), but instead it ends with the verbal form, which draws attention to this word and places it in correspondence with עֶלְיוֹן.

The opening stanza of Psalm 91 also contains a complex, macro-structural wordplay:

יֹשֵׁב בְּסֵתֶר עֶלְיוֹן	1a	The one who dwells in the shelter of the Most High
בְּצֵל שַׁדַּי יִתְלוֹנָן	1b	Will abide in the shadow of the Almighty.
לַיהוָה מַחְסִי וּמְצוּדָתִי אֹמַר	2a	I will say to the Lord, "My refuge and my fortress,
אֱלֹהַי אֶבְטַח־בּוֹ	2b	My God in whom I trust!"
כִּי הוּא יַצִּילְךָ מִפַּח יָקוּשׁ	3a	For he is the one who will deliver you from the trap of the fowler,
[מִדֶּבֶר] הַוּוֹת	3b	From a deadly sting.
בְּאֶבְרָתוֹ יָסֶךְ לָךְ	4a	With his pinions he will cover you,
וְתַחַת־כְּנָפָיו תֶּחְסֶה	4b	And under his wings you will seek refuge.
צִנָּה וְסֹחֵרָה אֲמִתּוֹ	4c	His faithfulness is a surrounding shield and a buckler.
לֹא־תִירָא מִפַּחַד לָיְלָה	5a	You will not be afraid of the terror of night,
מֵחֵץ יָעוּף יוֹמָם	5b	[Nor] of the arrow that flies by day,
[מִדֶּבֶר] בָּאֹפֶל יַהֲלֹךְ	6a	[Nor] of the plague that walks in the darkness,
מִקֶּטֶב יָשׁוּד צָהֳרָיִם	6b	[Nor] of the destruction that destroys at midday.

This abc-abc pattern suggests that all three word pairs are to be interpreted together. The first word pair is a paronomastic wordplay between בְּסֵתֶר ("in the shelter") in v. 1a and וְסֹחֵרָה ("and a surrounding shield") in v. 4c. Because only one letter is changed between the words (or between the roots, more specifically), this is an example of parasonancy. In addition to the shared consonants, this word pair is marked as a wordplay by the fact that סֹחֵרָה is a *hapax legomenon* with the probable meaning of "rampart" or "surrounding shield,"[23] when the author could have used

---

23. Goldingay, *Psalms*, 3:38; Keith N. Schoville, "סחרה," *NIDOTTE* 3:243; A. A. Macintosh, "Psalm XCI 4 and the Root *shr*," *VT* 23 (1973): 52–62. Based on cognates in Syriac and Akkadian that mean "fortress" and "surrounding" respectively,

more common words for the same (e.g., מָגֵן, which is also paired with צִנָּה in Ps. 35:2: מָגֵן וְצִנָּה). This wordplay connects the initial claim of the Most High being a shelter with the imagery of his faithfulness being a shield, a protective shelter for the one who dwells in him.

The second word pair is again linked through the use of parasonancy: מִפַּח ("from the fowler's trap") in v. 3a and מִפַּחַד ("[from] the terror")[24] in v. 5a. Despite the four intervening cola, the repetition of three consonants (מ-פ-ח) in the same order is striking. The use of the inseparable form of the preposition מִן in both the phrases יָקוּשׁ מִפַּח ("from [the] trap of [the] fowler") in v. 3a and לַיְלָה מִפַּחַד ("of [the] terror of night") in v. 5 further strengthens this wordplay. In v. 3, מִפַּח is the first in a series of two things from which the Lord will deliver the one who takes refuge in him. Verse 4 expands on this idea. Verse 5 is grammatically and thematically parallel to v. 3 and again offers the first of two direct objects, this time specifying what the faithful need not fear when they take refuge in the Lord.

The repetition of מִדֶּבֶר in vv. 3b and 6a contributes a third word pair to the pattern. There is compelling evidence to suggest that this example is more than key word repetition and that the words are actually homonyms, identical in appearance, but differing in meaning.[25] The two possible senses for דֶּבֶר include (1) a type of "sting" or "thorn," sometimes referring to the sting of death (Hos. 13:14);[26] and (2) "plague."[27] The first sense fits the context in v. 3, that the Lord delivers "from the sting of destruction,"

HALOT (750) lists only the sense of "wall" for Ps. 9:14 and mentions its parallel with צִנָּה; Erich Zenger suggests "protecting wall" in Frank-Lothar Hossfeld and Erich Zenger, *Psalms 2: A Commentary on Psalms 51–100*, ed. Klaus Baltzer, Hermeneia (Minneapolis: Fortress, 2005), 430; see also Kraus, *Psalms*, 2:223. Tate (*Psalms*, 448) interprets the collocation וְסֹחֵרָה צִנָּה as a hendiadys, translating it "shield of protection." The LXX may have interpreted it as a feminine participle modifying the noun (ὅπλῳ κυκλώσει).

24. Mitchell Dahood identifies פחד with a Ugaritic cognate meaning "pack," and thus interpreting the phrase as "a pack of dogs at night" (*Psalms I: 1–50, Introduction, Translation, and Notes*, AB [Garden City, NY: Doubleday, 1996], 331), which finds few if any modern supporters.

25. As mentioned above, homonyms are difficult to distinguish from polysemous words in Hebrew, and thus the former is classified as polysemy, irrespective of its etymology.

26. K. Lawson Younger, "דֶּבֶר," *NIDOTTE* 1:916; *HALOT* 212; Hossfeld and Zenger, *Psalms*, 2:427.

27. R. K. Harrison, "דֶּבֶר," *NIDOTTE* 1:915; *HALOT* 212. Several manuscripts read דָּבָר ("word" or "a deadly word") and some commentators follow suit; however, within the context of threatening dangers, the MT should not be emended. See VanGemeren, *Psalms*, 698.

whereas the second sense best fits the context of v. 6, that plague would stalk one in darkness. This sense fits the context well because the word is parallel with the following fear in v. 6b: "destruction" (קֶטֶב). If so, this wordplay would be an example of punning repetition. If, however, this word pair is better understood as turn or repetition, and not wordplay, its repetition in the abc-abc pattern reinforces the previous wordplay and adds two more things from which the Lord will deliver the worshipper and from which he/she need not fear.

The first and second stanzas of Psalm 91 are linked through parasonancy in vv. 6-7:

מִדֶּבֶר בָּאֹפֶל יַהֲלֹךְ	6a	[Nor] of the plague that walks in the darkness,
מִקֶּטֶב יָשׁוּד צָהֳרָיִם	6b	[Nor] of the destruction that destroys at midday.
יִפֹּל מִצִּדְּךָ אֶלֶף	7a	A thousand will fall from your side,
וּרְבָבָה מִימִינֶךָ	7b	And ten thousand from your right hand.
אֵלֶיךָ לֹא יִגָּשׁ	7c	To you they will not come near.

All three words share a פ and ל, and additionally two share either a defective holem or an א. The author also chose a far less common word for darkness (אֹפֶל, which occurs only nine times in the Old Testament) when he could have used a much more common word (חֹשֶׁךְ, which occurs 98 times). The graphic chiasm between the aleph and lamed in אֵלֶיךָ and לֹא in v. 7c reinforces this wordplay, as well as the repetition of shared phonemes in v. 7c (אֵלֶיךָ and לֹא). The effect of this parasonancy (אֹפֶל and יִפֹּל) on the surface level and root letter transposition (אֹפֶל and אֶלֶף) on the deep level is both aesthetic and structural, linking the final lines of the first stanza (v. 6) with the first lines of the second stanza (v. 7).

In v. 9, עֶלְיוֹן is again mentioned as a title for the Lord, and the retrospective reader will remember the similar wordplay in v. 1. However, instead of occurring as the object of the verb יִתְלוֹנָן ("he will abide"), עֶלְיוֹן is paired with a nominal form of abiding (מָעוֹן), creating alliteration. Both words share the three letters ע, ו, and נ, all in the same order:

כִּי־אַתָּה יְהוָה מַחְסִי	9a	For you, O Lord, are my refuge.
עֶלְיוֹן שַׂמְתָּ מְעוֹנֶךָ	9b	The Most High you have set [as] your dwelling place.

The syntax of v. 9a is particularly difficult. One could interpret the second person pronoun (אַתָּה) as a vocative, referring to the Lord (as translated above) or as a charge to the reader ("[If/Because] you [make] the Lord your refuge").[28] The latter option requires an emendation of מחסי to מחסך, and it also requires the verb of v. 9b to be implied in v. 9a. The meaning of v. 9b is likewise difficult and could be a conditional clause addressed to the reader ("[If] you make the Most High your refuge"), with the vv. 10-13 functioning as the apodosis of the statement, enumerating the various rewards of protection that come to those who make the Most High God their refuge. It could also be interpreted as a statement of fact, either with the Lord or the reader as the subject of שַׂמְתָּ.[29] The sense is quite different, but the translation above retains the ambiguity of the Hebrew.

The function of the wordplay depends largely on how one understands the syntax of these lines. It seems most natural to interpret a shift in addressee from the Lord in v. 9a to the reader/worshipper in v. 9b, in which case the wordplay serves a similar function to the wordplay in v. 1 between עֶלְיוֹן ("Most High") and יִתְלוֹנָן ("he will abide"), namely to draw an association between the two words, emphasizing that worshippers should seek the Most High as their dwelling place.

The next wordplay in Psalm 91 is a complex wordplay comprised of two alternating word pairs that conclude the main, central section of the poem (vv. 3-13). One pair builds on the root דרך, used first nominally דְּרָכֶיךָ, "your ways" (v. 11b), and then verbally תִּדְרֹךְ, "you will tread" (v. 13a), making it an example of root play. The second pair is comprised of the parasonantic words כַּפַּיִם ("[on their] hands," v. 12a) and כְּפִיר ("young lion," v. 13b), which differ in only one letter:

כִּי מַלְאָכָיו יְצַוֶּה־לָּךְ	11a	For he commands his angels for your sake,
לִשְׁמָרְךָ בְּכָל־דְּרָכֶיךָ	11b	To guard you in all of your ways.
עַל־כַּפַּיִם יִשָּׂאוּנְךָ	12a	On their hands they will carry you,
פֶּן־תִּגֹּף בָּאֶבֶן רַגְלֶךָ	12b	Lest you strike your foot on a stone.
עַל־שַׁחַל וָפֶתֶן תִּדְרֹךְ	13a	Upon the lion and the cobra you will tread.
תִּרְמֹס כְּפִיר וְתַנִּין	13b	You will trample the young lion and the serpent.

These word pairs are not merely staggered; the words in the first word pair conclude the lines immediately preceding the words in the second word pair, both of which constitute the second position of their respective

---

28. So Dahood, *Psalms II*, 333.
29. Tate (*Psalms*, 447–8) retains the MT in v. 9a and interprets v. 9b as a conditional clause.

lines.³⁰ In other words, the first of both word pairs are separated by only one word, and the second of both word pairs share this exact relationship, creating a parallelism. This complex wordplay, interspersing two wordplays in an alternating pattern, is reminiscent of the three-fold wordplay in vv. 1-6.

In addition to the patterning and similarity of the words, the author had at least nine other words for lion from which to choose, which helps to mark the use of כְּפִיר as wordplay.³¹ This complex wordplay has a structural effect, bookending what the faithful will be "upon" (עַל both times). First, she will be carried upon angels' hands (v. 12a), a powerful symbol of protection through trial. Second, she will trample upon the lion and the snake (v. 13), thus demonstrating the efficacy of being borne on angels' hands.

Wordplay in Psalm 92

In Psalm 92, the psalmist responds with thanksgiving to the Lord's promises in Psalm 91, thus uniting Psalms 90–92. In stark contrast to Psalms 90–91, however, Psalm 92 contains only two wordplays, both examples of paronomasia. The first is an implicit parasonancy marked by a rare word, while the second is a root letter play.

The first wordplay in Psalm 92 is a polysemantic implicit paronomasia in vv. 6b-7a:³²

מַה־גָּדְלוּ מַעֲשֶׂיךָ יְהוָה	6a	How great are your works, O Lord!
מְאֹד עָמְקוּ מַחְשְׁבֹתֶיךָ	6b	[How] very deep are your understandings!
אִישׁ־בַּעַר לֹא יֵדָע	7a	A brutish person does not know,
וּכְסִיל לֹא־יָבִין אֶת־זֹאת	7b	And a fool does not understand this.

30. The use of כַּפַּיִם in v. 12a is connected to the first word by a maqqef, making it the first, and not second, primary accent, but it is still the second word.

31. Robert C. Stallman, "אֲרִי," *NIDOTTE* 1:514.

32. Three poetic structures in Ps. 92 are near-wordplays, but do not contain the necessary marks of wordplay. Still, they deserve mention in order to prevent the misconception that because the psalm does not employ many wordplays, that it lacks poetic artistry. Three such cases deserve brief reference: (1) "light" alliteration (wherein only one consonant is repeated) in v. 2 that also serves to highlight and unite bracketing words (טוֹב and עֶלְיוֹן); (2) the leitmotif of the repeated verbal forms of פעל within the macrostructure of vv. 5-10, which is underscored by the three-fold repetition of the preposition עַל in v. 4; and (3) the repetition of verbal forms of פרח in vv. 8 and 13-14 to contrast the flourishing of the wicked and the righteous.

The break between these bicola mark the contrast between the Lord's works and understanding, and the works and understanding of the fool and the wicked. Verse 6b describes the Lord's understandings as "deep" (עָמְקוּ).[33] The following line states that the "brutish" or "ignorant" (בַּעַר) person does not know, or understand, a truth that the following line of synonymous parallelism underscores. The word for "brutish" or "ignorant" here (בַּעַר) is used only five times in the Old Testament, whereas other, more common words for foolish and ignorant abound (e.g., סכל, חלל, אֱוִיל, אִוֶּלֶת, or כְּסִיל [used in v. 7b]). Since the poet just mentioned the great depth of the Lord's understanding, and since he/she uses a rare word for ignorance, it seems likely that a very common near-homophone of בַּעַר may be implicitly alluded to here, namely, בְּאֵר, the noun for "well" or "pit," which occurs 47 times in the Old Testament.[34] If so, this is an example of implicit parasonancy or near-metaphony. In addition to the literal sense, in wisdom literature and the psalms בְּאֵר refers to a pit of corruption, according to Bryan E. Beyer, "a place from which one could not easily escape."[35] Thus, the depth of the Lord's understanding is contrasted with the depth (vastness) of the fool's lack of understanding. Another potential allusion is to another homophone, the verbal form of the root באר, which means "to explain, to elucidate (a law),"[36] resulting in a sarcastic play with the idea that the fool and brute without understanding could possibly explain that which they do not know.

---

33. According to Arnold A. Wieder, the meaning of עמק in this context may carry with it the Ugaritic meaning of the cognate 'mq and the Akkadian meaning of *emqu*, both of which have the sense of "strength" or "violence," "Ugaritic-Hebrew Lexicographical Notes," *JBL* 84 (1965): 160–4. This seems more probable in difficult passages wherein the attested Hebrew senses of the word עמק do not make sense, and it is possible here given that is parallel with גָּדְלוּ; however, "deep" is still an apt modifier of מַחְשְׁבֹתֶיךָ ("your understandings") and is thus to be preferred. Either way, the wordplay is still possible, since "deep" is a primary meaning of עמק and would readily come to the readers' minds.

34. בְּאֵר is related to the word בּוֹר, with the same meaning, which occurs 64 times in the Old Testament; see *HALOT* 106. While the sound correspondence between בּוֹר and בַּעַר is not as strong as that between בְּאֵר and בַּעַר, the fact that two words for "well/pit" sound very much like the word in the text (בַּעַר) only strengthens the likelihood that the poet's audience would call to mind this secondary meaning.

35. Beyer, "בְּאֵר" *NIDOTTE* 1:579.

36. *HALOT* 106.

Dahood identifies a "theological wordplay" between מָרוֹם ("exalted/on high") in v. 9 and וַתָּרֶם ("and you exalted") in v. 11a:[37]

וְאַתָּה מָרוֹם לְעֹלָם יְהוָה:	9a	But you are exalted forever, O Lord.
[...]		
וַתָּרֶם כִּרְאֵים קַרְנִי	11a	And you have exalted my horn like a wild ox.
בַּלֹּתִי בְּשֶׁמֶן רַעֲנָן:	11b	I have been anointed with fresh oil.

What Dahood calls a theological wordplay can also be classified as a root play because both the nominal מָרוֹם and the Hiphil וַתָּרֶם are from the root רום. Zenger notes how the metaphor of an exalted horn in the ancient Near East was an image of "divine dignity,"[38] which means that the wordplay may purport to show a comparison, rather than a contrast, between the Lord's exaltation and the psalmist's, which mirrors its source of exaltation. The intervening tricolon of v. 10c describes the contrasting demise of God's enemies. It is possible, therefore, that despite the separation, readers would have easily connected these words. Still, given their distance and the fact that they are from the same root, but differ little in meaning, we will classify this case as weak wordplay, weighing its significance accordingly.

Wordplay in Psalm 93

Even in this short psalm (five verses), the first of the Yahweh Malak psalms, there are two wordplays, one involving alliteration and the other, assonance. As with the wordplays of Psalm 92, the wordplays in Psalm 93 are admittedly not the strongest examples of the trope in Book IV, but they are included so that readers can evaluate their strengths and because they contain (if just barely) the criteria established in our methodological guidelines.

The first instance, in 93:1-2, shares only two similar sounds. However, the guttural followed immediately by the ז, the first two instances in close proximity, and the third also ending its line support its identification as wordplay:

---

37. Dahood, *Psalms II*, 337. Dahood compares this wordplay with a similar instance in Ps. 75:6, wherein the Lord's "exalted" status is again found in the context of man's exalted horn.

38. Hossfeld and Zenger, *Psalms*, 2:440.

יְהוָה מָלָךְ גֵּאוּת לָבֵשׁ	1a	The Lord reigns; he is clothed in majesty.
לָבֵשׁ יְהוָה עֹז הִתְאַזָּר	1b	The Lord clothes and equips himself with strength.
אַף־תִּכּוֹן תֵּבֵל בַּל־תִּמּוֹט	1c	Indeed the world is established; it will not be shaken
נָכוֹן כִּסְאֲךָ מֵאָז	2a	Your throne is established from old.
מֵעוֹלָם אָתָּה	2b	You are from everlasting.

The effect of this wordplay is the connection drawn between the Lord's "equipping himself" (הִתְאַזָּר)[39] with "strength" (עֹז) in v. 1b and the establishment of his throne and kingship "from old" (מֵאָז) in v. 2a. In other words, the Lord has been prepared to reign, and has been actively reigning, from the time of creation.[40]

In the second instance of wordplay in Psalm 93, the final two lines of the tricola in v. 3 end in words that share both assonance and a final letter:

נָשְׂאוּ נְהָרוֹת יְהוָה	3a	The seas have lifted up, O Lord!
נָשְׂאוּ נְהָרוֹת קוֹלָם	3b	The seas have lifted their voice!
יִשְׂאוּ נְהָרוֹת דָּכְיָם	3c	The seas lift up their pounding [waves]!

Although the words' initial vowels differ in length (the *holem waw* versus the *qamats hatuf*) they are both "o" class vowels with nearly identical phonetic value. Additionally, the parallelism of the three lines, especially the final two, and the shared ם and similar-sounding ק and כ suggest that these final words are being highlighted through wordplay. The syntactical parallelism in vv. 3b and 3c follows a verb-subject-direct object pattern, with the first two lexemes being identical. In fact, only the conjugation of the verb differs.[41] Moreover, in v. 2, only two lines before this wordplay,

---

39. According to Goldingay, the verb הִתְאַזָּר has the idea of "equipping oneself" for battle, thus elaborating on the previous phrase in v. 1a describing the majesty with which the Lord clothes himself (לָבֵשׁ גֵּאוּת). Goldingay (*Psalms*, 3:68) states, "The psalm refers not to a mere ceremonial robing in regalia but to Yhwh's taking up impressive battle equipment…in connection with asserting kingly authority."

40. Although the Lord is "from eternity" (v. 2b), his reign as king over "the world" (v. 1c) has an historical beginning at creation; see VanGemeren, *Psalms*, 708.

41. The shift in conjugation from perfect to imperfect in v. 3c is controversial and not entirely relevant here. For a discussion of the interpretive possibilities, see Tate, *Psalms*, 480. Dahood (*Psalms*, 2:341) also contends that the shift between perfect and imperfect is characteristic of Ugaritic poetry; cf. Goldingay, *Psalms*, 3:64; VanGemeren, *Psalms*, 709.

this same vowel pattern is used in the word מֵעוֹלָם(מֵ) ("everlasting"). The same lexeme (קֹל, "voice") that was used in v. 3b is again used in v. 4a, which draws attention to the wordplay in v. 3. A final mark of wordplay in this example is the fact that דָּכְיָ ("pounding [waves]") is a *hapax* in the Hebrew Bible.[42]

The function of this wordplay is emphatic, drawing attention to the words in play and emphasizing that the voice and the pounding waves of the seas are great. The three-fold repetition of the phrase, "the seas lift up," as well as the parallelism and assonance of קוֹלָם ("their voice") and דָּכְיָם ("their pounding [waves]"), also give the impression of the relentless beating and aggression of the waves. Indeed, it is unclear whether the waters are praising or threatening the Lord until the following strophe.[43] According to Ugaritic and Canaanite mythology, Baal defeats his opponent Yam, who was the god of the sea and manifestation of chaos. In Psalm 93, King Yahweh is likened as the true victor over chaos.[44] Yet this cosmogonic victory also symbolizes Yahweh's victory of Israel's enemies, the hostile surrounding nations.[45] Thus, the wordplay in v. 3 emphasizes the severity of the enemies' threatening voices, followed quickly in v. 4 by the assurance that the Lord of majesty outranks them all:

> More than[46] the sounds of the many waters,
> Majestic torrents of the sea,
> The Lord is majestic on high.

By using wordplay in v. 3 to heighten the intensity of the enemies' hostility, this assurance of the Lord's superiority is also heightened.

Wordplay in Psalm 94

Psalm 94 is comprised of a community lament (vv. 1-15) followed by an individual lament (vv. 16-21) and statements of trust (vv. 22-23). The

---

42. *HALOT* (221) gives the gloss "dashing (of waves)." Hossfeld and Zenger (*Psalms*, 2:446) translate the word, "roaring." An alternative explanation for the author's unique word choice is his desire to allude to the cognate *dkym* in the Ugaritic *UT* 49.5.1-3; see Tate, *Psalms*, 473; cf. Dahood, *Psalms*, 2:341; Kraus, *Psalms*, 2:235–6.

43. Goldingay, *Psalms*, 3:69.

44. Hossfeld and Zenger, *Psalms*, 2:449; Tate, *Psalms*, 479; Kraus, *Psalms*, 2:235–6.

45. Tate, *Psalms*, 479–80.

46. Note the mem of comparison, *IBHS* §11.2. 11e3; VanGemeren (*Psalms*, 709) offers a survey of possible renderings of this comparison.

psalmist uses four wordplays in the poem: two paronomastic wordplays and two *double entendres* within a complex wordplay. The first is a root letter transposition in 94:8b[47] that follows a three-fold case of alliteration:

בִּינוּ בֹּעֲרִים[48] בָּעָם	Understand, you senseless ones among the people!
וּכְסִילִים מָתַי תַּשְׂכִּילוּ	And you fools, when will you take heed?

For the root letter transposition in the second line, the fact that a ס is used in וּכְסִילִים ("and fools")[49] and a שׂ in תַּשְׂכִּילוּ ("[you] take heed/be wise") is incidental, as they have the same phonetic value. To split hairs, one could call this wordplay a parasonantic root letter transposition or, minimally, parasonancy. The identification of the wordplay is supported by the combination of literary devices used in these lines.

The function of this wordplay seems clear, especially within the rhetorical framework of the psalm. Verses 1-7 appeal to the Lord to take vengeance on Israel's enemies, who kill the innocent and even claim that the Lord himself neither sees nor understands. The repetition of the ב in the first colon binds that clause together, while the paronomasia between כְּסִיל and שְׂכִיל in the second colon invites the readers to consider those words together as well. The lines are semantically parallel, the first charging fools to understand, and the second asking when senseless people (i.e., fools) will act with insight (i.e., understand). In both lines, the wordplays are suggesting a connection between the foolish or senseless ones and their lack of understanding or insight. The fact that the literary devices bring these disparate concepts together (fools and that which they by definition do not have, insight) presents an irony: those who accuse God of lacking understanding themselves are only fools, incapable of insight.[50]

---

47. VanGemeren (ibid., 714) also observes the alliteration in the first cola and the play on words in the second.

48. The rare word בֹּעֲרִים is from the same root in the wordplay seen above in Ps. 92:7a and occurs only five times in the Old Testament; see Chou-Wee Pan, "בער" *NIDOTTE* 1:691.

49. "Fools" may be too gentle of a gloss here. *HALOT* (489) offers "stupid (in practical things), insolent (in religion)"; Kraus (*Psalms*, 2:240), among others, describes the word more pointedly: "a drastic expression for the blunt, insightless, and stupid."

50. This critique of foolishness is reminiscent of the similar wordplay in Ps. 92:6-7 (see above).

The next wordplay in Psalm 94 is found in v. 12a and involves metaphony between (יְ)אַשְׁרֵי ("blessed") and אֲשֶׁר ("whom"). Verses 10-11 help to set up this wordplay:

הֲיֹסֵר גּוֹיִם הֲלֹא יוֹכִיחַ	10a	The one who disciplines the nations, does he not reprove?
הַמְלַמֵּד [אָדָם] דָּעַת	10b	The one who teaches man knowledge?
יְהוָה יֹדֵעַ מַחְשְׁבוֹת [אָדָם]	11a	The Lord is the one who knows the thoughts of man,
כִּי־הֵמָּה הָבֶל	11b	That they are a breath.
אַשְׁרֵי הַ[גֶּבֶר] אֲשֶׁר־תְּיַסְּרֶנּוּ יָּהּ	12a	Blessed is the young man whom you discipline, O Lord,
וּמִתּוֹרָתְךָ תְ[לַמְּדֶ]נּוּ	12b	And from your law you teach him!

In the metaphony between (יְ)אַשְׁרֵי and אֲשֶׁר, the first letters differ only in vocalization and not consonants. This is technically the only wordplay in this section; the other word pairs are marked because they support the wordplay in some way. The use of תְּיַסְּרֶנּוּ heightens the wordplay by adding alliteration and underscoring the theme of discipline being a blessing for the faithful. In this case of alliteration, the ר is repeated three times, in each case it is preceded by either a ס or a שׁ, both of which are similar is sound.

Already in v. 10, the poet prepares his readers to think about the discipline (יסר) and teaching (למד) of the Lord.[51] He uses the lexeme אָדָם for "man" in vv. 10b and 11a and then switches to the synonym גֶּבֶר in v. 12a.[52] This switch may be influenced by his desire to use a ר in the alliteration with אַשְׁרֵי ("blessed" or "happy"), אֲשֶׁר ("whom"), and תְּיַסְּרֶנּוּ ("you discipline"). This deliberate word choice is supported by the similar collocation in Ps. 39:12, which uses the more common word for man, אִישׁ, in conjunction with יסר.

---

51. In fact, the same parallelism between discipline (יסר) and teaching (למד) in v. 10 is repeated in v. 12; cf. VanGemeren, *Psalms*, 714.

52. The poet's use of גֶּבֶר with אַשְׁרֵי is not unprecedented (three other times in the Psalter), but אִישׁ and אָדָם both serve as alternate objects in the singular (five times in the Psalter), as well as הָעָם to denote a community (two times).

The identification of this wordplay is also marked by the author's use of the relative pronoun אֲשֶׁר, which is not the most typical collocation with אַשְׁרֵי in the Psalter, and is used sparsely in poetry.[53] More often, אַשְׁרֵי is followed by a participle (ten times), a nominal clause (four times) or an imperfect (five times). Including this case of wordplay in Ps. 94:12, אַשְׁרֵי and אֲשֶׁר are used together five times.[54] Moreover, the use of the relative pronoun makes this colon the longest in the entire psalm and imbalanced in the meter of the couplet and strophe, leading some commentators to omit it.[55] However, the imbalanced meter might serve to draw attention to the wordplay.

The purpose of this wordplay is twofold. First, it contrasts the object of the Lord's discipline in v. 10a (the nations, as well as the "man" in vv. 10b and 11a) with the blessed man who learns from the Lord's law in v. 12a. This contrast is created by the repetition of יסר and למד and by the changed lexemes for "man." Up until v. 12, the text is ambiguous about whether or not the Lord's discipline is positive or negative, whether the object of his discipline is blessed or cursed or unaffected. This ambiguity is relieved in v. 12a, wherein the poet makes the development of his thoughts clear. The author also highlights his desire to contrast the foolish man with the blessed man by beginning both the stanza regarding the judgment of the fool in vv. 8-11 and the stanza regarding the wise man in vv. 12-15 with wordplays. The second purpose of the wordplay is to draw a tight connection between the first four words in v. 12a so that they are emphatically bound together: "*Blessed* is the *man whom* you *discipline...*" The wordplay leaves no doubt that the objects of the Lord's discipline are blessed, particularly if they choose to respond with learning and law-abiding hearts (v. 12b).

The third and fourth wordplays in Psalm 94 are both examples of polysemantic implicit paronomasia, and both words being played upon are the middle words in their respective lines and share similar sounds.

---

53. Watson, *Classical Hebrew Poetry*, 54.

54. Two occurrences, Pss. 40:5 and 127:5, are identical (אַשְׁרֵי הַגֶּבֶר אֲשֶׁר) and Pss. 1:1 and 33:2 are similar, using different lexemes for "man." Interestingly, the inseparable form of the relative pronoun (־שׁ) occurs with אַשְׁרֵי in two clusters: Pss. 137:8-9 and 144:15ab. What distinguishes the poet's use here and makes this wordplay unique (and not an incidental or stock wordplay) is the author's additional use of תְיַסְּרֶנּוּ.

55. David M. Howard (*The Structure of Psalms 93–100*, Biblical and Judaic Studies 5 [Winona Lake, IN: Eisenbrauns, 1997], 63–4) opts to maintain the relative pronoun precisely because of its use with אַשְׁרֵי. Tate (*Psalms*, 484) retains the pronoun as anacrusis, despite its position within the line.

Because these two wordplays are wordplays in their own right, and also working together through sound repetition, parallelism, and theological function; this is a complex wordplay, even if it is a concise one.

בְּרֹב שַׂרְעַפַּי בְּקִרְבִּי   19a   When my disquieting thoughts grow within me,

תַּנְחוּמֶיךָ יְשַׁעַשְׁעוּ נַפְשִׁי   19b   Your consolations delight my soul.

The second line breaks from the typical syntactical word order of <u>verb</u> → <u>subject</u> → <u>object or phrase</u>, and instead is ordered <u>subject</u> → <u>verb</u> → <u>object</u>, which emphasizes the subject[56] and links שַׂרְעַפַּי ("disquieting thoughts") and יְשַׁעַשְׁעוּ ("delight"). Besides both words sharing a שׂ/שׁ and an ע (which by itself would not be very impressive), the words also seem to be alluding to other, similar words. First, שַׂרְעַפַּי may allude to שׂרף ("to burn"), which shares the same consonants, in the same order, minus the ע. The immediate context of vv. 17-19 describes the Lord as a helping, sustaining, and delighting savior, so that an allusion to burning (something from which to be rescued and helped) might make sense. Also, an argument can be made that psychological turmoil has an emotional "burning" sense in that the sufferer feels similar anxiety and panic. Second, embedded in the Pilpel imperfect form of יְשַׁעַשְׁעוּ (from the root שעע) is the word for "to save" (ישע), which they thus may be intentionally alluded to, particularly given the context and intent of the stanza. The Lord's saving work has hitherto only been hinted at, as a helper (v. 17) and one with sustaining loving faithfulness (v. 18), and as consolations that delight the psalmist's soul when tormented by anxiety (v. 19). These wordplays implicitly allude to the Lord's salvation, which is ultimately paramount to his other works. That the verb שעע occurs in the Pilpel only three times in the Old Testament, and only nine times total in all stems, suggests that the author may have chosen this lexeme because of its similarity in form to ישע. Likewise, שַׂרְעַפַּי occurs only one other time in the Old Testament, which similarly supports its identification as wordplay. Because the reader's thoughts naturally jump to these second, far more common words and meanings, these *double entendres* maintain the reader's interest. They also reveal complexity in something that seems simple, emphasizing the theological point that the Lord saves his people from all dangers, from psychological anxiety to physical burning, and he does so in various ways, including consolation and support.

---

56. *IBHS* §8.3b; Joüon §155k.

Wordplay in Psalm 95

This short praise psalm contains three paronomastic wordplays. Two of these wordplays begin the two stanzas of the poem (vv. 1-2 and v. 6) and serve to emphasize the psalmist's exhortation to praise the Lord with both voice (vv. 1-2) and body (v. 6). Between these similar wordplays is an example of end rhyme which provides the reason for this call to praise: the greatness of the Lord.

Three of the four lines in vv. 1-2 exhibit a נר consonant sequence, creating alliteration between נְרַנְּנָה ("let us cry out!") and נָרִיעָה ("let us shout!"), which is then reinforced by the repetition of נָרִיעַ in v. 2b:[57]

לְכוּ נְרַנְּנָה לַיהוָה	1a	Come, let us cry out to the Lord!
נָרִיעָה לְצוּר יִשְׁעֵנוּ	1b	Let us shout to the rock of our salvation!
נְקַדְּמָה פָנָיו בְּתוֹדָה	2a	Let us come before him with thanksgiving!
בִּזְמִרוֹת נָרִיעַ לוֹ	2b	With songs let us shout to him!

These verbs occur together twice elsewhere in the Psalter (81:2 and 98:4), but both times in the imperative, yielding only light alliteration. Their occurrence in the cohortative here provides the extra phonetic similarity of the nun preformative that qualifies the word pair as wordplay. The effect of the word play is emphatic: worshippers are exhorted to vocalize their praise of the Lord with loud voices and song.

Another instance of wordplay in this psalm comes in v. 3b, wherein we find both assonance and rhyme in a classic paronomastic wordplay:

כִּי אֵל גָּדוֹל יְהוָה	3a	For the Lord is a great God,
וּמֶלֶךְ גָּדוֹל עַל־כָּל־אֱלֹהִים	3b	And a great king above all gods.

The attributive adjective גָּדוֹל ("great") and the phrase עַל־כָּל ("above all") have similar assonance. The only variance is that גָּדוֹל contains long "a" and "o" vowels, while עַל־כָּל has short "a" and "o" vowels. This in itself might not be suggestive of wordplay, but the author also employs end rhyme in that both forms end with the same sound (long "o" plus a lamed).[58] The repetition of ל in the couplet (seven times total) further

---

57. Casanowicz includes Ps. 95:1 in his list of wordplays, but he does not discuss it, *Paronomasia*, 91.

58. This use of assonance coupled with end rhyme is very similar to the wordplay in Ps. 93:3bc.

complements the similar sounds in גָּדוֹל and עַל־כָּל. This collocation also occurs in Ps. 47:3, which likewise describes the Lord as a מֶלֶךְ ("king"), specifically one to be feared above all of the earth: מֶלֶךְ גָּדוֹל עַל־כָּל־הָאָרֶץ. This combination of assonance and end rhyme, and the supporting alliteration, mark the wordplay as genuine.

This couplet (v. 3) serves as a justification for the psalmist's call to loud and joyful praise in vv. 1-2, as is clear from the use of the particle כִּי, being used here causally ("for/because"). It also serves as an introduction to vv. 4-5, which detail his sovereignty over his creation. Within this context, the effect of the wordplay is aesthetic and emphatic, highlighting both modifiers: the Lord's greatness and his transcendence above all god.[59]

The third wordplay occurs in v. 6, which begins the second of two stanzas in this poem. It is similar to the injunctions to worship in vv. 1-2, which introduced the first stanza, but the focus here shifts from vocal praise to physical prostration. The final word in the first line is semantically parallel with the first word in the second line, and both forms are phonetically similar, sharing four consonants:

| בֹּאוּ נִשְׁתַּחֲוֶה וְנִכְרָעָה | 6a | Come, let us worship and bow down! |
| נִבְרְכָה לִפְנֵי־יְהוָה עֹשֵׂנוּ | 6b | Let us kneel before the Lord who made us! |

Both words share a נ and ה, which is attributable to their common cohortative form, but the additional commonality of the ר and כ, coupled with their immediate proximity, suggest that this is indeed an instance of parasonancy. Moreover, these near-synonyms are surprisingly never used together.[60] The function of this wordplay is structural and emphatic. The author binds the two lines together tightly by using near-synonyms

---

59. Because גָּדוֹל is used in the preceding line and the meter is supposedly unbalanced, Kraus (*Psalms*, 2:235) recommends that the use of גָּדוֹל in the second line be omitted. We will not emend the text in this study for the sole purpose of meter, since its exact nature is contested and since it is not sufficient reason to challenge the reading. Indeed, if one counts only primary accents, it is v. 3a that has four accents versus v. 3b that has only three, since the phrase עַל־כָּל־אֱלֹהִים is all connected by maqqefs. Still, the meter should be considered balanced because the opening word in v. 3a is כִּי, which is functioning as anacrusis.

60. According to Dahood (*Psalms II*, 353), some scholars believe the third parallel verb in this series (נִבְרְכָה) to be an insertion, but Dahood affirms its originality, based on Ugaritic poetry with three parallel verbs. The likelihood of a wordplay here also supports the originality of the verb; in fact, the author may have intentionally used the unusual style of three parallel verbs in order to draw attention to his wordplay and to capture the interest of his readers.

in identical conjugations that are adjacent to each other and share more than half of their consonants. This naturally emphasizes the exhortation to worship the Lord physically, by both bowing and kneeling before him.

Wordplay in Psalm 96

Each of the three wordplays in Psalm 96 falls into the parasonancy subcategory of paronomasia. In two of these cases (vv. 2, 6) the psalmist uses word pairs composed of lexemes in the same semantic field, creating emphasis and nuance.

The first wordplay in Psalm 96 is between the first words in each of the four cola in vv. 1-2. The imperative שִׁירוּ ("sing!") is repeated three times (in addition to the one nominal use in v. 1a), followed by the similar-sounding imperative בַּשְּׂרוּ ("proclaim!"), creating through this wordplay an emphatic charge to worship the Lord:

שִׁירוּ לַיהוָה שִׁיר חָדָשׁ	1a	Sing to the Lord a new song!
שִׁירוּ לַיהוָה כָּל־הָאָרֶץ	1b	Sing to the Lord, all the earth!
שִׁירוּ לַיהוָה בָּרֲכוּ שְׁמוֹ	2a	Sing to the Lord, bless his name!
בַּשְּׂרוּ מִיּוֹם־לְיוֹם יְשׁוּעָתוֹ	2b	Proclaim his salvation from day to day!

The parallelism and three shared consonants (with the exchange of the שׂ for the שׁ) in שִׁירוּ ("sing!") and בַּשְּׂרוּ ("proclaim!") support the identification of this wordplay. Moreover, the verb בשר occurs in the imperative only here in the Psalter,[61] and rare forms are often indicators of wordplay. Since only one root letter varies (a י in שִׁירוּ and a ב in בַּשְּׂרוּ), this is an example of parasonantic paronomasia.

The effect of this wordplay is aesthetic and stylistic, starting each line with a similar-sounding word, thus accentuating the rhythm of the strophe and also emphasizing two important aspects of praise: singing praises to the Lord and proclaiming his salvation for all to hear.[62] In other words, this wordplay emphasizes the God-oriented aspect of praise as well as the evangelistic-oriented aspect of praise.[63]

---

61. Goldingay, *Psalms*, 3:103.

62. Goldingay (ibid.) describes the connection between these verbs as a "move from sound to content," providing the motive for song and praise, namely his deliverance, honor, and wonders.

63. Psalm 105:1 also uses wordplay to emphasize the relationship between praising God and proclaiming his saving deeds.

The second wordplay in Psalm 96 is an example of parasonantic paronomasia in the collocation הוֹד־וְהָדָר ("splendor and majesty") in v. 6a:[64]

| הוֹד־וְהָדָר לְפָנָיו | 6a | Splendor and majesty are before him |
| עֹז וְתִפְאֶרֶת בְּמִקְדָּשׁוֹ | 6b | Strength and beauty are in his sanctuary. |

Both words are adjacent and share two of their three root letters (excluding the conjunction). It also appears to be a stock wordplay, used primarily in the book of Psalms (here and the parallel passage in 1 Chr. 16:27; Pss. 21:6; 104:1; 111:3). The function of this wordplay is aesthetic and emphatic, using two near-synonyms to underscore the glory and majesty of the Lord, a hendiadys of emphasis.

Another wordplay exists between יִשְׂמְחוּ ("let them be glad!") and הַשָּׁמַיִם ("the heavens") in v. 11a and is strengthened by the end rhyme in the following line:

| יִשְׂמְחוּ הַשָּׁמַיִם וְתָגֵל הָאָרֶץ | 11a | Let the heavens be glad and the earth rejoice! |
| יִרְעַם הַיָּם וּמְלֹאוֹ | 11b | Let the sea and its fullness thunder! |

This wordplay uses three similar or identical letters (שׂ/שׁ, מ, and ח/ה) in the collocation יִשְׂמְחוּ הַשָּׁמַיִם, which only occurs in the parallel passage, 1 Chr. 16:31. This paronomastic wordplay would be a weak root letter transposition, but the ה in הַשָּׁמַיִם is the definite article and not part of the root. Therefore, it is best classified as parasonancy or alliteration. It may have been a stock wordplay, and certainly an easy one, but its impact is nonetheless significant as it adds emphasis to the psalmist's exhortation of praise.

Wordplay in Psalm 97

Psalm 97 expands on the final verses of Psalm 96, that King Yahweh is indeed coming to judge the world with faithfulness.[65] The four wordplays in Psalm 97 are all microstructure cases of paronomasia. Each is

---

64. Casanowicz (*Paronomasia*, 91) lists this as a wordplay, but he does not explain his reasoning.
65. According to Hossfeld and Zenger (*Psalms*, 2:477, citing S. Fuest), Ps. 97 sharpens this expectation with an eschatological perspective of the Lord's glorious coming in judgment and salvation.

composed of a word pair wherein some sort of connection is highlighted by the wordplay.

The first two examples[66] of wordplay in Psalm 97 are in vv. 3 and 4 and differ in syntax and function but can be discussed together as the word pairs are mutually reinforcing:

אֵשׁ לְפָנָיו תֵּלֵךְ 3a Fire goes before him,

וּתְלַהֵט סָבִיב צָרָיו 3b And it burns around his adversaries.

הֵאִירוּ בְרָקָיו תֵּבֵל 4a His bolts of lightning light up the world.

רָאֲתָה וַתָּחֵל הָאָרֶץ 4b The earth looked and writhed.

In the first couplet, the poet uses alliteration between the ת followed by the ל in תֵּלֵךְ ("it goes") וּתְלַהֵט ("and it burns").[67] This alliteration is strong enough to be classified as wordplay in its own right for three reasons. First, the words (in this case, both imperfect verbs) are adjacent. Second, the normal word order of a verbal clause (in v. 3a), and indeed the word order that would have created more syntactical parallelism with the following line, would have been <u>verb</u> → <u>subject</u> → <u>prepositional phrase</u> (used adverbially). Instead, the syntax is <u>subject</u> → <u>prepositional phrase</u> (used adverbially) → <u>verb</u>. The poet may have fronted the nominal אֵשׁ ("fire") to emphasize that word, but more likely the irregular syntax was used to link these alliterative verbs. Third, the words stand in syntagmatic and sequential relationship to one another, which is natural in the context. Fire first "goes" (הלך) and then "burns" (להט). The communicative effect of this parasonantic paronomasia is to bind the cola together structurally and thematically, enabling the reader to picture more vividly the raging fire that surrounds[68] God's enemies.

The very next couplet (v. 4) reinforces the wordplay in the first couplet in that it also plays on the letters ת and ל in תֵּבֵל ("world") and וַתָּחֵל ("and writhed"), making this a case of parasonancy. The words differ in only one

---

66. Casanowicz cites the theophany language of וְעֲרָפֶל עָנָן in v. 2 as a wordplay, but I do not see it, save for the repeated ע. For the theological significance of this common word pair, see Zenger, *Psalms*, 2:472–4. Goldingay (*Psalms*, 3:112) refers to this word pair as "paradoxical" because cloud and darkness would initially make us think of something hidden; and, yet, this is the way that God reveals his very real presence to his people.

67. The roots of both verbs also share two out of three consonants: הלך and להט.

68. Though not a wordplay proper, the repetition of the adverb סָבִיב in vv. 2a and 3b is significant because it first describes something natural (clouds) surrounding God and then describes something else natural (fire) surrounding God's enemies.

consonant but share an initial ת and a final ל, as well as a tsere in the final syllable. Not only are two near-synonyms used for the earth, or world, but the author uses a verb in its apocopated form with the third person feminine singular preformative, with the effect that it looks and sounds very similar to תֵּבֵל. This wordplay emphasizes the vast audience and witness to the Lord's reign. It also maintains the interest of the readers, who most likely would mistakenly hear or read תֵּבֵל instead of תָּחֵל in the second line until they were corrected by the use of הָאָרֶץ, forcing them to reconsider the couplet and sharpen their attention.

The wordplay in Ps. 97:7 is a case of paronomastic end rhyme between הַמִּתְהַלְלִים ("the ones who boast") and בָּאֱלִילִים ("in [the] vain things")[69] in the second line of the tricolon:

יֵבֹשׁוּ כָּל־עֹבְדֵי פֶסֶל	7a	Let all who serve an idol be ashamed!
הַמִּתְהַלְלִים בָּאֱלִילִים	7b	Those who boast in vain things!
הִשְׁתַּחֲווּ־לוֹ כָּל־אֱלֹהִים	7c	Worship him, all you gods!

End rhyme is often a natural byproduct of conjugational necessity, and thus incidental, but the end rhyme combined with the double ל, coupled with the proximity of the words, marks this wordplay as a true wordplay. The repeated use of ל in this strophe (nine total occurrences, five excluding the wordplay) further highlights the paronomasia between הַמִּתְהַלְלִים and בָּאֱלִילִים. Its function is probably aesthetic, structural, and theological. It binds the second line together in such a way as to show that the boasters themselves are much like the vain things they worship, drawing together two ideas in an ironic way.[70]

A final wordplay in Psalm 97 is an alliteration and root play paronomasia in v. 9:

כִּי־אַתָּה יְהוָה	9a	For you are the Lord,
עֶלְיוֹן עַל־כָּל־הָאָרֶץ	9b	Most High above all the earth,
מְאֹד נַעֲלֵיתָ עַל־כָּל־אֱלֹהִים	9c	Exceedingly exalted above all gods!

---

69. According to Hossfeld and Zenger (*Psalms*, 2:475), אֱלִילִים is "probably an artificially constructed diminutive of אל or אלהים, "God," and means, in an ironic sense, "little god." Its only other use in the plural is in Ps. 96:5. This may further support the intentionality of wordplay.

70. Dahood (*Psalms II*, 362) has also noticed this wordplay, referring to the "alliteration" and "theological wordplay" as "effective."

Zenger and Dahood identify the primary wordplay between עֶלְיוֹן ("Most High") and נַעֲלֵיתָ ("you are highly exalted"),[71] which are both derived from the root עלה.[72] The repetition of the ע and ל is four-fold. The repetition of ע, ל, and י in עֶלְיוֹן and נַעֲלֵיתָ, and the fact that both are followed by the preposition עַל with two shared letters,[73] are also marks of wordplay. The larger wordplay between all four words is a case of alliteration, whereas the wordplay between עֶלְיוֹן and נַעֲלֵיתָ is a root play. This wordplay effectively draws a connection between the Lord's title as "Most High" and the reason for that title, his exalted state above all gods, thus underscoring his exaltation at this high point in the psalm and as a conclusion to the stanza of vv. 7-9.[74]

Wordplay in Psalms 98–100

There is no evidence of wordplay in any of these three psalms.[75]

---

71. Hossfeld and Zenger, *Psalms*, 2:475; Dahood (*Psalms II*, 362) refers to this wordplay as "theological" as well.

72. VanGemeren, *Psalms*, 728.

73. VanGemeren (ibid., 153, following Dahood, *Psalms I*, 45–6) suggests that the preposition may be etymologically related to עֶלְיוֹן, making the wordplay encompass all four words.

74. Note too the affinity with the opening strophe of the stanza in v. 7 with its repetition of ל and double use of כֹּל, forming a nice *inclusio*.

75. Dahood identifies a "theological wordplay" (specifically, a *double entendre* using homonyms) with עַמִּים and הָעַמִּים in Ps. 99:1a and 2b, respectively:

יְהוָה מָלָךְ יִרְגְּזוּ עַמִּים	1a	The Lord reigns! Let the people tremble!
יֹשֵׁב כְּרוּבִים תָּנוּט הָאָרֶץ׃	1b	The one sitting above the cherubim, let the earth shake!
יְהוָה בְּצִיּוֹן גָּדוֹל	2a	The Lord is great in Zion,
וְרָם הוּא עַל־כָּל־הָעַמִּים׃	2b	And he is exalted above all the people!

Dahood claims that the use of הָעַמִּים in v. 2b is from the root עמם, meaning "to be strong," and thus renders the line, "exalted is he beyond all the strong ones." He considers these "strong ones" pagan deities, which would draw a theological connection between the people in v. 1 and the pagan gods they worship in v. 2 (*Psalms II*, 368). However, his theory receives little support from other scholars or versions, and the third person masculine subject of the following line (v. 3a) seems to be referring to the "people," which Dahood admits (368), suggesting that the closest antecedent (הָעַמִּים in v. 2b) is indeed the referent and should be rendered "people," as in v. 1a. Moreover, it is interesting that Dahood does not support his theory with the textual variant mentioned below or with the mention of the Lord's kingly "strength" in v. 4a.

Wordplay in Psalm 101

Psalm 101 is a royal psalm, shifting from a focus on the kingship of Yahweh to the kingship of his human representative and the expectations of integrity and righteousness fitting that office.[76] This theme is underscored by the sole wordplay in Psalm 101, which involves alliteration in the second line of the tricola of v. 3:

לֹא־אָשִׁית לְנֶגֶד עֵינַי דְּבַר־בְּלִיָּעַל	3a	I will not set before my eyes a worthless thing.
עֲשֹׂה־סֵטִים שָׂנֵאתִי	3b	I hate the work of transgressors.
לֹא יִדְבַּק בִּי	3c	It will not cling to me.

More than half of the consonants in the words סֵטִים and שָׂנֵאתִי share phonetic equivalents, with the initial infinitive עֲשֹׂה, as well as the verb אָשִׁית in the line above, reinforcing the wordplay. Moreover, every word in the line is either part of or contributes to the wordplay. Finally, the noun סֵט is a *hapax legomenon*,[77] even though several other words in the semantic field of evil works or evil-doers could have been chosen (e.g., פֹּעֲלֵי אָוֶן, עֹשֵׂה הָרָעָה).

This wordplay adds poetic beauty to the strophe and poem, and links together the words of this line, which is arguably the main idea of the strophe (vv. 3a-4b). It also emphasizes the psalmist's rejection of anything ungodly, which is further underscored by the *inclusio* of negatives (לֹא) in the preceding and following lines, viz., "I will not set before my eyes a worthless thing" (v. 3a) and "It will not cling to me" (v. 3c).[78] Use of the rare word סֵט also brings to mind the more common verb שׂוּט, meaning "to despise," thereby creating a polysemantic play emphasizing the depth of the psalmist's hatred toward evildoers.[79]

For the same reason, we should not emend the text to אֱלֹהִים in place of הָעַמִּים. A few manuscripts do so, but probably because of the influence of Pss. 95:3; 96:4; and 97:9; see Hossfeld and Zenger, *Psalms*, 2:483; cf., Tate, *Psalms*, 526.

76. Nancy deClaisse-Walford, Rolf A. Jacobson, and Beth LaNeel Tanner, *The Book of Psalms*, NICOT (Grand Rapids, MI: Eerdmans, 2014), 741.

77. According to *HALOT*, the form שֵׂטִים in Hos. 5:2 should be read סֵטִים (750), but the word is still a *hapax legomenon* in the unamended MT.

78. VanGemeren (*Psalms*, 746) refers to this string of negatives as "a manner of affirming devotion," cross-referencing Ps. 1:1-2 and Prov. 3:1-7.

79. This potential case of polysemy is worth noting, but will not be included in the final analysis due to lack of sufficient evidence.

Wordplay in Psalm 102

In this individual lament, the exilic psalmist describes his mortality in terms reminiscent of Psalm 90, and yet he hopes for the Lord's restoration of Zion. Like Psalm 90, Psalm 102 is steeped in wordplay. Like Psalms 90–91, the poet uses macro-structured, interlocking patterns of wordplay (vv. 5-6, 16-18). This affluence of wordplay abruptly breaks the relative poverty of wordplay in Psalms 98–101. The scholarly attention given to wordplay in this psalm is also noteworthy; Allen, Dahood, and Goldingay each recognize different wordplays in this psalm.

The following example of alliteration in v. 4 does not qualify as wordplay by our definition and standards, but the alliteration is striking enough to warrant mention, particularly because it sets the stage for the elaborate complex wordplay that follows. The syntax of Ps. 102:4 is chiastically parallel, the first line moving verb → prepositional phrase → subject, and the second line reversing that movement: subject → prepositional phrase → verb.[80]

כִּי־כָלוּ בְעָשָׁן יָמָי   4a   For my days cease like smoke,

וְעַצְמוֹתַי כְּמוֹ־קֵד נִחָרוּ   4b   And my bones burn like a glowing ember.

The double alliteration of the "k" sound is prominent in both lines. Although the first pair fronts its line while the second pair is in the middle, both pairs are composed of metrically and syntactically insignificant words (כִּי and כְּמוֹ) and are connected to the following word by a maqqef.[81] The noun קֵד is a *hapax* in the Old Testament. This case of "light alliteration" reinforces the similarity of the two similes: the poet's life ("days" and "bones") will be over imminently, being as short-lived as "smoke" (בְעָשָׁן) that "ceases to be" (כָלוּ) and "a glowing ember" (קֵד[־]כְּמוֹ) that "burns" (נִחָרוּ). That עָשָׁן ("smoke") and חרר ("burn") are semantically related also reinforces the similarity of the similes.

The following two verses contain three paronomastic wordplays that link the two bicola and their themes. Notice also the repetition of עַצְמִי

---

80. In the first line, the verb is preceded by the conjunction כִּי, but the two are connected by a maqqef so that the conjunction affects neither the metrical balance nor syntactical parallelism.

81. The editors of *BHS*, as well as several commentators (e.g., VanGemeren, *Psalms*, 751) and English versions (e.g., NIV and NEB), believe that the Leningrad codex erroneously added the maqqef to כְּמוֹ־קֵד, and that the words should be read together as כְּמוֹקֵד ("glowing embers" or "oven").

("my bone," singular here), which further binds these verses with the preceding couplet:[82]

הוּכָּה־כָעֵ֫שֶׂב וַיִּ֫בַשׁ לִבִּ֑י	5a	My heart was smitten like grass and dried up.
כִּי־שָׁכַ֫חְתִּי מֵאֲכֹ֥ל לַחְמִֽי	5b	Indeed, I have forgotten to eat my bread.
מִקּ֥וֹל אַנְחָתִ֑י	6a	On account of the sound of my groaning,
דָּבְקָ֥ה עַצְמִ֗י לִבְשָׂרִֽי	6b	My bone clings to my flesh.

The words מֵאֲכֹל ("to eat") in v. 5b and מִקּוֹל ("on account of the sound of") in v. 6a are nearly identical phonetically, with only the initial vowel(s) differing, and the כ and the ק being very similar in sound, making this paronomastic wordplay an example of near-metaphony, or at least parasonancy. The first word, מֵאֲכֹל, is an infinitive construct with the privative use of the prefixed preposition מִן,[83] a construction which is a *hapax legomenon*.[84] The second word, מִקּוֹל, also uses the preposition מִן inseparably for causation, which is a common construction.[85] The striking similarity in sound between the forms and their close proximity, coupled with the obscurity of the first form, supports the identification of this wordplay. The function of this wordplay seems to be structural, binding the couplets together.

The second paronomastic wordplay envelopes the first and is a case of alliteration that involves three words. The repetition of the שב/בש/בש combinations in כָעֵשֶׂב ("like grass"), וַיִּבַשׁ ("and dried up"), and לִבְשָׂרִי ("to my flesh") bind these cola, which lament how the psalmist's body is failing due to his despair. Specifically, the poet's description of his deteriorating physical body (with the use of לִבְשָׂרִי, "to my flesh") in the final line of the strophe calls to mind the sorry state of his inner self (with the use of כָעֵשֶׂב וַיִּבַשׁ, "like grass and dried up"); the poet is broken inside and out.

---

82. Allen also notes the first person common possessive suffix (י ָ) that ends each of the four lines in vv. 5-6 (and which dominates throughout vv. 6-12), *Psalms*, 9. Although this assonance may have influenced the author's choice of word order, it is difficult to discern whether or not the sound play is intentional or incidental, since the poet is speaking in first person and using many possessives.

83. Williams §321.

84. More common is the use of an infinitive by itself (אֲכֹל) or with the preposition -לְ (e.g., Pss. 27:2; 78:24; Prov. 25:27).

85. Williams §319; *IBHS* §11.2.11d.

The third component of this complex wordplay is the paronomasia between לִבִּי ("my heart"), which concludes the first line of v. 5, and לִבְשָׂרִי ("to my flesh"), which concludes the final line in v. 6, thus forming an *inclusio* around this section of the poem. All three consonants in לִבִּי are repeated in the prepositional phrase לִבְשָׂרִי, further solidifying this section of the stanza and emphasizing the connection between the poet's inner and outer turmoil.[86]

This complex wordplay clarifies and accentuates the rhetorical flow of these four lines, which read with the following rhetorical markers:

5a—The psalmist's heart is broken
5b—"Indeed" (כִּי־) the psalmist has even forgotten to eat
6a—"Because" (מִ־) of the psalmist's vocal sadness (groaning)
6b—The psalmist is therefore physically deteriorating

The causal marker of v. 6a (the affixed preposition מִן) connects vv. 5b and 6b: the psalmist's flesh clung to his body because he forgot to eat. Similarly, the parasonantic wordplay between מֶאֱכֹל and מִקּוֹל functions to connect the dots between vv. 5b and 6a: the psalmist is heartbroken and has even forgotten to eat (v. 5). This understandably leads to his groaning (v. 6a), and ultimately to the deterioration of his body (v. 6b).

The reason for the psalmist's suffering is given near the end of the stanza, in v. 11, where the poet uses two adjacent polysemantic wordplays in v. 11b. The psalmist has just depicted his low position of sadness and weeping, and he then attributes this misery to the Lord's "indignation" and "wrath" (v. 11a). He further explains that the Lord has "lifted" him up (נשׂא) and "cast" him away (שׁלך):

מִפְּנֵי־זַעַמְךָ וְקִצְפֶּךָ 11a Because of your indignation and wrath,
כִּי נְשָׂאתַנִי וַתַּשְׁלִיכֵנִי 11b or you have lifted me and cast me away.

While both of these words have negative connotations here, they also either have a secondary meaning of "forgiveness" or allude to a word with such a meaning, thus making the first a polysemantic *double entendre* and the second polysemantic implicit parasonancy (because it alludes to another, similar-sounding word). A secondary meaning of נשׂא is "to forgive," particularly when the Lord is the subject (as he is here

---

86. This wordplay hardly needs further support for identification, but note Job's similar lament in Job 19:20: "My bone clings to my skin and my flesh" (וּבִבְשָׂרִי עַצְמִי דָבְקָה), which uses the inseparable preposition -בְּ instead of -לְ, showing that the poet had other conventional means of expressing the same idea.

in Ps. 102:11) and often with a direct object of "sins" or "iniquity."[87] It is therefore possible that נְשָׂאתַנִי in this verse is alluding to the verb's meaning of "to forgive." The identification of a *double entendre* is strengthened when one considers that the root of the next word (וַתַּשְׁלִיכֵנִי) is שׁלך, which is phonetically similar to סלח, whose exclusive sense is "to forgive," occurring 47 times in the Hebrew Bible.[88] The frequency of the word and its sole reference to forgiveness means that the allusion and wordplay would have been an easy connection for the poet's readers or listeners. Both words have common secondary meanings (נשׂא) or allusions (שׁלך) and both mean forgiveness, supporting identification of the complex wordplay here.

But why would the psalmist allude to the Lord's forgiveness of sins when he is busy lamenting about the Lord's wrath? First, the poet seems to be showing, subtly, that even in the midst of the Lord's wrath there is mercy and forgiveness; not all hope is lost. Second, this subtle wordplay foreshadows the turn in the lament in vv. 13-18, which celebrates the Lord's mercy and forgiveness, wherein the psalmist offers confidence that the Lord will answer the prayer of the destitute and the prisoner.[89]

The next stanza explicitly celebrates the Lord's forgiveness and salvation and showcases two interlocking wordplays. These "theological wordplays," as Dahood identifies them, include paronomasia between וְיִירְאוּ and נִרְאָה in vv. 16a and 17b, respectively, as well as בָנָה and פָּנָה in vv. 17a and 18a, respectively.[90]

וְיִירְאוּ גוֹיִם אֶת־שֵׁם יְהוָה	16a	And the nations will fear the name of the Lord,
וְכָל־מַלְכֵי הָאָרֶץ אֶת־כְּבוֹדֶךָ	16b	And all of the kings of the earth, your glory,
כִּי־בָנָה יְהוָה צִיּוֹן	17a	For the Lord has built Zion.
נִרְאָה בִּכְבוֹדוֹ	17b	He has appeared in his glory.
פָּנָה אֶל־תְּפִלַּת הָעַרְעָר	18a	He has turned to the prayer of the destitute,
וְלֹא־בָזָה אֶת־תְּפִלָּתָם	18b	And he has not despised their prayer.

---

87. For נשׂא, *HALOT* (725) includes the meanings of "to receive someone in a friendly manner, be favourably disposed towards someone"; and "to take away someone's guilt," and "to rise up high" and "exalt" (726).

88. *HALOT*, 757.

89. This complex wordplay is reminiscent of Ps. 90:6b, which also employs both a *double entendre* and parasonantic allusion in a complex wordplay.

90. Dahood, *Psalms III*, 17–18.

All four words are verbs and front their lines (especially if כִּי is considered anacrusis in v. 17a).⁹¹ The first wordplay, between וְיִירְאוּ ("and they will fear")⁹² and נִרְאָה ("he has appeared"), is an example of paronomasia, specifically, alliteration on the surface level or parasonancy on the deep level, since the roots of וְיִירְאוּ (ירא) and נִרְאָה (ראה) differ only in one letter. This wordplay draws a connection between the nations' "fear" of the Lord and the cause of such reverence, namely that the Lord has "appeared" to them in his glory. Goldingay notes this similarity in form and describes its function as showing how "appearing leads to revering."⁹³

The second wordplay, between בָנָה ("he has built") and פָּנָה ("he has turned"), is similarly an example of parasonancy, with only the exchange of the ב and פ, both bilabial plosives that, according to Dahood, "often interchange with no semantic difference."⁹⁴ This wordplay draws a connection between the Lord's "building" Zion and his "turning towards" or regarding the "prayer of the destitute." In other words, the Lord's establishment of and presence in Jerusalem is both the prerequisite for his regard for the needy, as well as an answer to their prayer. Because both of these wordplays are so similar in classification and function, and because they are interlocking, readers are encouraged to see them together. The nations' reaction of fear and reverence for the Lord because of his appearance in glory is contrasted with the basis of the destitute's prayer, as well as the answer to it.

Leslie C. Allen identifies a wordplay between לִשְׁמֹעַ / שִׁמְעָה in vv. 2a and 21a, שֵׁם in vv. 16a and 22a, and מִשָּׁמַיִם / שָׁמַיִם in vv. 20b and 26b.⁹⁵ I am admittedly skeptical of some of these alleged wordplays that share only two phonemes and are separated by so many lines. At the very least, however, the words create alliterative wordplay in the stanza of vv. 20-23, the first three verses of which contain all three words in relatively close proximity:

---

91. The identification of כִּי as anacrusis is based on the definition given in Watson, *Classical Hebrew Poetry*, 110.

92. Several manuscripts read וְיִרְאוּ ("and they will see"), which makes sense in the context and is thus a plausible alternative. However, given the likelihood of wordplay, the MT's וְיִירְאוּ is to be preferred; see Dahood, *Psalms III*, 17.

93. Goldingay, *Psalms*, 3:156.

94. Dahood, *Psalms III*, 17.

95. Leslie C. Allen, *Psalms 101–150*, WBC 21 (Waco, TX: Word, 1983), 15, 21:10.

2. *Writing the Right Words*

כִּי־הִשְׁקִיף מִמְּרוֹם קָדְשׁוֹ	20a	For he looked down from his holy height,
יְהוָה מִשָּׁמַיִם אֶל־אֶרֶץ הִבִּיט	20b	The Lord gazed from heaven to earth,
לִשְׁמֹעַ אֶנְקַת אָסִיר	21a	To hear the groaning of the prisoner,
לְפַתֵּחַ בְּנֵי תְמוּתָה	21b	To free the sons of death,
לְסַפֵּר בְּצִיּוֹן שֵׁם יְהוָה	22a	So that they would recount the name of the Lord in Zion
וּתְהִלָּתוֹ בִּירוּשָׁלָםִ	22b	And his praise in Jerusalem.

This is an example of alliteration in that all three words share the שׁ and מ.[96] Allen cites Pss. 69:31-36 and 103:1-20 as other instances of the same use of this wordplay.[97] The proximity of and number of the words involved help to identify this wordplay. Its function is theological, emphasizing important thematic links between the glorious provenance of the Lord (heaven), his response to the needy (hearing them), and their response in praising his name in Zion.

One means by which the psalmist offers hope in the latter portion of the psalm is by contrasting the world's transience (v. 27) with the Lord's eternality (v. 28), themes which are reminiscent of Psalm 90. However, whereas Psalm 90 contrasted humanity's transience with God's eternality in an effort to wrestle through the sorry state of humanity, Psalm 102 contrasts the earth's transience with God's eternality, ensuring God's people that they will dwell before the Lord (v. 29). Within this context, the psalmist uses polysemantic punning repetition in v. 27c:

הֵמָּה יֹאבֵדוּ וְאַתָּה תַעֲמֹד	27a	They will perish, but you will stand.
וְכֻלָּם כַּבֶּגֶד יִבְלוּ	27b	And all of them will wear out like a garment.
כַּלְּבוּשׁ תַּחֲלִיפֵם וְיַחֲלֹפוּ	27c	You change them like clothing and they pass away.

---

96. Initially, I hesitated to identify this as genuine wordplay for three reasons: (1) the words are all very common; (2) the shared letters are common; and (3) there is no obvious purpose for this wordplay. However, the sheer proximity of these key words in this climactic stanza, coupled with their use exactly twice each in the psalm and their use together in other psalms, has led me to identify a wordplay at least within the words in vv. 20-22.

97. Allen, *Psalms*, 15.

In its final line, this tricolon contains the same root (חלף) in two different stems and two different senses.⁹⁸ First, the heavens and the earth are compared to a garment that the Lord "changes" (תַּחֲלִיפֵם). This is the usual sense of חלף in the Hiphil, and it fits the context well. After the Lord changes the heavens and earth like a garment, they naturally "pass away" (וְיַחֲלֹפוּ), which is the typical sense for the verb in the Qal stem. The imagery is of someone removing one garment in favor of another and leaving the old garment discarded.

The poet could have easily used another lexeme for either word, especially for the Qal sense of "passing away" (e.g., עבר or כלה), supporting the identification of this wordplay. The wordplay is also acknowledged by *HALOT* in the entry for the root חלף.⁹⁹ Moreover, this wordplay occurs in one of only three tricola in Psalm 102, compared to 26 bicola, which draws attention to the pun. The effect of the wordplay maintains reader interest and adds emphasis before the contrasting bicolon of v. 28. Theologically, the wordplay shows how closely the two ideas are related: just as a garment that is changed is easily discarded forever, so also can those who are removed from Zion into exile be discarded forever if they do not dwell before the Lord (v. 29).

The final wordplay in Psalm 102 concludes the psalm in v. 29, and emphasizes the certitude that the Lord will indeed establish his servants to dwell before him:

בְּנֵי־עֲבָדֶיךָ יִשְׁכּוֹנוּ	29a	The children of your servants will dwell,
וְזַרְעָם לְפָנֶיךָ יִכּוֹן	29b	And their descendants will be established before you.

The repetition of two root letters (ן and כ) and an unchangeably long vowel (וֹ) in יִשְׁכּוֹנוּ ("they will dwell") and יִכּוֹן ("it will be established") make this an example of parasonancy since really only one letter is missing from כן (namely, שׁ), and it has no other letter in its place because it is a hollow verb. Both words are imperfect verbs, so they also share a preformative yod, and they are syntactically parallel and conclude their respective lines, offering a sense of rhyme. An additional factor that helps to mark this as a wordplay is the fact that the author could have used other lexemes

---

98. Because both words are in the same word class (verb), this wordplay is classified as a polysemantic punning repetition, rather than a paronomastic root play, which would involve different word classes.

99. *HALOT* 321.

(especially the common word for "dwell," יָשַׁב).¹⁰⁰ By ending both lines with a similar sound, this wordplay both underscores the semantic and syntactic parallelism and emphasizes the author's final point: that the servants of the Lord and their descendants will dwell securely before the Lord.

Wordplay in Psalm 103

Psalm 103 is a thanksgiving psalm complementing Psalm 102 with its language of mortality and its confidence in the Lord's love and forgiveness.¹⁰¹ It contains three paronomastic wordplays, including alliteration and parasonancy. The psalm begins in vv. 1-2a with a paronomastic wordplay between בָּרֲכִי ("bless!") and קְרָבַי ("within me"):

לְדָוִד	1a	Of David
בָּרֲכִי נַפְשִׁי אֶת־יְהוָה	1b	Bless the Lord, O my soul!
וְכָל־קְרָבַי אֶת־שֵׁם¹⁰² קָדְשׁוֹ	1c	And all that is within me, [bless] his holy name!
בָּרֲכִי נַפְשִׁי אֶת־יְהוָה	1d	Bless the Lord, O my soul!

Technically, this is a parasonantic wordplay because the כ and ק are exchanged, but phonetically, it is a root letter transposition because the כ and ק sound very similar. Moreover, the root letters are chiastically transposed, and both words end with י.¹⁰³ Both words contain the first

---

100. Compare 147 occurrences of שׁכן with 1077 occurrences of ישׁב. It is possible that the psalmist chose the former for theological reasons, namely, to allude to God's abiding glory in the tabernacle and temple; even so, such theological motives (which are very uncertain) do not exclude the possibility of wordplay, but only complement it.

101. Hossfeld and Zenger (*Psalms*, 3:28) describe this relationship saying, "Thus, the two psalms augment each other in mirror fashion and justify being placed in sequence."

102. Allen (*Psalms*, 22) again identifies wordplay between שֵׁם and שָׁמַיִם, though the latter is only alluded to in this psalm. I find this unconvincing, since he does not adequately explain why one could assume a wordplay in this use of שֵׁם and not in any other use of the common word.

103. Although the words differ in vocalic ending (*hiriq yod* versus *patach yod*) there remains ample similarity to confirm the wordplay. The editors of the *BHS* and Kraus (*Psalms*, 2:289) suggest the emendation of a singular pronominal suffix for the second word (i.e., קִרְבִּי) which is unnecessary; cf., Hossfeld, *Psalms*, 3:31; Allen, *Psalms*, 18.

primary accents in their respective lines and share a striking similarity in sound. The repetition of בְּרָכִי in v. 2a, which encloses קְרָבַי, also supports the identification of this wordplay. Functionally, the play with קְרָבַי has the effect of alluding to בְּרָכִי, which brackets קְרָבַי in the preceding and following verses and is elided in v. 1c.

A case of paronomasia begins the lines of vv. 11a and b:

כִּי כִגְבֹהַּ שָׁמַיִם עַל־הָאָרֶץ	11a	(So) strong is his steadfast love for those who fear him.
גָּבַר חַסְדּוֹ עַל־יְרֵאָיו׃	11b	For as high as the heavens are above the earth,

Since כִּי stands outside the meter of v. 11a as anacrusis, כִגְבֹהַּ ("high") should be understood as the first word, syntactically parallel with the first word in the following line, גָּבַר ("strong"). Both adjectives share the consonants ג and ב, making this a case of alliteration. This parallel wordplay connects two words in the simile with the effect of emphasizing the strength of the Lord's steadfast love.

The use of simile continues into vv. 12-13, where paronomasia is again used in syntactically parallel words in order to draw connections between components in the similes. This use of paronomasia links[104] two couplets (and four consecutive lines) by repetition in the initial words:

כִּרְחֹק מִזְרָח מִמַּעֲרָב	12a	As far as east is from west,
הִרְחִיק מִמֶּנּוּ אֶת־פְּשָׁעֵינוּ	12b	He has removed from us our rebellions.
כְּרַחֵם אָב עַל־בָּנִים	13a	As a father has compassion for his children,
רִחַם יְהוָה עַל־יְרֵאָיו	13b	The Lord has compassion for those who fear him.

The repetition of the רח sequence in the first word of each line is an example of parasonancy. Both word pairs are derived from the same root. כִּרְחֹק ("as far") and הִרְחִיק ("he has removed") are derived from רחק, and כְּרַחֵם ("as he has compassion") and רִחַם ("he has compassion") are derived from רחם. Viewed as individual word pairs, כִּרְחֹק and הִרְחִיק would constitute root play and כְּרַחֵם and רִחַם would constitute turn (not a wordplay by definition). However, the four words together constitute

---

104. The psalmist also uses alliteration in vv. 10-14 to bind that stanza together. Each couplet begins with a כ (except for v. 10, in which the כ is necessarily preceded by לֹא); see Goldingay, *Psalms*, 3:171.

parasonancy and function to group these bicola of comparisons and emphasize the message of God's forgiveness and compassion.

Wordplay in Psalm 104

Psalm 104 praises the power, faithfulness, and grace of the creator God. It is filled with beautiful imagery of the Lord's work in creation and providence, and the poet uses four paronomastic wordplays to enhance his message. Most of these tropes go unmentioned in scholarly discussion, which typically revolves around the psalm's ancient Near Eastern connections or polemics.

Casanowicz identifies the wordplay הוֹד וְהָדָר in v. 1c, which also occurs in Ps. 96:6. This collocation qualifies as parasonantic paronomasia. Its function is aesthetic and emphatic, using two near-synonyms, a hendiadys of emphasis, to make prominent the glory and majesty of the Lord's reign.

In the following verse, the psalmist presents a wordplay between עֹטֶה ("wrapping") and נוֹטֶה ("stretching out"):

עֹטֶה־אוֹר כַּשַּׂלְמָה   2a   Wrapping yourself with light like a garment,

נוֹטֶה שָׁמַיִם כַּיְרִיעָה   2b   Stretching out the heavens like a curtain.

The assonance in both initial words is identical, and all but the initial consonants are also identical, making this a paronomastic wordplay, specifically employing assonance, end rhyme, and parasonancy.[105] In addition to their striking similarity, both words begin their respective lines and both lines end with ה ָ . The parallel use of -כְּ, functioning adverbially in the parallel similes, further binds the lines and draws attention to the wordplay. In addition to linking the cola, this example of paronomasia draws attention to the action words of these lines, emphasizing the imagery of Lord's "splendor and majesty" (v. 1b) in which he adorns himself and his dwelling place.

---

105. This is now the third case of assonance used in conjunction with end rhyme (cf., Pss. 93:3bc; 95:3b). Dahood (*Psalms*, 3:33) notes the "fine rhyme and assonance" as well, arguing that the emendations to both words suggested by the editors of *BHS* (and continued by *BHS*) and Kraus (*Psalms*, 3:297) and Allen (*Psalms*, 26) are unfounded. Moreover, the switch from an indicative verb in v. 1 to a participle is not problematic, as the poet is at liberty to make such a change, and it does not damage the style or quality of the poetry. Hossfeld (*Psalms*, 3:44) agrees, stating "Verse 2 creates a fluid transition from the so-called majesty sayings in v. 1 to the chain of determinate participles in v. 3, which are elucidated by means of self-abbreviating parallel clauses with an indeterminate participle and ellipsis in v. 4."

Verse 12 presents another wordplay:

עֲלֵיהֶם עוֹף־הַשָּׁמַיִם יִשְׁכּוֹן	12a	With them the birds of the heavens dwell.
מִבֵּין עֳפָאיִם יִתְּנוּ־קוֹל	12b	From among the foliage they lift up a voice.

Both words share a ע and a פ, making this a case of alliteration. Both words are also second in their lines and syntactically parallel in that both lines begin with a prepositional phrase and end with the verb. The middle phrase in the first line (עוֹף־הַשָּׁמַיִם, "bird[s] of the heavens") is the subject whereas the middle word in the second line (עֳפָאיִם, "foliage") is the object of the preposition, making it a ballast variant, corresponding to the subject.[106] As is common in wordplay, עֳפָאיִם, from עֳפִי, is a *hapax legomenon*, even though the poet could have used other words, such as שִׂיחַ ("bush" or "shrub") as he does in v. 34. This wordplay serves effectively to connect the subjects (birds of the heavens) with their setting (the foliage).

Psalm 104:27-28 uses complex, chiastic wordplay to connect two actions of God's creatures: they hope in the Lord (יְשַׂבֵּרוּן) and are satisfied (יִשְׂבְּעוּן) by him:

כֻּלָּם אֵלֶיךָ יְשַׂבֵּרוּן	27a	All of them put their hope in you,
[לָתֵת] אָכְלָם בְּעִתּוֹ	27b	To give [them] their food in its season.
[תִּתֵּן] לָהֶם יִלְקֹטוּן	28a	You give [it] to them; they gather [it].
תִּפְתַּח יָדְךָ יִשְׂבְּעוּן טוֹב	28b	You open your hand; they are satisfied with goodness.

The verbs יְשַׂבֵּרוּן ("they put their hope in") and יִשְׂבְּעוּן ("they are satisfied") share all but one consonant. Of course, the words are also both imperfect third person masculine plural, so some similarity is expected, but they also share root letter שׂ and ב. They both hold the third position in their lines and seem to function as an *inclusio* for the poetic unit. It is also significant that שׂבר in the Piel is the least common means of communicating the action of hope and expectation, occurring only five other times in the Old Testament (Ruth 1:13; Est. 9:1; Pss. 119:166; 145:15; Isa. 38:18). The Qal form, which has the meaning of "to test" or "to investigate," occurs two

---

106. The *hapax* עֳפָאיִם is usually translated as "foliage" based on the Aramaic cognate; however, Dahood (*Psalms*, 3:38–9) proposes the meaning of "ravens" based on the parallelism with עוֹף־הַשָּׁמַיִם and similar Hebrew roots meaning "dark" or "black"; cf., Hossfeld, *Psalms*, 3:51.

times, while the nominal form, meaning "a hope," occurs twice as well. Other lexical options, such as יחל or קוה, would be expected if the poet were not making a wordplay.

The second word pair could be an example of polysemantic implicit paronomasia: לָהֶם in v. 28a sounds much like לֶחֶם ("bread, food"), which is elided in v. 28a and which alludes to אָכְלָם ("their food") in v. 27b. If this allusion is too far-fetched, the terms at the very least share a lamed and mem, making the word a case of parasonancy.

The key word repetition of the verbal forms לָתֵת and תִּתֵּן, both from נתן, is not wordplay, but its parallel structure strengthens the patterning of this complex wordplay. The substantival use of טוֹב ("goodness") standing outside of this structure does not compromise its effectiveness. The word is also outside of the metrical balance of the two couplets, as it is the fourth primary syllable, whereas each succeeding line has only three tone syllables. Its imbalanced inclusion functions to draw attention to the object of the Lord's provision for his creatures: goodness.[107]

This complex wordplay serves a structural and theological function, highlighting the flow of thought of these verses: God's creatures hope in the Lord (v. 27a) for their food (v. 27b), and the Lord then provides food for them (v. 28a) so that all they must do is receive what his open hand offers (v. 28b). In short, God's creatures *hope* in their creator, and he *satisfies* them with what they need. The chiastic and alternating progression of the words involved in or contributing to this complex wordplay can be seen below:

    a—יְשַׂבֵּרוּן—God's creatures *hope* in the Lord (parasonantic paronomasia)
      b—לָתֵת—*to give* them (key word repetition)
        c—אָכְלָם—*food* (implicit paronomasia)
      b'—תִּתֵּן—The Lord *gives* to his creatures (key word repetition)
        c'—לָהֶם—*to them* (implicit paronomasia)
    a'—יִשְׂבְּעוּן—and God's creatures are *satisfied* (parasonantic paronomasia)

Although the key word repetition in lines b/b' in not technically wordplay, and even if the implicit wordplay in lines c/c' are dubious, these pairs nonetheless help to support the identification of the wordplay between יְשַׂבֵּרוּן and יִשְׂבְּעוּן by binding the strophe together and by highlighting the poetic *inclusio* created by the wordplay.

---

107. Dahood (*Psalms*, 3:46) translates טוֹב as a vocative ("O Good One!") and argues for its inclusion, despite the unbalanced meter and its omission in the Peshitta.

This wordplay serves both a structural function, by forming an *inclusio* around the strophe, and also a theological function, by drawing a connection between the *hope* of the Lord's creatures and his consequent *satisfaction* of their needs, thus underscoring the main theme of the strophe with the poetic device of wordplay.

Wordplay in Psalm 105

Just as Psalm 104 celebrated the Lord's faithfulness in creation, Psalm 105 highlights his faithfulness in Israel's early history. Each of the four paronomastic wordplays in this psalm are micro-structural and are contained within one colon or one bicolon. The two cases that encompass two lines are syntactically parallel and chiastically parallel word pairs, and the two cases that are contained in one line are adjacent words creating alliteration.

The psalm opens in v. 1 with a paronomastic wordplay found also in Isa. 12:4b in which the poet employs parasonancy to begin two consecutive lines of a couplet:

הוֹדוּ לַיהוָה קִרְאוּ בִשְׁמוֹ   1a   Give thanks to the Lord! Call upon his name!

הוֹדִיעוּ בָעַמִּים עֲלִילוֹתָיו   1b   Make known his deeds among the nations!

Not only do הוֹדוּ ("give thanks!") and הוֹדִיעוּ ("make known!") share four common consonants, but they also share the same stem (Hiphil), conjugation (imperative), inflection (2mp), and weak verb class (I-yod); and they both are syntactically parallel. The wordplay binds the couplet and emphasizes the syntagmatic, causal relationship, viz., giving thanks (ידה) to the Lord should lead to the proclamation (ידע) among the nations of his great works. This use of paronomasia to emphasize a syntagmatic relationship of praise and proclamation recalls the similar wordplay in and 96:1-2.

The next wordplay involves the middle words in the chiastic parallelism of Ps. 105:15:

אַל־תִּגְּעוּ בִמְשִׁיחָי   15a   Do not afflict my anointed ones!

וְלִנְבִיאַי אַל־תָּרֵעוּ   15b   And to my prophets do no evil!

These adjacent words share the same assonance (with the exception of the prefixed waw conjunction). The words are also syntactically and chiastically parallel: <u>jussive</u> → <u>object</u> // <u>object</u> → <u>jussive</u>, which enables them to be adjacent and thus more noticeably played upon. This paronomastic wordplay binds these two lines, and specifically the two objects. The Lord's anointed and his prophets are to be protected from evil and affliction, and the Lord himself will ensure their safety.

Psalm 105:22 offers an example of alliteration between לֶאְסֹר ("to bind") and שָׂרָיו ("his princes"):

> לֶאְסֹר שָׂרָיו בְּנַפְשׁוֹ 22a To bind (instruct?) his princes in his soul,
>
> וּזְקֵנָיו יְחַכֵּם 22b So that he could make his elders wise.

The ס and שׂ have the same sound, and because the repeated sounds themselves are adjacent and constitute half of their words' consonants (minus the prefix and suffix), this alliteration qualifies as a genuine wordplay. It functions to draw the attention of the readers to the unique imagery in this line. But what is that imagery?

The first line is problematic because the use of לֶאְסֹר ("to bind") in the MT does not make much sense in the context. This stanza recounts God's sovereignty over Joseph's life in Egypt, and how the pharaoh gave Joseph great authority. Verse 22 provides the reason why Joseph was given this authority. If the MT is retained, the line could have the sense that Joseph had royal authority in order to maintain control over the other nobility, i.e., that he could secure ("bind") their loyalty and obedience his own will ("soul"). A more physical sense of "binding" could also be in view, as the NET Bible demonstrates: "giving him authority to imprison his officials and to teach his advisers." The LXX (and Peshitta), however, reflect a *Vorlage* of ליסר ("to instruct"), which better fits the context of v. 22b, making these two lines together about Joseph's teaching of the Egyptian nobility, which is the reason why he was given authority (v. 21).[108] While this textual difficulty is important to note for the exegesis and understanding of the line, it has no bearing on the identification of the wordplay. Both לאסר and ליסר retain the shared consonantal sounds of שָׂרָיו. If the MT is to be retained, the wordplay would serve to show how Joseph had authority for two, complementary reasons: to restrain wayward leaders when necessary, and to instruct leaders with ears to hear. If the supposed *Vorlage* LXX is to be preferred, then the wordplay emphasizes Joseph's role of teaching wisdom to the nobility and leadership of Egypt.

---

108. English translations are divided. Some retain the MT reading (ESV, JPS), and some favor the LXX (NIV, NRS). Most commentators follow the *BHS* suggestion to read with the LXX and Peshitta, deClaissé-Walford, Jacobson, and Tanner, *The Book of Psalms*, 785; VanGemeren, *Psalms*, 775.

The following stanza in Psalm 105 focuses on the next leader and deliverer of God's people, Moses, as he performs God's miracles for judgment on Egypt and the deliverance of his people. Verse 30a is another example of alliteration with two consonants:

שָׁרַץ אַרְצָם צְפַרְדְּעִים 30a Their land swarmed with frogs,
בְּחַדְרֵי מַלְכֵיהֶם 30b [Even] in the chambers of their kings.

In this case of alliteration, שָׁרַץ ("swarmed") and אַרְצָם ("their land") are separated by another letter (א), but their repetition (in reverse order and separated) for a third time in צְפַרְדְּעִים ("frogs") serves to strengthen the case for wordplay here. The wordplay unites the three words in the colon and perhaps underscores the sense of the initial verb, שָׁרַץ. Just as Egypt swarmed with frogs, so also this line swarms with sound repetition!

Wordplay in Psalm 106

Psalm 106 complements and contrasts Psalm 105 by highlighting the Lord's disappointment with Israel and yet faithfulness throughout her early history of perennial infidelity. Though different in genre and theme from its corresponding bookend, Psalm 90, the psalms share similarities in their abundant use of wordplay and in the diversity of subcategories, structures, and functions employed. The most common function of wordplay in Psalm 106 is the reinforcement of parallelism in adjoining lines or bicola.

Wordplay first emerges in Psalm 106 with parasonancy in v. 3:

אַשְׁרֵי שֹׁמְרֵי מִשְׁפָּט 3a Blessed are those who observe justice,
עֹשֵׂה צְדָקָה בְכָל־עֵת 3b The one who does righteousness in every season.

The opening words אַשְׁרֵי ("blessed/happy") and שֹׁמְרֵי ("those who observe") differ only in one letter, א and מ, respectively, as well as the initial vowel and vocalization of the shewa. The opening vowel is short in אַשְׁרֵי, causing the following shewa to be silent and resulting in a bi-syllabic word, whereas the opening vowel in שֹׁמְרֵי is long, causing the following shewa to be vocal and resulting in a tri-syllabic word. The phonetic resemblance is still significant and creates a wordplay that emphasizes the blessedness of those who keep justice (מִשְׁפָּט, which also contains a שׁ).

The next wordplay in Psalm 106 is found in the third colon of v. 7:

אֲבוֹתֵינוּ בְמִצְרַיִם לֹא־הִשְׂכִּילוּ נִפְלְאוֹתֶיךָ	7a	Our fathers in Egypt did not understand your wonders.
לֹא זָכְרוּ אֶת־רֹב חֲסָדֶיךָ	7b	They did not remember the multitude of your lovingkindnesses,
וַיַּמְרוּ[109] עַל־יָם בְּיַם־סוּף	7c	And they rebelled by the sea, by the Red Sea.

This three-fold repetition of the closed syllable "yam," each with a י, מ, and an "a" class vowel, occurs in each of the three metrical sections of this line. After the waw consecutive וַיַּמְרוּ ("and they rebelled"), the author mentions יָם ("sea") twice. The last instance of יָם could be construed as a means of balancing the meter of the final line, and indeed some versions (such as the LXX) and some scholars[110] omit one instance of the word. This omission is supported by the possibility of dittography. However, the use of the word וַיַּמְרוּ, in which the full word יָם is imbedded, supports the more likely explanation that the sound is repeated for phonetic and wordplay reasons. Moreover, if metrical balance was the poet's primary objective, he likely would have added another tone syllable to this three-accent line in order for it to conform to the four-accent lines preceding it in the tricolon.

This wordplay underscores the initial word וַיַּמְרוּ in order to emphasize Israel's rebellion. Thus, while at first glance the tricolon appears to emphasize the place of Israel's rebellion (the Sea), the wordplay in fact subtly and cleverly emphasizes the rebellion itself by repeating the same sound found in the word.

By saving Israel from the Sea, God also saved them from their enemies because he caused that same Sea to destroy the Egyptians. The psalmist emphasizes this subsequent redemption by using repetition and assonance in parallel in v. 10:

---

109. Allen (*Psalms*, 49) identifies a macro-structural wordplay between וַיַּמְרוּ ("and they rebelled"), מִהֲרוּ ("they hastened"), הִמְרוּ ("they rebelled/embittered"), and יַמְרוּ ("they rebelled") in vv. 7, 13, 33, and 43 respectively. His argument is based largely on his strophication of the psalm and the placement of these words at key junctures. However, three of the four words are from the same root, being used in essentially the same way, which more accurately constitutes turn or *leitmotif*, and the words occur at only some of the many (at least 16) strophic junctures in Allen's strophication. Thus, these words will not be analyzed as wordplay in this study.

110. Kraus, *Psalms*, 2:315; Allen, *Psalms*, 45.

יוֹשִׁיעֵם מִיַּד שׂוֹנֵא	10a	And he saved them from the hand of the hater
וַיִּגְאָלֵם מִיַּד אוֹיֵב	10b	And he redeemed them from the hand of the enemy

The final words in each line correspond in assonance by virtue of their shared inflection (Qal, active participle, masculine singular). However, שׂנא ("to hate") is usually transitive,[111] while איב ("to be hostile to") is usually intransitive, which means that the former would most naturally take at least an objective suffix. The object ("them") is elided, suggesting that this wordplay is genuine and an example of using assonance to reinforce strong syntactical and semantic parallelism.

In the next stanza (vv. 13-15), Israel again is rebelling against the Lord, but instead of deliverance, the Lord sends punishment, ironically in the form of something they wanted. The background is probably Numbers 11, when the Israelites complained about their humdrum diet of manna and wanted meat as well. God sent them quail, which they greedily devoured, and then he struck them down for their craving (Num. 11:33). The poet recounts this episode using a polysemantic implicit paronomasia in the final verse of the stanza:

וַיִּתֵּן לָהֶם שֶׁאֱלָתָם	15a	And he gave to them their request,
וַיְשַׁלַּח רָזוֹן בְּנַפְשָׁם	15b	And he sent a wasting (disease) among their souls.

In its context, the primary sense of רָזוֹן is "a wasting," which most English translations rightly render as "a wasting disease."[112] The nominal form occurs only two other times in the Old Testament. The LXX (followed by the Vulgate and Peshitta) reads πλησμονήν ("satisfaction"), perhaps misreading the rare word as רָצוֹן ("goodwill, favor")[113] or, according to the editors of *BHS*, מָזוֹן ("food, provisions"), which fits the context well but is likewise rare (two occurrences in the Hebrew Bible) and thus an unlikely choice.[114] The LXX translator probably did not read or misread רָזוֹן as רָצוֹן because in v. 4 he translates it with εὐδοκίᾳ ("good pleasure"), and not πλησμονήν, as we have in v. 15. If the LXX translator was reading

---

111. *HALOT* 1339–40.

112. *HALOT* (1209) gives the meaning of "consumption" for the use of רָזוֹן in this verse.

113. *HALOT* 1282–3.

114. *HALOT* 565. Allen (*Psalms*, 48) also interprets the LXX, as well as the Peshitta, as a "misreading."

or misreading מָזוֹן, we would expect a standard translation equivalent, such as אֹכֶל or לֶחֶם.

The translators might have been surprised by the Hebrew רָזוֹן because the previous line reads, "And [the Lord] gave to them their request," that is, what they "lusted for," in the wilderness in v. 14a. However, it is possible that the author was purposefully shocking his readers by highlighting that the people's "lusting" was as destructive as a wasting disease. Thus, the MT should be retained, and there are several possibilities for other words to which רָזוֹן could be alluding, creating a *double entendre*.[115]

The first interpretive possibility is that רָזוֹן could allude to the verbal form from which it is derived, רזן, which is only used substantively in the Old Testament of judicious rulers, meaning "to be weighty, judicious, commanding."[116] The Arabic cognate has a similar meaning of "to be weighty, firm; to be reliable in judgment."[117] This has the effect of presenting multiple, related ideas at once: the Lord afflicted Israel with a wasting disease (the primary meaning of the text) for the purpose of commanding judgment (the implicit, secondary meaning). This use of polysemy would explain the author's unique word choice and would fit the context.

The second and even more likely possibility is that רָזוֹן is alluding to the more common and similar-sounding רָצוֹן ("pleasure, favor") either in itself or specifically its use in v. 4a. רָצוֹן is common enough in the Hebrew Bible (56 occurrences) that this near-homophone would likely have come to the minds of the readers or listeners. This would constitute polysemantic implicit paronomasia, specifically parasonancy, and it would create an ironic connection: in v. 4 the psalmist is pleading faithfully for the Lord's favor that he shows towards his people; in v. 15b he is recounting Israel's unfaithfulness and the Lord's disfavor with them.[118] Nearly five centuries ago, John Calvin noted this implicit paronomasia with רָצוֹן (without reference to its use in v. 4) interpreting the wordplay in what this project would call paronomastic, implicit parasonancy. He interprets the רָזוֹן as "leanness," referring to the quail, which satisfied the people's lustful desire for meat, but resulted in only leanness, or a wasting away (Num. 11:33). He describes the poet's purpose of this "fine paronomasia," saying:

---

115. Many critics disagree, arguing that the MT was probably corrupted because the psalm contains much more synonymous parallelism than antithetical parallelism. Dahood (*Psalms*, 3:71) cites this prevailing opinion but opts for interpreting רָזוֹן as a Ugaritic cognate meaning "leanness."
116. BDB, 931.
117. *HALOT* 1210; cf., BDB, 931.
118. Goldingay mentions the paronomasia between רָזוֹן and רָצוֹן, *Psalms*, 3:229.

> The prophet, therefore, in allusion to their lusting, by a word which is very similar to good pleasure or desire, says that God sent leanness into their souls; meaning by that, that he had indeed gratified the inordinate desires of the people, in such a way, however, as that those who had loathed the manna, now received nothing but leanness.[119]

This allusion to God's favor in the midst of judgment is reminiscent of the similar wordplays in Ps. 102:11b. The allusion could function to contrast God's favor with his judgment, or it could (as in Ps. 102:11) hint towards hope and the constancy of God's character even in the midst of judgment.

Judgment continues in the next stanza, which recounts the rebellion of Korah, Dathan, and Abiram, prominent Levites who were jealous of Moses and Aaron and challenged their authority and holiness (cf., Num. 16). In Ps. 106:17-18, the psalmist uses a paronomastic wordplay to draw a connection between דָּתָן ("Dathan") and בַּעֲדָתָם ("within their assembly"):

תִּפְתַּח־אֶרֶץ וַתִּבְלַע דָּתָן	17a	The earth opened and swallowed up Dathan,
וַתְּכַס עַל־עֲדַת אֲבִירָם	17b	And it covered the assembly of Abiram,
וַתִּבְעַר־אֵשׁ בַּעֲדָתָם	18a	And a fire burned within their assembly.
לֶהָבָה תְּלַהֵט רְשָׁעִים	18b	A flame set ablaze the wicked.

Both words end the first lines of their respective couplets, which tightens the correspondence of these couplets. In addition to the shared ד and ת, the מ and נ are both nasal letters. The wordplay functions to emphasize that it was not only Dathan and Abiram (and Korah) who were destroyed by God's wrath, but all of their 250 followers as well.

The following stanza of Psalm 106 (vv. 19-23) recounts Israel's famously tragic idolatry with the golden calf and Moses' intercession for mercy on Israel's behalf (Exod. 32:1-14). In vv. 23-24, the poet employs alternating pairs of similar sounds:

וַיֹּאמֶר לְהַשְׁמִידָם	23a	And he said [that he would] destroy them
לוּלֵי מֹשֶׁה בְחִירוֹ	23b	Had not Moses, his chosen one,
עָמַד בַּפֶּרֶץ לְפָנָיו	23c	Stood in the breach before him
לְהָשִׁיב חֲמָתוֹ מֵהַשְׁחִית	23d	To turn his wrath from destroying [them]

---

119. John Calvin, *Commentary on the Book of Psalms*, trans. James Anderson (Grand Rapids: Baker, 2005), 4:218–19.

וַיִּמְאֲסוּ בְּאֶרֶץ חֶמְדָּה 24a And they despised the delight of the land.

לֹא־הֶאֱמִינוּ לִדְבָרוֹ 24b They did not believe his word.

The four-fold repetition of the ש/ה combination marks this as a wordplay. Additionally, the poet chose two words for "destroy," שמד and שחת, both of which employ the ש/ה combination in the Hiphil, and both of which bracket the verse and stand in contrast, the first as a reference to God's determination to destroy Israel and the second as the retraction of that destruction because of Moses' intercession. Thus, four key words in this verse are highlighted through alliterative paronomasia: לְהַשְׁמִידָם ("to destroy them"), מֹשֶׁה ("Moses"), לְהָשִׁיב ("to turn back"), and מֵהַשְׁחִית ("from destroying [them]").

Similarly, the words חֲמָתוֹ ("his wrath") and חֶמְדָּה ("delight") are related through sharp contrast. This two-fold repetition of the ח/מ in vv. 23d and 24a is a weak example of wordplay, since the words share only two phonemes, are not adjacent, are repeated only once, and span two stanzas. Watson cites the word pair as paronomasia,[120] and its use in conjunction with the four-fold wordplay above makes it more viable. The poet could be using the sound similarity between חֲמָתוֹ and חֶמְדָּה to highlight the sharp contrast between the mercy God shows to Israel in v. 23 and Israel's relentless unfaithfulness as they despise that in which they should delight, the land. Thus, emphasizing these key theological concepts through wordplay, the poet is able to highlight the Lord's turning of his wrath only for Israel to reject what was actually pleasant. Just as Israel desired something destructive (v. 15), she also rejected something good (v. 24).

Verse 27 is part of a prophetic threat that follows from Israel's faithlessness in refusing to enter the land. In the previous line, v. 26b, God promises to let this first generation of the exodus fall in the wilderness. The next couplet links that generation with the exilic generation, who cry out at the end of the psalm for restoration (v. 47). The poet describes the scattering of God's faithless people by using parasonancy:

וּלְהַפִּיל זַרְעָם בַּגּוֹיִם 27a And to make their seed fall among the nations,

וּלְזָרוֹתָם בָּאֲרָצוֹת 27b And to scatter them throughout the lands.

All of the consonants of זַרְעָם ("their seed") are repeated in the next line in the word וּלְזָרוֹתָם ("and to scatter them"), except for the ע, and several

---

120. W. G. E. Watson, *Traditional Techniques in Classical Hebrew Verse*, JSOTSup 170 (Sheffield: Sheffield Academic, 1994), 381.

other words for "scatter" could have been used (such as פוץ, בזר, or נדח). In the Piel this verb is commonly used to refer to the Lord's scattering of Israel or other kingdoms among the nations; however, it is never used with words for offspring or seed, so this wordplay is unique to this psalm. The poet is probably seeking to emphasize and draw together the imagery of scattered seed: just like plant seed is scattered throughout the ground, so also were God's people scattered among the nations.

Another case of parasonancy occurs in Ps. 106:32, which records the account of Israel's complaining for water and Moses' punishment for hitting (and not speaking to) the rock (Num. 20:2-13):

| וַיַּקְצִיפוּ עַל־מֵי מְרִיבָה | 32a | And they provoked [him] to wrath by the waters of Meribah, |
| וַיֵּרַע לְמֹשֶׁה בַּעֲבוּרָם | 32b | And he brought punishment to Moses on their account. |

Aside from the inseparable preposition בְּ- on בַּעֲבוּרָם ("on their account") and the exchange of ה for ע, both words share three of the same consonants, only in reverse, chiastic order: ר, מ, and ב (מ-ר-ב//ב-ר-מ). Both words also have an unchangeably long vowel (*hireq yod* and *shureq*). This wordplay has a structural function, ending each line with similar sounds. This wordplay binds the cola, and possibly emphasizes placement of blame on the Israelites, who embittered Moses and caused him to speak and act rashly (v. 33), thus incurring punishment.

Psalm 106:42 presents the next wordplay, a complex wordplay composed of two cases of paronomasia:

וַיִּשְׁפְּכוּ דָם נָקִי	38a	And they poured out innocent blood,
דַּם־בְּנֵיהֶם וּבְנוֹתֵיהֶם	38b	Blood of their sons and their daughters,
אֲשֶׁר זִבְּחוּ לַעֲצַבֵּי כְנָעַן	38c	Whom they sacrificed to the idols of Canaan,
וַתֶּחֱנַף הָאָרֶץ בַּדָּמִים	38d	And the land was defiled by the blood.
[...]		
וַיִּלְחָצוּם אוֹיְבֵיהֶם	42a	And their enemies oppressed them,
וַיִּכָּנְעוּ תַּחַת יָדָם	42b	And they were humbled under their hand.

Not only is the three-fold repetition of דָם ("blood") significant in v. 38, but the verse is also rare in that it is a quatrain, when all but seven of the 48 verses of Psalm 106 are bicolons. The use of a quatrain in v. 38 slows down the narrative drama and draws attention to the horrors of what God's people were capable of doing, namely, spilling the blood of their own children for idols.¹²¹ This is arguably the climax of the historical review of Israel's faithlessness in Psalm 106. The poet understandably waits until v. 42 to play on the word דָּם since it is the point in the poem that describes the ironic effects of Israel's rebellion, namely, that the nations whom they were emulating in turn oppressed and humbled them. Thus, v. 42 describes how Israel's enemies carried out the Lord's judgment under "their hand" (יָדָם).

This case of parasonancy draws the readers' attention back to the horrific imagery of Israel's child sacrifice in v. 38 as a bountiful warrant for their own blood spilled by the hand of their enemies in v. 42; the spilling of innocent blood was repaid by the spilling of their own guilty blood.¹²² This is God's justice. And, yet, the very next verse, and final tricolon of the stanza (v. 43), begins to recount how God sought to deliver them, in spite of their sin, and in light of his grace: "Many times he delivered them, but they were rebellious in their counsel and were brought low through their iniquity." Thus, the wordplay between vv. 38 and 42 further highlights the Lord's merciful grace and just punishment.¹²³

The wordplay between the three-fold use of דָּם in v. 38 and יָדָם in v. 42b is complemented by another wordplay in these verses, that between כְּנָעַן ("Canaan") and וַיִּכָּנְעוּ ("and they humbled themselves"). This wordplay is another example of parasonancy, in that the נ, כ, and ע are all shared, even in the same order. Its function is theological, as Dahood describes: "The Israelites were brought into subjection precisely because they

---

121. The editors of *BHS*, as well as some commentators, believe that the second and third line in this quatrain (v. 38bc) are a gloss due to their disruption of the meter, the repetition of "their sons and daughters," and the geographical identification of "Canaan," and believe that the lines should therefore be deleted. Kraus (*Psalms*, 2:316, 321) argues that this section "clearly breaks up the meter and interprets נקי דם incorrectly."

Most scholars maintain that the lines are original. Allen (*Psalms*, 49) considers the MT's text "vindicated by its stylistic role in the context" as well as its parallel in Ezek. 20:30-31 and the wordplay between כְּנָעַן and וַיִּכָּנְעוּ. Hossfeld (*Psalms*, 3:92) also argues that the quatrain can be divided into two bicola and that "this localization of 'Canaan' fits well within the Priestly-suffused Psalm 106." Dahood (*Psalms*, 3:74) likewise argues that the deletion of these lines would remove the wordplay between כְּנָעַן and וַיִּכָּנְעוּ and damage the rhetorical flow.

122. Robert B. Chisholm, Jr. ("Wordplay in the Eighth Century Prophets," 52) also notes how the prophets often used wordplay to make connections between Israel's sin and God's judgment saying, "The prophets used wordplay to draw attention to the appropriate or poetic nature of divine justice."

123. God's mercy is highlighted even more in the following stanza (vv. 44-46), which is almost shockingly gracious in the context.

adopted Canaanite mores."[124] Allen adds that this wordplay "ironically makes the punishment fit the crime."[125] This is similar to the irony in Ps. 106:15 (when Israel got what she wanted, but it turned out to be a wasting punishment), which likewise was emphasized through wordplay.

Summary of Findings

While Casanowicz identifies eight wordplays in Book IV of the Psalter, this study has identified 74. This disparity is attributable to the differences in methodology and scope between the projects. Casanowicz's study is relatively brief, 93 pages, including appendices and index. The first portion, 44 pages, explains the phenomenon of paronomasia and wordplay, citing select examples from the Old Testament. The second section is 41 pages long and lists, in alphabetical order, each wordplay that Casanowicz identified in the entire Old Testament. Because Casanowicz devotes only half of his project to identifying individual wordplays, and because his analysis included a much larger corpus, it is understandable that his findings were more conservative than those in the present study. Moreover, not all of the wordplays identified in this study are equally persuasive, which is why each wordplay is assigned a numerical rating in an effort to portray the data as objectively and honestly as possible. However, even if some of the 74 wordplays identified in this study are considered dubious to the reader, the sheer number of instances, many of which contain a high degree of certitude, reflect a profuse use of the trope in Book IV.

In her important work on Hebrew parallelism, Adele Berlin discusses how the use of sound pairs "enhances the perception of correspondence" between parallel lines.[126] We have noted this function in numerous wordplays discussed in this chapter. Berlin's criteria for identifying sound pairs differs from our criteria of identifying wordplays insofar as she excludes assonance and looks only for consonant repetition, and she limits sounds pairs to those found in parallel lines. Her exclusion of assonance is based on the uncertainty of the ancient pronunciation, and her focus on parallel lines is due to her focus on parallelism and the effect of phonetic similarity on that trope.[127] However, although our concerns and criterion differ in these matters, our caution regarding the subjective nature of

---

124. Dahood, *Psalms III*, 74, 75. It is unfortunate that Dahood does not recognize the additional wordplay between vv. 38 and 42, as the pairing of these wordplays strengthen each other.
125. Allen, *Psalms*, 49.
126. Berlin, *The Dynamics of Biblical Parallelism*, 111.
127. Ibid., 104.

identifying phonetic correspondences between words and of overstating our conclusions reflects a similar methodology:

> There is always a risk of subjectivity in identifying sound correspondence. What rings loudly in my ears may only echo silence in the ears of others. I can only hope that out of the large number of illustrations that I have brought, a sufficient number will be acceptable proof that sound must also be considered an aspect of parallelism... Although some of this correspondence may have been accidental...the quantity of examples strongly suggests that sound pairing is no less significant than are other types of linguistic equivalence.[128]

Like Berlin, I acknowledge that some of the instances of wordplay analyzed above are less persuasive or may not have been clear to the emic, original readers or listeners; however, having cast the net wide, I have erred on the side of possibly including some cases that are not wordplays in order to safeguard against excluding any that are in fact genuine wordplays. Thus, readers are asked to forgive any overstatement in this analysis, given the inherent subjectivity and challenge of identifying a phenomenon such as wordplay.

The above analysis identified 74 individual wordplays, employing 78 total subcategories. There are four more subcategories (78) than wordplays (74) because three of the wordplays employ a combination of two or three subcategories of wordplay (Pss. 95:3ab; 97:9bc; 104:2ab). These wordplays all combine various subcategories of paronomasia. For example, the wordplay between the collocated words גָּדוֹל עַל־כָּל in Ps. 95:3b employs both end rhyme and assonance.

In order to draw some conclusions, it will be helpful to synthesize our findings according to the strength of the data, the categories and subcategories of wordplay, the distribution of wordplays within Book IV, and other observations. Table 1 displays the quality rankings of each wordplay, as well as the average ranking of each psalm. It is important to keep in mind that we are not evaluating the quality of the psalm's use of wordplay, but are rather evaluating the surety with which we have identified the wordplays for analysis. In other words, this is a vital element of methodology and not a reflection of the quality of the text. Where a rating of 1 denotes a very high degree of certainty or strength, a rating of 2 denotes a moderate amount of certainty, and a 3 denotes a lower amount of certainty. While those wordplays receiving a 3 are considered weaker examples of the trope, they nonetheless exhibit enough criteria (e.g., multiple shared phonemes, proximity, or juxtaposition with another wordplay) to qualify.

128. Ibid., 125.

Table 2. Rating of Confidence in the MT Wordplay

Reference	Category	Strength	Average Rating Per Psalm
90:1b, 17a	Paronomasia	1	1.79
90:3ab	Polysemy	3	
90:4b, 6b	Paronomasia	2	
90:4c, 6a	Paronomasia	1	
90:6a	Polysemy	2	
90:6b	Polysemy	2	
90:8b, 9a	Paronomasia	1	
90:9a, 10b, 11b	Paronomasia	1	
90:10ab	Paronomasia	1	
90:10c	Polysemy	3	
90:12ab	Paronomasia	2	
90:14b, 15a	Polysemy	2	
90:15b, 16a	Polysemy	2	
90:15b, 16a	Paronomasia	2	
91:1ab	Paronomasia	2	1.50
91:1a, 4c	Paronomasia	1	
91:3a, 5a	Paronomasia	1	
91:3b, 6a	Polysemy	2	
91:6a, 7b	Paronomasia	1	
91:9b	Paronomasia	3	
91:11b, 13a	Paronomasia	1	
91:12a, 13b	Paronomasia	1	
92:6b, 7a	Polysemy	2	2.50
92:9a, 11a	Paronomasia	3	
93:1b, 2a	Paronomasia	3	3.00
93:3bc	Paronomasia	3	
94:8b	Paronomasia	1	1.50
94:12a	Paronomasia	1	
94:19a	Polysemy	2	
94:19b	Polysemy	2	
95:1ab, 2b	Paronomasia	2	1.67
95:3ab	Paronomasia	2	
95:6ab	Paronomasia	1	
96:1ab-2ab	Paronomasia	2	1.33
96:6a	Paronomasia	1	
96:11a	Paronomasia	1	
97:3ab	Paronomasia	1	1.25
97:4ab	Paronomasia	1	
97:7b	Paronomasia	2	
97:9bc	Paronomasia	1	
101:3ab	Paronomasia	2	2.00

102:5a, 6b	Paronomasia	1	1.30
102:5b, 6a	Paronomasia	1	
102:5b, 6a	Paronomasia	1	
102:11b	Polysemy	2	
102:11b	Polysemy	2	
102:16a, 17b	Paronomasia	2	
102:17a, 18a	Paronomasia	1	
102:20b, 21a, 22a	Paronomasia	1	
102:27c	Polysemy	1	
102:29ab	Paronomasia	1	
103:1bc, 2a	Paronomasia	1	1.33
103:11ab	Paronomasia	2	
103:12ab, 13ab	Paronomasia	1	
104:1c	Paronomasia	1	1.2
104:2ab	Paronomasia	1	
104:12ab	Paronomasia	1	
104:27a, 28b	Paronomasia	1	
104:27b, 28a	Polysemy	2	
105:1ab	Paronomasia	2	1.75
105:15ab	Paronomasia	3	
105:22a	Paronomasia	1	
105:30a	Paronomasia	1	
106:3a	Paronomasia	1	1.64
106:7c	Paronomasia	2	
106:10ab	Paronomasia	2	
106:15b	Polysemy	2	
106:17a, 18a	Paronomasia	1	
106:23abd	Paronomasia	2	
106:23d, 24a	Paronomasia	3	
106:27ab	Paronomasia	2	
106:32ab	Paronomasia	1	
106:38abd, 42b	Paronomasia	1	
106:38c, 42b	Paronomasia	1	
Overall Average		1.59	

Several general conclusions and specific patterns can be seen from this data. The overall average of all 74 wordplays is 1.59, meaning that most wordplays are somewhere between the spectrum of certain and moderate; in other words, they exhibit an above average strength. There are a total of 38 wordplays that have a rating of 1, meaning that 51.4 percent of the wordplays have the highest degree of certainty. Twenty-eight wordplays have a rating of 2, meaning that 37.8 percent of the total wordplays have a moderate amount of certainty. Combining these groups, 89.2 percent of the wordplays above are either certain or moderately strong. Only eight of the wordplays are weak, meaning that 10.8 percent are less persuasive.

These data conform to the methodology established in the first chapter, which offered specific criteria for identifying wordplay and also a balanced openness towards potential wordplay.

The rating of individual psalms largely reflects this overall average. Psalms with fewer wordplays do not offer enough data points from which to draw a sound conclusion, so although Psalms 92, 93, and 101 appear to have more dubious wordplays based on their average ratings, such conclusions cannot be drawn because they have only one or two cases of wordplay. Two psalms with sufficient data and greater certainty are Psalms 102 and 104.

Looking at the distribution between categories, the average rating for polysemy is 2.00, while the average rating for paronomasia is 1.44. This variance is not surprising given the more interpretative nature of identifying polysemy; polysemy can rarely be definitively proven, whereas paronomasia is often more obvious and straight forward.

Having established the methodological effectiveness of the analysis and the overall confidence that the data provides, the following tables synthesize various components of the analysis. The following table summarizes the distribution of the categories and subcategories of wordplays in Book IV:

Table 3. Distribution of Categories and Subcategories of Wordplay

Category	Subcategory	Total	% in Category	Total %
Paronomasia	Alliteration	22	34.9	28.2
	Assonance	6	9.5	7.7
	Rhyme	3	4.8	3.8
	Metaphony	1	1.6	1.3
	Parasonancy	24	38.1	30.8
	Root Play/Transposition	7	11.1	9.0
Total in Paronomasia		63	100.0	80.8
Polysemy	*Double entendre*	2	13.3	2.6
	Implicit Paronomasia	8	53.3	10.3
	Punning Repetition	5	33.3	6.4
Total in Polysemy		15	100.0	19.2
Total		78		100

Of the 78 wordplay subcategories in Book IV of the MT Psalter, 80.8 percent of them are types of paronomasia while 19.2 percent are examples of polysemy. The prominence of paronomasia reflects the relative ease of playing on sound as compared to playing on meaning. Within the paronomasia category, the largest subcategory is parasonancy, with 38.1 percent of all examples of paronomasia. Alliteration is the second most common type of paronomasia, used in 34.9 percent of the paronomastic wordplays. The relative difficulty of parasonancy, as compared to alliteration and assonance, for example, makes the extensive use of parasonancy impressive. Root letter plays and transpositions account for 11.1 percent of paronomasia. Assonance and rhyme (which often work in tandem) are used in 9.5 percent and 4.8 percent of paronomastic wordplays, respectively. The sole case of metaphony accounts 1.6 percent.

Of the polysemantic wordplay, implicit paronomasia and *double entendre* are implicit wordplays, wherein the word is mentioned only once and the reader must discern from the context whether or not the author is alluding to a secondary meaning or similar-sounding word. Punning repetition, however, makes the polysemy explicit by repeating the word and providing contexts to make each distinct meaning clear. Of the three polysemantic subcategories, implicit paronomasia had the greatest attestation in that category, 53.3 percent. This is not surprising given that the second word alluded to only shared key sounds, giving the poet more options. *Double entendre* is a relatively more difficult trope because the poet is limited to the meanings within a word's semantic range. Of the polysemantic wordplays, only 13.3 percent were *double entendres*. Punning repetition accounted for 33.3 percent of the polysemantic wordplays.

The following table summarizes the number of wordplays within each psalm, as well as the number of subcategories employed:

Table 4. Distribution of Wordplay Subcategories in Each Psalm of Book IV

Psalm	Paronomasia						Polysemy			Total
	Alliteration	Assonance	Rhyme	Metaphony	Parasonancy	Root Play/Trans.	*Double entendre*	Implicit Paronomasia	Punning Repetition	
90	3	1			2	2	1	2	3	14
91	2				4	1			1	8
92						1		1		2
93	1	1								2
94				1		1		2		4
95	1	1	1		1					4
96					3					3
97	2		1		1	1				5

98									
99									
100									
101	1								1
102	4				3	1	1	1	10
103	1				1	1			3
104	1	1	1		3			1	7
105	2	1			1				4
106	4	1			5			1	11
Total	22	6	3	1	24	7	2	8	5	78

The following table summarizes these data further, focusing on the category (paronomasia vs. polysemy) rather than the subcategory. It also includes the percentage of total wordplay categories used in each psalm.

Table 5. Distribution of Wordplay Categories in Each Psalm of Book IV

Psalm	Paronomasia	Polysemy	Total	Total %
90	8	6	14	17.9
91	7	1	8	10.3
92	1	1	2	2.6
93	2		2	2.6
94	2	2	4	5.1
95	4		4	5.1
96	3		3	3.8
97	5		5	6.4
98			0	0
99			0	0
100			0	0
101	1		1	1.3
102	7	3	10	12.8
103	3		3	3.8
104	6	1	7	9.0
105	4		4	5.1
106	10	1	11	14.1
Total	63	15	78	100

One important observation is that the four psalms with the most wordplays are all connected in the larger shaping of the Psalter. According to Gerald Wilson, Psalms 90, 91, 92, 94, 102, 105, and 106 are all part of the "Mosaic Frame" of Book IV.[129] Of these, Psalms 90, 91, 102,

---

129. Gerald H. Wilson, "Shaping the Psalter: A Consideration of Editorial Linkage in the Book of Psalms," in *Shape and Shaping of the Psalter*, ed. J. Clinton McCann, Jr., JSOTSup 159 (Sheffield: JSOT, 1993), 76; cf., Wilson, *The Editing of the Hebrew Psalter*, SBLDS 76 (Chico, CA: Scholars Press, 1985 [1981]), 214–19.

and 106 each contain more than 10 percent of the total wordplays in Book IV, and together they contain 55.1 percent of the total wordplay subcategories in Book IV. It is not surprising that Psalms 90 and 102 correspond in number and type of wordplay, since they are strongly connected theologically through the theme of human transience. The numerous wordplays in Psalm 91 also fits the style of Psalm 90, which complements their shared relationship of lament over human transience and the responding reassurance of the Lord's protection and love. What is surprising, however, is that Psalm 92, which is likewise closely tied to Psalms 90 and 91 only provides 2.6 percent of the total wordplays in Book IV. Moreover, the prevalence of wordplay in Psalm 106 stands in (slight) contrast to its neighboring Psalm 105, which likewise recounts the Lord's faithfulness in Israel's history and yet uses roughly one-third of the number of wordplays in Psalm 106.

The ratio of paronomasia to polysemy in each psalm in Book IV also corresponds roughly to the same relationship in the whole corpus of Book IV. Because there is one polysemantic play for every 4.13 paronomastic plays in all, one would expect that each psalm with over four paronomastic wordplays would have at least one polysemantic play, and that is approximately the case. The data for some psalms are too scarce to draw firm conclusions; for example, Psalm 94 seems to exhibit a higher than average tendency towards the use of polysemy, while the poet who wrote Psalm 97 appears to have favored paronomasia. It does seem clear, however, that Psalms 90 and 102 share a preference for both wordplay categories and a higher percentage of polysemy than the other books in Book IV. Conversely, Psalm 106 exhibits a higher ratio of paronomasia.

Of the 323 verses in Book IV, 82 exhibit wordplay, thus constituting 25.4 percent of the corpus. The distribution of these verses is telling. Looking first at literary genres, the psalms in Book IV may be grouped into five broad categories: Wisdom, Lament, Enthronement/Royal, Praise/Thanksgiving, and Historical.[130] The following table summarizes the distribution of these genres and the wordplays within them:

---

130. These five categories are similar to those of Gunkel, which are hymn, lament, royal/enthronement, thanksgiving, and wisdom. The key difference is that I have combined the hymn and thanksgiving category and added a category for history psalms, which Gunkel considers a smaller genre, but is well represented in Book IV. See Hermann Gunkel, The *Psalms: A Form-Critical Introduction*, trans. T. M. Horner (Philadelphia: Fortress, 1967); *An Introduction to the Psalms*, completed by Joachim Begrich and trans. James D. Nogalski (Macon, GA: Mercer University Press, 1998).

Table 6. Distribution of Wordplay in Book IV by Genre

Genre	Psalms	Total Number of Verses	Number of Wordplays	Number of Verses Containing Wordplays
Wisdom	91	16	8	10
Lament	90, 94, 102	69	28	26
Enthronement/Royal	93, 95–101	72	13	16
Praise/Thanksgiving	92, 103–104	73	10	14
Historical	105–106	93	15	16
Total		323	74	82

The following table shows both the percentage of verses containing wordplay within each genre and compares this figure to the total percentage of verses within the genre in Book IV:

Table 7. Summary Distribution of Wordplay in Book IV by Genre

Genre	Total Number of Verses	Percentage of Genre in Book IV	Number of Verses Containing Wordplays	Percentage of Genre Containing Wordplay
Wisdom	16	5	10	62.5
Lament	69	21	26	37.7
Enthronement/Royal	72	22	16	22.2
Praise/Thanksgiving	73	23	14	19.2
Historical	93	29	16	17.2

The most telling distributional figure in the above tables is the final, highlighted column, "Percentage of Genre Containing Wordplay." If wordplay constitutes 25.4 percent of the total verses in Book IV, any percentage below that figure evinces a below-average use of wordplay, while any figure greater than 25.4 percent exhibits an above-average use of wordplay. Two genres exhibit significantly above-average wordplay use: wisdom and lament.

Of the 69 verses in Book IV's lament psalms, 37.7 percent contain wordplay. Dahood recognizes the prevalence of wordplay in lament psalms, listing the following examples: Pss. 5:10; 7:16; 44:19; 56:9; 60:5; 69:30; 74:19; 80:10; 86:1; 88:10, 16, 18; and 137:5 (regrettably disregarding Book IV!).[131] Holladay also notes, "It has become more and more apparent that early laments exhibit word-play," as his study on one

---

131. Dahood, *Psalms II*, 78.

of the earliest laments (2 Sam. 1:18-27) supports.[132] With only one psalm representing the wisdom genre (only 5 percent of the corpus), one cannot draw too many conclusions on this trend, despite how impressive it may be that nearly two thirds of the psalm (62.5 percent) involves wordplay.

According to J. M. Sasson, wordplay should be expected in "divine revelation" because the trope "promoted a certain aura of ambiguity, which was intended to excite curiosity and to invite a search for meanings that were not readily apparent."[133] Despite the limited data sample under consideration in this study, a comparison of wordplay within divine and human discourse is worth mentioning. We have already noted that 82 of 323 verses within Book IV, or 25.4 percent, contain wordplay. Of these 323 verses, only ten are either quotations of God's words or divine oracles (Pss. 90:3; 91:14-16; 95:8-11; 105:11, 15). This constitutes only 3.1 percent of Book IV. Only one of these verses contains wordplay, Ps. 90:3, which is not a divine oracle, but a direct quotation by the psalmist. Thus, only 10 percent of divine discourse contains wordplay, as compared to 25.7 percent of the total verses in Book IV which contain wordplay. Although the data sample in this study is too small to draw a strong conclusion, additional study outside of Book IV could help to determine whether wordplay is more or less prevalent in divine discourse.

Conclusion

This chapter has shown the importance of establishing solid methodology for identifying Hebrew wordplay. Ranking the persuasiveness of each wordplay adds important quantitative and qualitative elements to the research. This means that the data and the conclusions drawn from these data are based on both *specific statistics* (rather than the interpreter's gut feelings about what he/she see in the text) and also *objective criteria for evaluating the quality of each data point*, lest the numbers overstate the case. While methodology does not eradicate all subjectivity from the enterprise, it helps to make the research as consistent and reproducible as possible.

With less than 11 percent of the wordplays ranking as "weak" or "unpersuasive," we can have a fairly high level of confidence about the findings presented above. Of the primary categories (paronomasia and polysemy), paronomasia is by far the more common (over 80 percent), of

---

132. Holladay, "Form and Word-Play in David's Lament over Saul and Jonathan," 156.
133. Sasson, "Wordplay in the O.T.," 968.

which the subcategories parosonancy and alliteration accounted for over half. As for psalm distribution, a higher percentage of wordplays was found in psalms integral to the editorial frame of the fourth book (Pss. 90, 102, 106) as well as the genres of wisdom and lament.

With these data in place, we can now to turn the LXX translation of these psalms, exploring when and how the translator was able to represent the Hebrew wordplay in his/her target language.

Chapter 3

LXX Translation of Wordplay in Book IV
of the Psalms:
Writing the Right Words from Left to
Right

"A foreign tongue in fact, as in the pun,
is language itself experienced as foreign."[1]

Having analyzed each wordplay in Book IV of the MT Psalter, we can now move on to the LXX translation of these passages. In order to determine whether the LXX is exhibiting true wordplay or just chance correspondence, we must consider the translational norms of the LXX Psalter. As a whole, we noted that it consistently follows the syntax of the MT and renders the semantic equivalents of the Hebrew as closely as possible. This has been the general consensus of LXX scholarship and has been confirmed by the meticulous work of Frank Austerman in his (now published) dissertation, *Von der Tora zum Nomos: Untersuchungen zur Übersetzungsweise und Interpretation im Septuaginta-Psalter*.[2]

This characterization of the translational technique of the LXX Psalter has at least two implications for the present study. First, we have a clear, reliable witness to the *Vorlage* and can thus be more confident in our

---

1. This is Redfern's translation of Jean-Paul Sartre (*L'Idiot de la famille*, vol. 2 [Paris: Gallimard, 1971]; cited in *Puns*, 1). As scholar of both French studies and linguistics, Redfern is duly qualified to both adequately render Sartre's meaning as well as speak to the relation between inter-linguistics and wordplay.

2. Frank Austerman, *Von der Tora zum Nomos: Untersuchungen zur Übersetzungsweise und Interpretation im Septuaginta-Psalter* (Göttingen: Vandenhoeck & Ruprecht, 2003), 102; but see also Austermann's full argument in Chapter 2 of his book (41–106), which reviews the qualitative and then quantitative correspondences between the LXX and the Hebrew *Vorlage*.

claims about the nature of the translator's rendering of wordplay. Second, we have the standard against which to evaluate LXX representation of wordplay, especially with regard to transformations in the LXX. For example, if the LXX stays close to the MT in word order and word choice, any deviation from those translation norms may suggest the presence of wordplay. Given the close correspondence to the MT, it is not surprising that the LXX translator rarely creates wordplays independently from the source text (eight times total) and the vast majority of LXX wordplay is used to render that from the source text.

Scholars like Randall Gauthier, Eberhard Bons, and Thomas Kraus have shown that the translator of Psalms also exhibits a degree of flexibility, particularly with regards to varying translation equivalents.[3] Thomas Kraus characterizes the LXX Psalms translation as both a "close if not verbatim translation of the Hebrew '*Vorlage*'" that nonetheless exhibits "striking differences,"[4] claiming that "a translator dared to cut his own path, especially in relation to word choice; and by leaving the trail of simply translating a text from one language into another a translator could put his own mark on it."[5] To continue Kraus' metaphor, we will attempt to follow the LXX off the beaten track, bushwacking through each pertinent passage and attempting to examine each translational choice on its own, considering the alternative options and employing a descriptive approach to the translation technique.

So how do we put these two characterizations together? If the LXX Psalms is primarily literal in its translation technique, but also occasionally flexible, how do we proceed to evaluate which occurrences of wordplay were deliberate creations of the translator and which are incidental byproducts of translation? For the purpose of this study, we will keep our initial criteria to the phenomena level; if wordplay exists in the Greek, it will be analyzed below, regardless of what is going on in the Hebrew *Vorlage*. In summary, that criteria is alliteration of two or more words in close proximity and no more than one line separating the Greek wordplay from the Hebrew wordplay it is possibly rendering. However, we will rate the strength and certainty of each wordplay representation using the stricter criteria espoused by Joosen. Joosten contends that wordplay renderings cannot be proven from literal translations that follow the syntax and semantic equivalents of the Hebrew, and any change in the

---

3. Gauthier, "Examining the 'Pluses' in the Greek Psalter," 45–76; Bons, "Rhetorical Devices in the Septuagint Psalter," 69–82.
4. Kraus, "Translating the Septuagint Psalms," 67.
5. Ibid., 62–3.

LXX made to accommodate different conventions in the target language are likewise dubious. A rating system of 1 (strong), 2 (moderate), or 3 (weak or unproveable) will thus be assigned and the results tabulated at the end of this chapter. Unless otherwise noted, renderings that involve at least two markers of wordplay representation (e.g., a transformation or a deviation from a translational norm) will receive a rating of 1, renderings with one such marker will receive a rating of 2, and renderings that do not have these marks but nonetheless exhibit strong sound correspondence, clear function, or are reinforced with other wordplays will receive a rating of 3.

Analysis of the LXX's Translation Technique of Hebrew Wordplay

The LXX translation technique of Hebrew wordplay can be classified under two broad categories: either the translator rendered the wordplay in some way or he did not. The first broad category includes cases where the translator was able to represent the Hebrew wordplay. Within this category are two subcategories: (1) the translator was able to replicate the same subcategory of wordplay using the same words employed by the Hebrew poet, and (2) the translator was able to represent a similar wordplay, using either a different subcategory of wordplay or different words in the immediate context.

The second broad category of translation technique includes cases where the LXX does not represent the wordplay. Again, this category contains two subcategories: (1) the translator rendered the sense of the Hebrew but did not (or could not) represent the poetic device of the wordplay, and (2) the LXX contains a variation that results in not representing the wordplay.

Wordplays Represented in the LXX

The first category of LXX translation technique includes Hebrew wordplays that were represented in the Greek target text. Of the 74 Hebrew wordplays in Book IV, the LXX represents 23, or 31.1 percent. We will first address the cases in which the LXX translator was able to replicate the same type of wordplay using the same words, and then we will turn to the more numerous examples in which the translator represented the wordplay by either using a different type of wordplay or using the same type of wordplay with different words in the immediate context. For the sake of clarity and consistency with the previous chapter, the Hebrew chapter and verse numbering system will be used for the LXX.

LXX Replicates the Same Wordplay

In this first subcategory of translation technique, the translator was able to render the same type of wordplay using the same words (or the majority of the words) used in the Hebrew source language. All four cases are examples of paronomasia, three involving alliteration, and one involving root play. These instances are evenly distributed throughout Psalms 90–106.

Psalm 92:9a and 11a exhibit theological wordplay in the MT between מָרוֹם ("high") with reference to the Lord's natural exalted state and וַתָּרֶם ("and you exalted") with reference to the state in which the Lord graciously lifts his people:

9a   וְאַתָּה מָרוֹם לְעֹלָם יְהוָה׃
     [...]
11a וַתָּרֶם כִּרְאֵים קַרְנִי   And you have exalted my horn like a wild ox.
11b בַּלֹּתִי בְּשֶׁמֶן רַעֲנָן׃   I have been anointed with fresh oil.

9a   But you are exalted forever, O Lord.

This is an example of root play in the MT, and it is replicated in the LXX by the use of ὕψιστος ("highest") and ὑψωθήσεται ("it shall be exalted"), both of which are also from the same root:

9a.   σὺ δὲ ὕψιστος εἰς τὸν αἰῶνα κύριε
      [...]
11a. καὶ ὑψωθήσεται ὡς μονοκέρωτος τὸ κέρας μου

9a.   But you are Most High forever, O Lord!
      [...]
11a. And my horn is exalted like a single-horned creature.

The translator uses transformations of syntactic function by rendering a noun with an adjective in v. 9 and then rendering an active verb with a passive verb.[6] Of its 25 uses in the LXX Psalms, the translator uses ὕψιστος only two other times to render מָרוֹם (71:19; 149:1). His preference by far (and the standard translation equivalent throughout the LXX) is עֶלְיוֹן (e.g.,

---

6. According to F. C. Conybeare and St. George Stock (*Grammar of Septuagint Greek, with Selected Readings, Vocabularies, and Updated Indexes* [Boston: Hendrickson, 1995], §24), "The Greek of the LXX displays a preference for the strong verb over the weak tenses of the passive." The may suggest that the LXX translator chose a passive form in order to represent the MT wordplay; see Daniel B. Wallace, *Greek Grammar: Beyond the Basics. An Exegetical Syntax of the New Testament* (Grand Rapids: Zondervan, 1996), 437.

Ps. 90:1). He also uses a specification transformation by rendering מָרוֹם with a superlative, a modulation that makes contextual and theological sense in the target language. The translator's use of three transformations and a deviation from his standard translation equivalent, along with the alliteration between the Greek word pair, are marks of true wordplay and justify a high rating (1) for the strength of this wordplay translation.

Another example of wordplay replication is in Ps. 95:1-2, wherein the Hebrew text exhibits alliteration between נְרַנְּנָה and נָרִיעָה:

לְכוּ נְרַנְּנָה לַיהוָה	1a	Come, let us cry out to the Lord!
נָרִיעָה לְצוּר יִשְׁעֵנוּ	1b	Let us shout to the rock of our salvation!
נְקַדְּמָה פָנָיו בְּתוֹדָה	2a	Let us come before him with thanksgiving!
בִּזְמִרוֹת נָרִיעַ לוֹ	2b	With songs let us shout to him!

The LXX contains alliteration using the same words:

1a. δεῦτε ἀγαλλιασώμεθα τῷ κυρίῳ
1b. ἀλαλάξωμεν τῷ θεῷ τῷ σωτῆρι ἡμῶν[7]

2a. προφθάσωμεν τὸ πρόσωπον αὐτοῦ ἐν ἐξομολογήσει
2b. καὶ ἐν ψαλμοῖς ἀλαλάξωμεν αὐτῷ

1a. Come! Let us rejoice in the Lord!
1b. Let us cry out to God, our savior!

2a. Let us come before his presence with praise!
2b. And with psalms let us cry out to him!

---

7. The LXX's avoidance of physical metaphors (such as "Rock") for God is best explained by the cultural context of the LXX translator, who was most likely influenced by the Greek petition and religious language found in the documentary papyri of Egypt. James Aitken ("Jewish Worship Amid the Greeks," 68) explains, "The similarity between the Psalms and the documentary papyri of the appeal language is striking. It accounts for the choice of words by the translator and why he diverges from the Hebrew where it refers to physical objects, such as rock, fortress or shield. The translator is not merely avoiding unfamiliar metaphors in the Hebrew, but translating them into culturally specific and resonant terms." See also Staffan Olofsson, *God Is My Rock: A Study of Translation Technique and Theological Exegesis in the Septuagint*, ConBOT 31 (Stockholm: Almqvist & Wiksell International, 1990).

The repetition of αλ is significant, as well as the translator's use of the same type of wordplay to render the same words. The verbs ἀγαλλιάω ("to rejoice") and ἀλαλάζω ("to cry out") are used together two other times in the LXX Psalms (81:2 and 98:4), both times as imperatives to render רוע and רנן in the imperative. While all three cases of word pairs in the LXX may potentially be wordplays in their own right, the only instance of wordplay in the MT is in Ps. 95:1-2 because the cohortative form provides the terms the additional phonetic similarity to constitute wordplay. The translator may be using stock equivalent wordplays for the Hebrew word pair, which does not weaken the evidence for wordplay here, but simply suggests that the translator used an already existing wordplay at a particularly apt time. This is similar to the stock wordplays in the Hebrew that have already been noted, such as הוֹד־וְהָדָר ("splendor and majesty") in Pss. 96:6 and 104:1. Even these words share strong enough sound correspondence and close enough proximity to qualify them as wordplay for this study, they do not contain any deviations from the translational norms of the LXX translator and thus it is impossible to determine whether this wordplay is the product of the LXX translator or our own imaginations. This is a good example of a rating of 3 (weak) for our confidence in the surety of this wordplay rendering.

In Ps. 101:3b, the MT uses two-consonant alliteration between three words:

לֹא־אָשִׁית לְנֶגֶד עֵינַי דְּבַר־בְּלִיָּעַל	3a	I will not set before my eyes a worthless thing.
עֲשֹׂה־סֵטִים שָׂנֵאתִי	3b	I hate the work of transgressors.
לֹא יִדְבַּק בִּי	3c	It will not cling to me.

The LXX creates alliteration between two of these equivalent words, as well as four of the words in the preceding line. This passage is included in this section because the LXX uses two out of the three (and thus a majority) of the same words:

3a. οὐ προεθέμην πρὸ ὀφθαλμῶν μου πρᾶγμα παράνομον
3b. ποιοῦντας παραβάσεις ἐμίσησα

3a. I have not set before my eyes an unlawful thing.
3b. I have hated those who commit transgressions.

The five-fold repetition of the π and the four-fold repetition of the π and ρ together help mark this as a wordplay. The verb προτίθημι ("to set before")⁸ is not the standard translation equivalent for שִׁית. It only occurs twelve times in the entire LXX and is only used here to render שִׁית (which occurs 97 times). It is used two other times in Psalms, both times to render שִׂים (Pss. 54:5; 86:14). Likewise, παράβασις ("transgression")⁹ is a *hapax legomenon* in the Hebrew Bible and occurs only two other times in the apocryphal books.¹⁰ In addition, παράνομον ("lawless")¹¹ and ποιοῦντας ("those who do/work") are not standard translation equivalents, and they could even be construed as variants were the translator not making a purposeful transformation in order to create a wordplay. The former word, παράνομον, is used to render the MT's דְּבַר־בְּלִיָּעַל ("a worthless thing"), and the latter participial phrase is used to render the MT's nominal use of the infinitive construct עֲשֹׂה־סֵטִים ("works of transgression/faithless men"), thus shifting focus from the deeds to the doers.¹² Finally, the use of πρὸ ("before") to render לְנֶגֶד is unique in the LXX Psalter, where it far more often is used adverbially to render temporal primacy. The LXX translator of Psalms renders לְנֶגֶד and נֶגֶד with ἐνώπιον, ἐναντίον, or κατέναντι, but never with πρὸ, suggesting that the translator chose this preposition for its sound correspondence in the wordplay. These lexical and syntactic choices enabled the translator to create as much alliteration as possible and should thus be explained as style, compensation, accidence, and word class transformations rather than true variants.

In Ps. 104:12, the Hebrew poet plays on עוֹף ("birds") and their dwelling place עֳפָאיִם ("foliage") by using alliteration:

| עֲלֵיהֶם עוֹף־הַשָּׁמַיִם יִשְׁכּוֹן | 12a | The birds of the heavens dwell with them. |
| מִבֵּין עֳפָאיִם יִתְּנוּ־קוֹל | 12b | From among the foliage they lift up a voice. |

The LXX translator is able to replicate this same wordplay, translating the same Hebrew words with the same alliterative device:

---

8. J. Lust, E. Eynikel, and K. Hauspie, *A Greek–English Lexicon of the Septuagint*, 2 vols. (Stuttgart: Deutsche Bibelgesellschaft, 1992), 407 (hereafter Lust).
9. Ibid., 350.
10. 2 Macc. 15:10; Wis. 14:31.
11. Lust, 355.
12. VanGemeren (*Psalms*, 746) also notes this variant. It is unclear whether the *hapax legomenon* סֵטִים refers to the unfaithful acts or perpetrators of those acts. For interpretive options, see Goldingay, *Psalms*, 3:138; Allen, *Psalms*, 2.

12a. ἐπ' αὐτὰ τὰ πετεινὰ τοῦ οὐρανοῦ κατασκηνώσει
12b. ἐκ μέσου τῶν πετρῶν δώσουσιν φωνήν

12a. The birds of the heaven[s] will dwell among them.
12b. From the midst of the rocks they will lift up a voice.

Just as in the MT, the Greek word pair directly follows the prepositional phrase. Both words begin with the syllable πετ, ending (or nearly ending) with ν. The translator's choice of πετρῶν ("rocks") suggests that he either did not recognize the Hebrew *hapax* עְפָאיִם, or was intentionally using a different word for the sake of creating a parallel wordplay. If the translator did not recognize the word and was merely using the context to make an educated guess, as Hossfeld suggests,[13] then one might expect a better guess, since trees and foliage are more obvious dwelling places for birds.[14] In fact, just a few verses later, the psalmist describes the homes of the birds as cedars and firs (Ps. 104:16-17), whereas the smaller ground animals prefer to den in the rocks, where the LXX predictably renders סֶלַע with πέτρα (Ps. 104:18). It is more likely that this is in fact a wordplay, making it an example of a modification transformation, substituting a word of equivalent specificity for the original, in this case for the purpose of making a compensational transformation and wordplay.

LXX Represents a Similar Wordplay

In this subcategory of translation technique, the LXX is able to represent the Hebrew wordplay by creating a wordplay of a different type, or involving different words in the immediate context (an adjacent line) of the Hebrew wordplay. With the greater flexibility inherent in this technique comes a greater number of wordplay representations. Twenty-one wordplays are represented with similar wordplays in the LXX, accounting for 27.6 percent of the total Hebrew wordplays in Book IV. These wordplays represent a variety of wordplay subcategories and are also fairly evenly distributed throughout Book IV. The only exceptions are Psalms 93, 103, and 105, which also have relatively few Hebrew wordplays (two, three, and four, respectively). Nor did the translator render the ten Hebrew wordplays in Psalm 102, though he used an impressive wordplay to render what we deemed "light alliteration" in Ps. 102:4.

---

13. Hossfeld, *Psalms*, 3:59.
14. Goldingay (*Psalms*, 3:186) even sees a chiastic connection between the mention of birds and trees in vv. 12-13 and then in vv. 16-17.

Wordplay Represented in Psalm 90

Of the 14 Hebrew wordplays in Psalm 90, the LXX represents six (42.9 percent) with a similar wordplay. Three of these are polysemantic wordplays. In Ps. 90:3ab, the psalmist uses the same Hebrew root (שׁוב) in two different stems (Hiphil and Qal) with a similar sense.

תָּשֵׁב אֱנוֹשׁ עַד־דַּכָּא 3a You return a mortal to dust,

וַתֹּאמֶר שׁוּבוּ בְנֵי־אָדָם 3b And you say, "Return, O sons of humanity!"

The LXX translator used two near-synonyms for שׁוב that are paronomastic and an additional, third paronomastic word to make the wordplay more explicit:

3a. μὴ[15] ἀπο|στρέψῃς ἄνθρωπον εἰς ταπείνωσιν[16]

3b. καὶ εἶ|πας ἐ|πισ|τρέψατε υἱοὶ ἀνθρώπων

3a. Do not return humanity to humiliation!

3b. And say, "Return, O sons of humanity!"

The verbs ἀποστρέψῃς ("turn back") and ἐπιστρέψατε ("return") are nearly identical phonetically and εἶπας ("you said") shares the π and σ.[17] The three-fold repetition of the π-vowel-ν syllables in ἄνθρωπον, ταπείνωσιν, and ἀνθρώπων also support the identification of the wordplay. Granted, these Greek equivalents are used in close proximity elsewhere, such as Pss. 78:38-39 and 85:4-5, in order to render שׁוב and other similar Hebrew words.[18] The only place within the Psalter where both words occur in the same verse is in Ps. 104:29. However, in this case, ἀποστρέφω is used

---

15. This line in the MT contains no negative particle. Most likely, the translators read the final word in v. 2c as אַל ("no/not") instead of אֵל ("God"), which also explains why the translators omit the divine reference v. 2c: καὶ ἀπὸ τοῦ αἰῶνος ἕως τοῦ αἰῶνος σὺ εἶ; see Dahood, *Psalms II*, 323. According to Hossfeld and Zenger (*Psalms*, 2:425), the translators chose to create a petition in order not to attribute such active violence to God. However, the minus in the previous line suggests the former option.

16. Again, Hossfeld and Zenger (*Psalms*, 2:425) suggest that this variant is due to the translator's desire to remove violence from this description of God, rather than a transformation of specification, which seems more likely.

17. According to James K. Aitken, alliteration using π was "particularly favored" in antiquity, which is supported by its use in so many wordplays in this study (90:10c; 91:12b; 101:3ab; 104:12ab), "Rhetoric and Poetry in Greek Ecclesiastes," 64.

18. Aejmelaeus, "Characterizing Criteria for the Characterization of the Septuagint Translators," 70–1.

to render the idiom תַּסְתִּיר פָּנֶיךָ ("you hide your face"), which is also a common equivalent (13 times in the Psalter). Therefore, although these paronomastic Greek words were both common equivalents for translating שוב within different contexts and stems, the translator chose these and not other lexemes, and nowhere else in the Psalter are these words used within the same verse to render שוב.

While stereotyping, or rendering the same Hebrew word consistently with the same Greek equivalent, is notable in the work of some LXX translators, Anneli Aejmelaeus has shown that the translators of the Psalter regularly chose to "reduce the number of synonymous or nearly synonymous expressions" in their translation.[19] Takamitsu Muraoka notes, for example, that for the seven terms for "anger" used by the Hebrew psalmists, the LXX translator uses only two Greek equivalents.[20] However, there also appears to be an affinity for lexical variation, as John A. L. Lee explains, "the most readily noticeable and widespread feature [of LXX translation technique] is μεταβολή, variatio, 'elegant variation', that is, the avoidance of repeating, within a short space, a noticeable word."[21] The Greek rhetorician Quintilian taught his students that both styles had their place in Greek rhetoric; in some cases terse reduction of semantic repetition was preferred, in other cases exact verbal repetition was effective, but most often rhetoricians favored lexical variety as a way of ornamenting and emphasizing their message, and also showcasing their vocabulary.[22] Thus, the translator's choice of different lexemes to render the same word in Hebrew may only be attributable to his desire for lexical variation, but his use of two phonetically similar synonyms in addition to other phonetic repetitions in close proximity qualify this as wordplay translation according to our criteria.

The wordplay serves to underscore and fill out the idea of returning. While ἐπιστρέψατε primarily has the sense of turning or returning to a spiritual or physical place,[23] ἀποστρέψῃς has the additional possible sense

---

19. Anneli Aejmelaeus, "Faith, Hope and Interpretation: A Lexical and Syntactical Study of the Semantic Field of Hope in the Greek Psalter," in *Studies in the Hebrew Bible, Qumran and the Septuagint Presented to Eugene Ulrich*, ed. Peter W. Flint, Emanuel Tov, and James C. VanderKam, VTSup 101 (Leiden: Brill, 2006), 375. See also Aejmelaeus, "Translation Technique and Intention," 83.

20. Takamitsu Muraoka, "Pairs of Synonyms in the Septuagint Psalms," in Hiebert et al., eds., *The Old Greek Psalter*, 36–43.

21. Lee, "Translations of the Old Testament: I. Greek," 776.

22. Quintilian, *The Orator's Education* 9.3.31, 45.

23. Frederick William Danker, ed., *A Greek–English Lexicon of the New Testament and Other Early Christian Literature*, 3rd ed. (Chicago: University of Chicago

of turning something with the purpose of rejecting it,[24] which fits the context here. Thus, the translator was able to specify that the Lord could return man to his state of humiliation, thereby rejecting him.

The LXX translator again represents wordplay a few verses later in Ps. 90:6b, corresponding to the *inclusio* portion of the complex Hebrew wordplay between אֶתְמוֹל ("yesterday") and יְמוֹלֵל ("withers") in 90:4b and 6b:

כִּי אֶלֶף שָׁנִים בְּעֵינֶיךָ	4a	For a thousand years in your eyes
כְּיוֹם אֶתְמוֹל כִּי יַעֲבֹר	4b	[Are] like a day, yesterday, when it passes,
וְאַשְׁמוּרָה בַלָּיְלָה	4c	And like a watch in the night.
זְרַמְתָּם שֵׁנָה יִהְיוּ	5a	You swept them away [while] they were sleeping.
בַּבֹּקֶר כֶּחָצִיר יַחֲלֹף	5b	In the morning [they are] like grass being renewed.
בַּבֹּקֶר יָצִיץ וְחָלָף	6a	In the morning, it flourishes and is renewed
לָעֶרֶב יְמוֹלֵל וְיָבֵשׁ	6b	Until evening, it withers and dries up.

The translator's necessary use of ἡ ἐχθές for "yesterday" limited his ability to render the same type of wordplay as that found in the Hebrew. However, he was able to represent the second Hebrew word (יְמוֹלֵל) by adding an additional, paronomastic Greek word to the string of verbs that describe the withering of the grass:

6a. τὸ πρωὶ ἀνθήσαι καὶ παρέλθοι
6b. τὸ ἑσπέρας ἀποπέσοι σκληρυνθείη καὶ ξηρανθείη

6a. [In] the morning it flourishes and may pass away.
6b. [In] the evening it may fall, harden, and dry up.

In the second line of the couplet, the phonetic similarity between σχ and ξ and the repetition of the ηρ, and ν and the passive aorist optative ending

---

Press, 2000), 382; Takamitsu Muraoka (*A Greek–English Lexicon of the Septuagint* (Louvain: Peeters, 2009), 282 [hereafter Muraoka]) describes the transitive use of the verb thus: "to reverse the direction of movement and return to the point of origin." J. Lust (1:175) notes that the meaning is "return" when used intransitively, as it is here.

24. BAGD, 122–3; Muraoka, 84–5; Lust, 1:56.

-νθείη in σκληρυνθείη ("it hardens")[25] and ξηρανθείη ("it dries up/withers")[26] is striking. The alliterative repetition of π and σ in ἑσπέρας and ἀποπέσοι complements and accentuates the wordplay between σκληρυνθείη and ξηρανθείη. Finally, the use of a third, paronomastic word (a plus in the LXX) also marks the Greek wordplay. Here again is an example of a transformation that is best understood as an effort to represent the poetic style of the Hebrew original.

Another reason for the LXX's additional verb (ἀποπέσοι) in 90:6b is that it creates an additional wordplay to correspond to the polysemantic wordplay in the MT between חָלַף and יָבֵשׁ in v. 6ab.[27] Just as the MT created polysemantic *double entendre* and implicit parasonancy with the double and alluded meanings of חָלַף and יָבֵשׁ (which have general meanings of "transgress" in addition to "pass away"), so too the LXX creates *double entendres* using not two, but three words. In addition to the primary sense of "pass away," παρέρχομαι can also mean "to transgress, neglect, disobey."[28] Likewise, ἀποπίπτω can mean both literally "to fall from a point or location" or "to depart from a norm, to deviate"[29] or "to fail."[30] The LXX's use of σκληρύνω, meaning "to be hardened" in the passive, could also have dual referents of the grass as well as humanity's hearts. In fact, σκληρύνω is used almost exclusively in the LXX to describe the hardening of one's heart against the Lord's will.[31]

The strength of this second wordplay representation is marked by the uncommon use of all three words. The first term, παρέρχομαι, is not the standard translation equivalent for חָלַף and is used only one other time in the Psalter (and never outside of the Psalter) to render חָלַף. It is much more commonly used to render עבר (five times in Psalms and 87 times in the LXX). The second term, ἀποπίπτω, is used only this once to translate מלל, and the third term in the wordplay (σκληρύνω) is a plus in the LXX.

---

25. Muraoka, 625; Lust, 2:429.

26. Muraoka, 480; Lust, 2:321.

27. Although the translators are able to use *double entendres* in very close proximity to where the Hebrew used the same type of wordplay, this Greek wordplay is discussed here rather than with the previous category of instances wherein the translators were able to render the same Hebrew words using the same type of wordplay because the same words are not used. The Hebrew poet played on the final words in each line, whereas the translators did not.

28. BAGD, 776; Muraoka, 534; Lust (2:358) additionally offers the senses "to reject, to rush."

29. BAGD, 118.

30. Muraoka, 80; Lust, 1:54.

31. See, e.g., Ps. 94:8. Muraoka, 625; Lust, 2:429.

Thus, all three words involve some kind of transformation and deviation from the translational norms of the LXX translator, strongly suggesting that the LXX chose these words to render both the sense and the style of the Hebrew. In this way, the translator was thus able to retain even the dual meaning of the MT, that the underlying cause of humanity's transience is its sinful nature.[32] This is one of only two cases in Book IV where the LXX translator was able to render a complex (multi-faceted) Hebrew wordplay with a complex/overlapping wordplay in in his target language; the other example is Ps. 106:38-42, below.[33]

We noted in the previous chapter that Casanowicz identifies the phrase עָמָל וָאָוֶן as a wordplay in Ps. 90:10c, and yet the apparent alliteration involves only one (different) guttural in each word and a qamats.[34] Because this phonemic similarity does not consist of two consonants with additional support, it does not qualify as wordplay in this study. The translator did, however, use wordplay to represent the alliterative Hebrew wordplays in v. 10ab:

יְמֵי־שְׁנוֹתֵינוּ בָהֶם שִׁבְעִים שָׁנָה	10a	The days of our years, in them are seventy years,
וְאִם בִּגְבוּרֹת שְׁמוֹנִים שָׁנָה	10b	Or, if with strength, eighty years.
וְרָהְבָּם עָמָל וָאָוֶן	10c	Yet their extent is toil and sorrow,

The LXX represents this wordplay in near proximity by patterned alliteration:

10c. καὶ τὸ πλεῖον αὐτῶν κόπος καὶ πόνος
10c. And the majority of them is labor and toil

Κόπος is a standard translation equivalent for עָמָל; ten of its twelve uses in the LXX Psalter are used to render עָמָל. However, πόνος renders עָמָל only four out of twelve times, suggesting that the translator might have chosen it for its phonetic correspondence with κόπος. The letters κ, π,

---

32. This example does not belong in the category of wordplay replication because the translator replicates the *double entendre* of יָבֵשׁ, but uses surrounding translation equivalents to create a parallel *double entendre*.

33. In Ps. 92:7, the LXX translator renders a single Hebrew wordplay with two Greek wordplays, thus making a complex wordplay in place of an individual wordplay.

34. These words are catalogued on 45 and implicitly explained on 30 in Casanowicz, *Paronomasia*.

and final ς repeat in that same order, and in very close proximity, add additional support for the identification of this wordplay. Moreover, both nouns are graphically similar in that both employ three consonants alternating with two omicrons, which adds assonance to the wordplay. The wordplay serves to emphasize this word pair, much like the "hendiadys of emphasis" in the Hebrew wordplay הוֹד־וְהָדָר of Ps. 96:6 and Ps. 104:1.[35]

We also noted in the previous chapter that the wordplay in Ps. 90:10c of the MT is implicit parasonancy because the best reading is probably וְרָבָּם ("and their extent") rather than the MT's וְרָהְבָּם ("and their pride"), and the poet is alluding to the latter word:

וְרָהְבָּם עָמָל וָאָוֶן   10c Yet their extent is toil and sorrow,
כִּי־גָז חִישׁ וַנָּעֻפָה   10d For it quickly passes and we fly away.

The LXX reads τὸ πλεῖον αὐτῶν ("the majority of them"), which supports the emendation to וְרָבָּם. The translator, however, might have been aware of the Hebrew poet's allusion to וְרָהְבָּם ("pride") as he was able to play on the idea of "pride," albeit in the following colon, v. 10d:[36]

10c. καὶ τὸ πλεῖον αὐτῶν κόπος καὶ πόνος
10d. ὅτι ἐπῆλθεν πραΰτης ἐφ' ἡμᾶς καὶ παιδευθησόμεθα

10c. And the majority of them is labor and toil,
10d. For humility comes against us and we will be disciplined.

Whereas the MT reads in v. 10d "for it quickly passes and we fly away," the LXX brings in the ideas of humility (πραΰτης) and discipline (παιδευθησόμεθα) with the alliterative repetition of π and the repetition of the similar-sounding syllables της and θης. The verb גז ("to pass away") occurs only twice in the Old Testament and the adverb חִישׁ ("quickly") is a *hapax legomenon*. The LXX is interpreting גז as being from the root גז or גזה, both of which usually mean "to cut off" or "to destroy," which would explain the use of παιδευθησόμεθα. The use of πραΰτης has been influenced

---

35. The collocation κόπος καὶ πόνος is also used in Ps. 9:28 to render the same Hebrew word pair, עָמָל וָאָוֶן, as well as in Ps. 10:7, where the Greek wordplay does not appear to be representing a Hebrew wordplay.

36. Regarding the LXX wordplays in 90:10c and 90:10d, it is difficult to determine which, if not both or neither, were employed to represent the Hebrew wordplays in 90:10ab and 90:10c. Their proximity makes such a dissection difficult. What is clear (and sufficient for this study) is that the LXX has created two separate wordplays for the MT's two wordplays.

by the wordplay in v. 10c between "extent" and "pride." Regardless of whether or not the LXX translator understood the Hebrew *Vorlage* in v. 10d, it seems that he recognized the wordplay in v. 10c and then tried to represent a similar play in his own language in v. 10d. This might explain why the LXX version of Ps. 90:10d is interpreted as an irreconcilable variant by scholars such as Thomas Kraus, who argues that the translator was attempting to resolve textual difficulties in the Hebrew *Vorlage*.[37] Here again, a better explanation for textual variance is provided by a close analysis of the poetic features of the text, their rhetorical function, and importance of transformations for the LXX translator.

Wordplay Represented in Psalm 91

In Psalm 91, the LXX represents two cases of Hebrew parasonancy using alliteration in the immediate context. In Ps. 91:6a and 7a, the Hebrew poet uses parasonancy between בָּאֹפֶל ("in the darkness"), יִפֹּל ("will fall"), and אֶלֶף ("one thousand"):

מִדֶּבֶר בָּאֹפֶל יַהֲלֹךְ	6a	[Nor] of the plague that walks in the darkness,
מִקֶּטֶב יָשׁוּד צָהֳרָיִם	6b	[Nor] of the destruction that destroys at midday.
יִפֹּל מִצִּדְּךָ אֶלֶף	7a	A thousand will fall from your side,
וּרְבָבָה מִימִינֶךָ	7b	And ten thousand from your right hand.
אֵלֶיךָ לֹא יִגָּשׁ	7c	To you they will not come near.

The LXX translator had the opportunity to represent this wordplay in v. 7a by rendering מִצִּדְּךָ יִפֹּל אֶלֶף ("a thousand may fall from your side") thus:

7a. πεσεῖται ἐκ τοῦ κλίτους σου χιλιὰς
7a. One thousand will fall from your side.

Both words share a λ and final ς, and the phonetic similarity between κ and χ suggests that the translator chose κλίτους ("side")[38] for its phonetic similarity to χιλιὰς ("one thousand"). This is supported by the fact that the translator could have used πλευρά, which most often refers to the side of

---

37. Kraus ("Translating the Septuagint Psalms," 66–7) describes the MT and LXX of Ps. 90:10d saying that they "differ absolutely from each other"; cf., Hossfeld, *Psalms*, 2:425.

38. Lust, 1:258.

a human, whereas κλίτους is used almost exclusively of a region or side of an inanimate object, often referring to articles or areas in the Temple.[39] The unexpected use of κλίτους thus draws attention to the wordplay and also explains the variant lexical choice.

In Ps. 91:11-13, the MT exhibits interlocking wordplays using repetition of similar sound:

כִּי מַלְאָכָיו יְצַוֶּה־לָּךְ	11a	For he commands his angels for your sake,
לִשְׁמָרְךָ בְּכָל־דְּרָכֶיךָ	11b	To guard you in all of your ways.
עַל־כַּפַּיִם יִשָּׂאוּנְךָ	12a	On their hands they will carry you,
פֶּן־תִּגֹּף בָּאֶבֶן רַגְלֶךָ	12b	Lest you strike your foot on a stone.
עַל־שַׁחַל וָפֶתֶן תִּדְרֹךְ	13a	Upon the lion and the cobra you will tread.
תִּרְמֹס כְּפִיר וְתַנִּין	13b	You will trample the young lion and the serpent.

The LXX does not precisely emulate any of these wordplays, but it evinces recognition of this cluster by employing heavy alliteration in v. 12:

12b. μήποτε προσκόψῃς πρὸς λίθον τὸν πόδα σου
12b. Lest you strike your foot against a rock.

This alliteration may seem incidental at first, especially since μήποτε, προσκόψῃς, and πόδα are the standard translation equivalents of the corresponding Hebrew terms,[40] but one would not expect the preposition πρὸς to render the Hebrew preposition בְּ־ in this context, but rather ἐπί[41] or ἐν, as in the similar phrase in Sir. 32:20 (καὶ μὴ προσκόψῃς ἐν λιθώδεσιν).[42] According to Eberhard Bons, "the tendency of creating paronomastic formulations between a verb and prepositional phrase" is a common rhetorical device in the LXX Psalter.[43] Thus, this four-fold repetition exhibits marks of genuine wordplay.

---

39. BAGD, 824–5; Muraoka, 401; Lust, 2:379.
40. The citations of this verse in Matt. 4:6 and Luke 4:11 use the exact wording indicating that the Gospel writers are probably citing the LXX verbatim (and not making the same wordplay, independently from the LXX translator).
41. BAGD, 366.
42. Bons, "Rhetorical Devices in the Greek Psalter," in Bons and Kraus, eds., *Et Sapienter et Eloquenter*, 77.
43. Ibid.

Wordplay Represented in Psalm 92

One of the two Hebrew wordplays in Psalm 92 is represented in the Greek translation. The polysemantic wordplay between עָמְקוּ and בַּעַר in 92:6b and 7a functioned to underscore the inability of the ignorant to understand.

מַה־גָּדְלוּ מַעֲשֶׂיךָ יְהוָה	6a	How great are your works, O Lord!
מְאֹד עָמְקוּ מַחְשְׁבֹתֶיךָ	6b	[How] very deep are your understandings!
אִישׁ־בַּעַר לֹא יֵדָע	7a	A brutish person does not know,
וּכְסִיל לֹא־יָבִין אֶת־זֹאת	7b	And a fool does not understand this.

The LXX translator was able to represent this wordplay using two, overlapping Greek wordplays. This is the only instance in Book IV where the LXX translator used more wordplays in the target text to account for the wordplay in the source text:

7a. ἀνὴρ ἄφρων οὐ γνώσεται
7b. καὶ ἀσύνετος οὐ συνήσει ταῦτα

7a. A foolish man will not know
7b. And somone without understanding will not understand this.

The translator uses *alpha privativum* to create alliteration between ἀνήρ, ἄφρων, and ἀσύνετος,[44] which binds the cola together and also reflects the Hebrew wordplay. The choice of ἀνήρ to render אִישׁ is not surprising in the context, but it is not the most standard translation equivalent either. Most often in the Psalter, the LXX translator uses a form of ἄνθρωπος (used 26 times to render אִישׁ). The translator uses ἀνήρ fifteen times, but there are some clear patterns associated with his preference. For example, seven (nearly half) of these times are restricted to Book V. In fact, ἀνήρ only occurs this once in Book IV. Also, and more significantly, the LXX uses the collocation ἀνδρῶν αἱμάτων five times to translate the Hebrew אַנְשֵׁי דָמִים ("men of bloodshed"), making it a stereotyped expression. Outside of Book V and aside from this stereotyped expression, the LXX translator used ἀνήρ only four times for אִישׁ, which suggests at the very least that was not the most expected translation equivalent.

The LXX may have also deviated from his translational norms by rendering בַּעַר with ἄφρων. It is difficult to determine the translator's preferred lexical equivalent for the attributive use of בַּעַר, but the closest

44. Ibid., 72.

expression in the Psalter to the one in Ps. 92:7 is in Ps. 73:22 וַאֲנִי־בַעַר וְלֹא אֵדָע ("And I was brutish and I did not know"), which the LXX renders καὶ ἐγὼ ἐξουδενωμένος καὶ οὐκ ἔγνων ("And I was of no account and I did not know"). At the very least, the translator had other options and was not constrained by convention or habit to use ἄφρων, but may have chosen it for its phonetic contribution to the wordplay.

The translator uses a second, overlapping wordplay in v. 7b, using the same root for both the noun and verb in play, even though the Hebrew uses different roots for the noun and verb. If this movement away from lexical variety is uncharacteristic of the LXX translation technique in the Psalter, the deviation here might further support the authenticity of this wordplay. Eberhard Bons identifies this and several other instances wherein the LXX renders two Hebrew words of different roots with two Greek words of the same root for the sake of wordplay. In other words, the LXX translator uses root play in the Greek to render a different wordplay in the Hebrew.[45]

Wordplay Represented in Psalm 94

While the LXX shows no evidence of representing the three Hebrew wordplays in Psalm 93, one paronomastic wordplay is represented in Psalm 94. In Ps. 94:8ab, the Hebrew poet uses three-fold alliteration in v. 8a followed by a root letter transposition between וּכְסִילִים and תַּשְׂכִּילוּ in v. 8b:

בֹּעֲרִים בָּעָם בִּינוּ	8a	Understand, you senseless ones among the people!
וּכְסִילִים מָתַי תַּשְׂכִּילוּ	8b	And you fools, when will you take heed?

The LXX translator could not emulate these wordplays exactly, but he shows evidence of recognition by creating his own root play between ἄφρονες ("foolish [ones]") and φρονήσατε ("understand!"):

8a. σύνετε δή ἄφρονες ἐν τῷ λαῷ
8b. καί μωροί ποτὲ φρονήσατε

8a. Understand, therefore, foolish ones among the people!
8b. And, stupid ones, at last understand!

---

45. Ibid., 74.

The LXX heightens the contrast between these words by using similar-sounding antonyms; fools by definition inherently lack understanding. Moreover, the translator uses a transformation of accidence, changing the Hebrew interrogative (מָתַי תַּשְׂכִּילוּ) to an aorist imperative, which heightens the similarity in sound by virtue of the σ case ending.[46] The verb φρονέω is used only this once to translate שׂכל and occurs only seven times in the LXX, which suggests that it was specifically selected for its use in this wordplay. The adjective ἄφρων is used only twice in the Hebrew Bible to render words from the root בער (here and in Ps. 92:7 above). More often, the LXX uses ἄφρων to translate נָבָל (five times in the Psalms).

Using two terms that are not standard translation equivalents strongly supports the identification of this wordplay representation, which would typically warrant a strong rating of a 1. However, one might expect the translator to have exchanged ἄφρονες ("foolish ones") in v. 8a and μωροί ("stupid ones") in v. 8b in order to create greater proximity between the words being played upon. The translator's decision to keep ἄφρονες in the first line when he could have easily moved it closer to φρονήσατε makes this wordplay a bit less certain, landing it a moderate rating of 2.

Wordplay Represented in Psalm 96

The LXX translator of Psalm 95 was able to replicate the same wordplay in one instance, but there is no evidence of representing wordplay using similar wordplays or wordplays within the context. The translator of Psalm 96 was able to represent one case of paronomasia. In Ps. 96:2ab, the psalmist uses parasonancy between שִׁירוּ and בַּשְּׂרוּ, both of which begin their respective lines.

שִׁירוּ לַיהוָה שִׁיר חָדָשׁ	1a	Sing to the Lord a new song!
שִׁירוּ לַיהוָה כָּל־הָאָרֶץ	1b	Sing to the Lord, all the earth!
שִׁירוּ לַיהוָה בָּרֲכוּ שְׁמוֹ	2a	Sing to the Lord, bless his name!
בַּשְּׂרוּ מִיּוֹם־לְיוֹם יְשׁוּעָתוֹ	2b	Proclaim his salvation from day to day!
סַפְּרוּ בַגּוֹיִם כְּבוֹדוֹ	3a	Recount among the nations his glory!

The LXX translator likewise uses verbal repetition in vv. 1ab-2a, with a three-fold repetition of ᾄσατε, underscored by the similar-sounding

---

46. Even if the LXX translator's rendering of the interrogative particle מָתַי is a result of misunderstanding, this issue is peripheral to the wordplays in both texts.

nominal ᾆσμα. These are standard translation equivalents and do not constitute wordplay, but (as with the Hebrew wordplay), they support the paronomastic wordplay in vv. 2ab-3a:

1a. ᾄσατε τῷ κυρίῳ ᾆσμα καινόν
1b. ᾄσατε τῷ κυρίῳ πᾶσα ἡ γῆ
2a. ᾄσατε τῷ κυρίῳ εὐλογήσατε τὸ ὄνομα αὐτοῦ
2b. εὐαγγελίζεσθε ἡμέραν ἐξ ἡμέρας τὸ σωτήριον αὐτοῦ
3a. ἀναγγείλατε ἐν τοῖς ἔθνεσιν τὴν δόξαν αὐτοῦ

1a. Sing to the Lord a new song!
1b. Sing to the Lord, all the earth!
2a. Sing to the Lord! Bless his name!
2b. Proclaim his salvation from day to day!
3a. Declare among the nations his glory!

All three words share a λ and at least one γ, and the middle word, εὐαγγελίζεσθε ("Proclaim!"), additionally shares the ευ of εὐλογήσατε ("Bless!") and the αγγελ of ἀναγγείλατε ("Declare!"). The three imperatives are also consecutive exhortations to worship, creating an escalating emphasis, mirroring the rhetorical effect of the Hebrew wordplay. Two of these three words are standard translation equivalents, but ἀναγγέλλω is used to render ספר only six of its 20 occurrences in the LXX Psalms. Far more often, it is used to render נגד (15 times in the LXX Psalms). This may suggest the translator used ἀναγγέλλω rather than the more typical equivalents like διηγέομαι or ἐξαγγέλλω in order to represent the Hebrew wordplay.

Wordplay Represented in Psalm 97

The LXX translation of Psalm 97 exhibits two wordplays that are similar to those of the Hebrew text, in addition to the same wordplay noted in the category above. Casanowicz identifies a wordplay in Ps. 97:2a between עָנָן ("cloud") and וַעֲרָפֶל ("and darkness/heavy cloud"), and yet he only lists it as a case of paronomasia, leaving his reasoning for identifying it as such unclear.[47] Even if this wordplay were equally obscure to the LXX translator (as it is to us) he may have used a wordplay for this phrase in order to acknowledge the MT's paronomastic wordplay in the following lines in v. 3 (תְּלַהֵט תֵּלֵךְ):

---

47. Casanowicz, *Paronomasia*, 70.

עָנָן וַעֲרָפֶל סְבִיבָיו	2a	Clouds and thick darkness surround him
צֶדֶק וּמִשְׁפָּט מְכוֹן כִּסְאוֹ	2b	Righteousness and justice are the foundation of his throne
אֵשׁ לְפָנָיו תֵּלֵךְ	3a	Fire goes before him,
וּתְלַהֵט סָבִיב צָרָיו	3b	And it burns around his adversaries.

The LXX contains a paronomastic wordplay between νεφέλη ("cloud") and γνόφος ("darkness") in v. 2a:

2a. νεφέλη καὶ γνόφος κύκλῳ αὐτοῦ
2a. Cloud and darkness are round about him.

Because the γ is quiescent before the ν, both words vocalize the ν and φ as their beginning two consonant sounds, creating alliterative paronomasia. The translator chose the typical Greek translational equivalents, but the similarity in sound and immediate proximity of the lexemes identify it as a wordplay, even if its certainty rating is low.[48]

Another representation of wordplay in Psalm 97 occurs in v. 7, wherein the translator attempted his own paronomasia in the place of the Hebrew rhyme in v. 7b:

יֵבֹשׁוּ כָּל־עֹבְדֵי פֶסֶל	7a	Let all who serve an idol be ashamed!
הַמִּתְהַלְלִים בָּאֱלִילִים	7b	Those who boast in vain things!
הִשְׁתַּחֲווּ־לוֹ כָּל־אֱלֹהִים	7c	Worship him, all you gods!

Whereas the Hebrew paronomasia is condensed in the second cola, the LXX translator used alliteration throughout the tricolon:

7a. αἰσχυνθήτωσαν πάντες οἱ προσκυνοῦντες τοῖς γλυπτοῖς
7b. οἱ ἐγκαυχώμενοι ἐν τοῖς εἰδώλοις αὐτῶν
7c. προσκυνήσατε αὐτῷ πάντες οἱ ἄγγελοι αὐτοῦ

---

48. At first glance, it may appear that the translator is using alliteration to render the alliterative wordplay in Ps. 97:4 between תֵּלֵךְ and וּתְלַהֵט by using the phrase πῦρ ἐναντίον αὐτοῦ προπορεύσεται ("fire goes before him"). However, if the translator were trying to play with the π and ρ repetition, he most likely would have used a construction with even greater alliteration like the one in Ps. 89:15: προπορεύσεται πρὸ προσώπου σου ("they shall go before you").

7a. Let anyone who bows down to carved images be ashamed!
7b. Those who boast in their idols!
7c. Worship him, all his angels!

The three-fold repetition of the κυν/χυν syllable is reinforced by the similar-sounding χωμ syllable. The translator's choice of προσκυνοῦντες ("those who bow down/worship")[49] in v. 7a to render עֹבְדֵי ("those who serve") is unique in the LXX. Of its 288 occurrences, it is almost exclusively used to render שחה ("to bow down") and occasionally the similar סגד ("to do homage/bow down") in Aramaic. The translator's desire to simulate the Hebrew wordplay would also explain the explicating transformation in the LXX, that is, the rendering of the vague (though conventional) בָּאֱלִילִים with εἰδώλοις, which would have been more understandable to Greek readers.[50] This wordplay has the effect of emphasizing and explicating the contrast between idolatrous worship (v. 7a) and Yahwistic worship (v. 7c).

Wordplay Represented in Psalm 102

No Hebrew wordplays were used in Psalms 98–100, and the sole wordplay of Psalm 101, as noted above, was replicated in the same way in the LXX. The Hebrew psalmist uses ten wordplays in Psalm 102, none of which are represented in the LXX. The translator was, however, able to use wordplay to represent what we categorized as "light alliteration" in Ps. 102:4. Because the sound repetition only involves one sound per word, this case does not meet the criteria for wordplay in Hebrew, but it is included in the discussion (and not the analysis) because this example of Greek wordplay does not appear to be an independent wordplay, but rather an attempt to represent the style of the Hebrew *Vorlage*.

The Hebrew poet uses four-fold alliteration in Ps. 102:4ab:

כִּי־כָלוּ בְעָשָׁן יָמָי 4a For my days cease like smoke,

וְעַצְמוֹתַי כְּמוֹ־קֵד נִחָרוּ 4b And my bones burn like a glowing ember

While this trope does not technically qualify as wordplay for this study, the strong repetition of sound in such immediate literary context did not go unnoticed by the LXX translator, who rendered the couplet using alliteration of adjacent words v. 4b:[51]

---

49. Muraoka, 596; Lust, 2:403.

50. The many variants in the verse between the MT and LXX (including grammatical and semantic) are well-known and not pertinent to the relevant wordplays. For a good discussion of these, see Tate, *Psalms*, 517.

51. Lust, 2:508 and 452.

4b. καὶ τὰ ὀστᾶ μου ὡσεὶ φρύγιον συνεφρύγησαν
4b. And my bones are like firewood burned

Both of these lexemes are *hapax legomena* in the LXX. Both are also from the same root, making it a root play in the LXX. This shows the translator's acknowledgment of the Hebrew style and admirable attempt at replicating it as well as possible.

Wordplay Represented in Psalm 104

Psalm 103 shows no evidence of wordplay representation in the LXX, which is not surprising given that the poet used only three wordplays. The LXX represents a similar wordplay in Psalm 104, in addition to the one already discussed above.

The psalmist uses what was probably a stock wordplay in Ps. 104:1c:

בָּרֲכִי נַפְשִׁי אֶת־יְהוָה 1a Bless the Lord, O my soul!
יְהוָה אֱלֹהַי גָּדַלְתָּ מְּאֹד 1b O, Lord, my God, you are very great!
הוֹד וְהָדָר לָבָשְׁתָּ 1c With splendor and majesty you clothe yourself!

This stock Hebrew wordplay also occurs in Pss. 21:6; 96:6 (and its parallel 1 Chr. 16:27); and Ps. 111:3. In all five contexts, the phrase has the same basic sense, describing God's splendor and majesty. It is interesting, therefore, that it is rendered five different ways in each instance in the LXX:[52]

---

52. Hossfeld (*Psalms*, 3:59) interprets the translator's choice of ἐξομολόγησιν for הוֹד as a misunderstanding, arguing that the translator must have understood the root of הוֹד to be from ידה ("to praise"). This is possible but unlikely given the frequency of the Hebrew word (25 times in the LXX) and the fact that ἐξομολόγησις is used in three of the five instances of the expression, as well as in Ps. 148:13 where it is also used to translate הוֹד. More likely the translator considered their ranges of meanings to overlap in such a way as to justify his word choice. Moreover, Lust (162) identifies this phrase in the LXX as a "semiticism" and "stereotyped rendition of הוֹד וְהָדָר." One wonders how the phrase ἐξομολόγησιν καὶ εὐπρέπειαν could be stereotyped, since the LXX translators use different words in other contexts, but his affirmation of the translator's understanding of the Hebrew phrase is another argument against Hossfeld's critique.

Stefan Seiler ("Theologische Konzepte in der Septuaginta," in *Der Septuagint-Psalter: Sprachliche und Theologische Aspekte*, ed. Erich Zenger, Herders Biblische Studien [Freiburg: Herder, 2001], 202–3) discusses the collocation used to translate רָדְהוּ דוֹה.

Ps. 21:6   δόξαν καὶ μεγαλοπρέπειαν
Ps. 96:6   ἐξομολόγησις καὶ ὡραιότης[53]
1 Chr. 16:27 δόξα καὶ ἔπαινος
Ps. 104:1   ἐξομολόγησιν καὶ εὐπρέπειαν
Ps. 111:3   ἐξομολόγησις καὶ μεγαλοπρέπεια

Although none of these word pairs by themselves constitute a wordplay, the translator of Ps. 104:1 represented the Hebrew wordplay by using ἐμεγαλύνθης ("you are great") and ἐξομολόγησιν ("praise") in the same verse:

1b. κύριε ὁ θεός μου ἐμεγαλύνθης σφόδρα
1c. ἐξομολόγησιν καὶ εὐπρέπειαν ἐνεδύσω

1b. O Lord, my God, you were made very great!
1c. With praise and beauty you clothe yourself!

Both words share μ, γ, λ, σ, and ν, in addition to the vowels ε and η. They are also in close proximity, separated by only one word. The wordplay draws a connection between the greatness of the Lord and our expectant response of praise. The LXX choice of ἐξομολόγησιν ("praise") to render הוֹד ("splendor") is unique outside the Psalter, where the LXX generally uses ἡ δόξα ("glory").[54] Within the Psalms, it is used four times to render הוֹד, and only slightly more often (five times) to render תּוֹדָה ("thanksgiving"). Thus, while the expression was not stereotyped for the Psalms translator, he he did not have to go out of his way to create the wordplay, which diminishes the strength of our identification, but not to the point of excluding it from the study. It is retained in this study because of the proximity of the terms, the other options available to the translator (e.g., he renders הוֹד with ἡ δόξα in Ps. 21:6), and the number of phonemes shared.

Wordplay Represented in Psalm 106

There is no evidence of wordplay representation for the six Hebrew wordplays in Psalm 105. However, there are four represented wordplays

---

53. Although the translator does not appear to create a similar wordplay in Ps. 96:6a, in the second line (96:6b), he does use the same root twice, whereas the MT does not, possibly playing on the root, or possibly misunderstanding the meaning of עֹז: עֹז וְתִפְאֶרֶת בְּמִקְדָּשׁוֹ, ἁγιωσύνη καὶ μεγαλοπρέπεια ἐν τῷ ἁγιάσματι αὐτοῦ.

54. 1 Chr. 16:27; 29:25; Job 37:22; 39:20; Pss. 21:6; Isa. 30:30.

in Psalm 106, the same number as were represented in Psalm 90. All six are cases of Hebrew paronomasia and are represented by alliteration in the LXX.

In Ps. 106:7c, the Hebrew poet creates a paronomastic play with וַיַּמְרוּ ("and they rebelled") by repeating יָם ("sea"):

וַיַּמְרוּ עַל־יָם בְּיַם־סוּף   7c   And they rebelled by the sea, by the Red Sea.

The LXX omits the second reference to "sea" but compensates by adding ἀναβαίνοντες ("while going up"):

7c.   καὶ παρεπίκραναν ἀναβαίνοντες ἐν τῇ ἐρυθρᾷ θαλάσσῃ⁵⁵
7c.   And they rebelled while going up to the Red Sea.

Semantically, the participle ἀναβαίνοντες is unnecessary in the context of the line, so its insertion could be compensation for the omission of a second reference to the sea, or the translator could be reading the MT's prepositional phrase עַל־יָם as a Qal active participle עֹלִים ("going up").⁵⁶ While the LXX's misreading of the MT's repetition of יָם may weaken the identification of this wordplay, the participle's inclusion contributes three additional instances of ν, totaling six occurrences within three consecutive words, suggesting that the LXX may offer not just a variant, but an attempt at representing the Hebrew wordplay, an exchange that would alter the meaning of the source text little if at all. If this is indeed the case, this is another example of how an apparent error in translation or transmission is possibly better explained by the translator's sensitively to the author's wordplay.

In Ps. 106:23, the poet uses alliteration (with הֹשׁ and שֶׁה) employing four different lexemes:

---

55. The inverted word order in the Greek (literally "the Red Sea" rather than "the Sea of Red") is probably influenced by the word order used in the Pentateuch and Joshua (e.g., Exod. 10:19; 13:18; 15:4; 23:31; Deut. 1:40; Josh. 2:10; 4:23); see Olofsson, *Translation Technique and Theological Exegesis*, 129.

56. Some scholars, including the editors of *BHS*, emend the text to read וְעֶלְיוֹן so that the line reads, "but rebelled against the Most High by the Reed Sea," cross-referencing Ps. 78:17 (Allen, *Psalms*, 45; Kraus, *Psalms*, 2:315). However, this suggestion assumes the omission (perhaps due to haplography) of an adversative preposition and finds no support from the versions.

וַיֹּאמֶר לְהַשְׁמִידָם	23a	And he said [that he would] destroy them
לוּלֵי מֹשֶׁה בְחִירוֹ	23b	Had not Moses, his chosen one,
עָמַד בַּפֶּרֶץ לְפָנָיו	23c	Stood in the breach before him
לְהָשִׁיב חֲמָתוֹ מֵהַשְׁחִית	23d	To turn his wrath from destroying [them]

The MT uses two different words for "destroy," both of which include this consonant cluster. The LXX attempts a similar wordplay, rendering both שמד and שחת with ἐξολεθρεύω, but making transformations in order to create four-fold sound repetition:

23a. καὶ εἶπεν τοῦ ἐξολεθρεῦσαι αὐτούς
23b. εἰ μὴ Μωυσῆς ὁ ἐκλεκτὸς αὐτοῦ
23c. ἔστη ἐν τῇ θραύσει ἐνώπιον αὐτοῦ
23d. τοῦ ἀποστρέψαι τὴν ὀργὴν αὐτοῦ τοῦ μὴ ἐξολεθρεῦσαι

23a. And he said that he would destroy them,
23b. Had not Moses, his chosen one,
23c. Stood in the destruction before him,
23d. In order to turn his wrath to not destroy them.

Although ἐξολεθρεύω suitably translates שמד and שחת, the translator had other options in the semantic field of destruction, such as καταφθείρω or ἀπόλλυμι, that he could have used to maintain the variety of the Hebrew and preference for variety evinced in the LXX. Moreover, ἐξολεθρεύω is not the standard translation equivalent for either Hebrew verb. Of its 22 uses in LXX Psalms, it is used only six times to render and שמד, and it renders שחת only in this verse. More often, the LXX translator uses ἐξολεθρεύω to translate כרת (nine times).

Most importantly, the translator renders בַּפֶּרֶץ ("in the breach") with ἐν τῇ θραύσει[57] ("in the destruction"), which creates a wordplay with ἐξολεθρεῦσαι by repeating the θρ blend. θραύσει is used twice in the LXX Psalms, and it only renders פֶּרֶץ in this verse. It is unlikely that the LXX was unfamiliar with the Hebrew *Vorlage*, as פֶּרֶץ occurs 83 times in the Hebrew Bible.[58] More likely, the translator is trying to replicate the MT's

---

57. The word θραύσις is also used to describe plague and slaughter, Lust, 1:207.

58. According to Hossfeld (*Psalms*, 3:94), "the LXX does not know what to do with the 'breach.' Throughout the verse it stays within the verbal field of 'rooting out.'" What Hossfeld attributes to the translator's ignorance may be better understood as his attempt at creating a wordplay similar to that in the MT and his theological understanding of what the "breach" signified, showing his recognition of and skill with wordplay, as well as his knowledge of Hebrew semantics.

alliteration with his own repetition of θρ.⁵⁹ His choice of τῇ θραύσει should also be understood as a transformation of explication. VanGemeren aptly explains the Hebrew expression:

> The metaphor "stood in the breach" derives from military language and signifies the bravery of a soldier who, standing in the breach of the wall, is willing to give his life to ward off the enemy (cf. Eze 22:30). So Moses stood bravely in the presence of Almighty God on behalf of Israel... The Lord responded to Moses' intercession by not destroying the people.⁶⁰

Thus, the LXX word choice is not only an apt decision to communicate the wordplay, but a helpful clarification for his readers. The translator's willingness to (mildly) sacrifice sense for style in this compensation and explication transformation is further supported by his use of μή instead of the more literal ἀπό (see Jer. 13:14; Lam. 2:8), a choice that better suits the Greek verse.

The next example of a similar wordplay rendered by the LXX is in Ps. 106:27ab. The MT plays on the words זַרְעָם ("their seed") and וּלְזָרוֹתָם ("and to scatter them"), which share several letters:

וּלְהַפִּיל זַרְעָם בַּגּוֹיִם 27a And to make their seed fall among the nations,

וּלְזָרוֹתָם בָּאֲרָצוֹת 27b And to scatter them throughout the lands.

The LXX may have tried a similar wordplay in v. 27b:

27a. καὶ τοῦ καταβαλεῖν τὸ σπέρμα αὐτῶν ἐν τοῖς ἔθνεσιν
27b. καὶ διασκορπίσαι αὐτοὺς ἐν ταῖς χώραις

27a. And to strike down their seed among the nations,
27b. And to scatter them in the lands.

Although χώραις ("lands") exchanges a χ and ω for the κ and ο of διασκορπίσαι ("to scatter"), the phonetic similarity of the syllable is suggestive of paronomasia.⁶¹ The effect of this wordplay links the verb with the indirect object, highlighting where the unfaithful will be scattered.

---

59. This repeated consonant blend is also followed by a diphthong in each case, which may be an additional, albeit weak, correspondence in sound.

60. VanGemeren, *Psalms*, 786.

61. Although ἐν ταῖς χώραις is the standard equivalent for the phrase בָּאֲרָצוֹת (and used numerous times in the LXX) the verb זרה is rendered by seven different Greek equivalents in the LXX, evincing that the translator had several other options from which to choose.

Neither of these words are standard translation equivalents. Of its ten uses in LXX Psalms, διασκορπίζω is only used here to render זרה. Of its four occurrences in Psalms, χώρα is used each time to render אֶרֶץ. However, the LXX translator far prefers to render אֶרֶץ with γῆ. The psalmist uses אֶרֶץ two hundred times and nearly all of those times (190) the LXX prefers γῆ. Moreover, there may be additional thematic reasons for the LXX translator's choice of χώρα. Three of its four occurrences highlight the changing status of land in Israel's history: God gave the promised land to Israel (105:44); God scattered Israel throughout other, foreign lands (106:27); and God gathered them from those lands (107:3). This potential thematic connection could also undercut the possibility of χώρα being chosen for the sake of wordplay in Ps. 106:27, but its sound correspondence and its deviation from the standard translation norms for both terms still support the certainty of the wordplay.

The next instance of LXX wordplay is an example of complex wordplay—three paronomastic wordplays within the same context that the MT contains one paronomastic and one polysemantic wordplay. In Ps. 106:38 and 42, the Hebrew poet plays on three repetitions of דָּם ("blood") with the phrase יָדָם ("their hand") as well as the similarity between כְּנַעַן ("Canaan") and וַיִּכָּנְעוּ ("and they subdued"):

וַיִּשְׁפְּכוּ דָם נָקִי	38a	And they poured out innocent blood,
דַּם־בְּנֵיהֶם וּבְנוֹתֵיהֶם	38b	Blood of their sons and their daughters,
אֲשֶׁר זִבְּחוּ לַעֲצַבֵּי כְנָעַן	38c	Whom they sacrificed to the idols of Canaan,
וַתֶּחֱנַף הָאָרֶץ בַּדָּמִים	38d	And the land was defiled by the blood.
וַיִּטְמְאוּ בְמַעֲשֵׂיהֶם	39a	Thus they became unclean in their acts
וַיִּזְנוּ בְּמַעַלְלֵיהֶם׃	39b	And played the whore in their deeds.
וַיִּחַר־אַף יְהוָה בְּעַמּוֹ	40a	And the anger of the Lord kindled against his people,
וַיְתָעֵב אֶת־נַחֲלָתוֹ׃	40b	And he abhorred his inheritance.
וַיִּתְּנֵם בְּיַד־גּוֹיִם	41a	And he gave them into the hands of the nations;
וַיִּמְשְׁלוּ בָהֶם שֹׂנְאֵיהֶם׃	41b	And those who hated them ruled over them.
וַיִּלְחָצוּם אוֹיְבֵיהֶם	42a	And their enemies oppressed them,
וַיִּכָּנְעוּ תַּחַת יָדָם	42b	And they were humbled under their hand.

The LXX translator does an exemplary job of creating his own complex wordplay using three word pairs, two of which underscore causal relationships between Israel's sin and its consequences, and the third word pair uses co-referential terms to paint the picture of Israel's subjugation under her enemies, similar to the wordplay between דָּם and יָדָם in the MT.

38a. καὶ ἐξέχεαν αἷμα ἀθῷον
38b. αἷμα υἱῶν αὐτῶν καὶ θυγατέρων
38c. ὧν ἔθυσαν τοῖς γλυπτοῖς Χανααν
38d. καὶ ἐφονοκτονήθη ἡ γῆ ἐν τοῖς αἵμασιν

39a. καὶ ἐμιάνθη ἐν τοῖς ἔργοις αὐτῶν
39b. καὶ ἐπόρνευσαν ἐν τοῖς ἐπιτηδεύμασιν αὐτῶν
40a. καὶ ὠργίσθη θυμῷ κύριος ἐπὶ τὸν λαὸν αὐτοῦ
40b. καὶ ἐβδελύξατο τὴν κληρονομίαν αὐτοῦ

41a. καὶ παρέδωκεν αὐτοὺς εἰς χεῖρας ἐθνῶν
41b. καὶ ἐκυρίευσαν αὐτῶν οἱ μισοῦντες αὐτούς

42a. καὶ ἔθλιψαν αὐτοὺς οἱ ἐχθροὶ αὐτῶν
42b. καὶ ἐταπεινώθησαν ὑπὸ τὰς χεῖρας αὐτῶν

38a. And they poured out innocent blood,
38b. Blood of their sons and daughters,
38c. Whom they sacrificed to the carved images of Canaan,
38d. And the land was defiled by the blood.

39a. And they became unclean in their practices,
39b. And they committed fornication with their deeds.
40a. And the anger of the Lord was furious against,
40b. And he abhorred his inheritance.

41a. And he delivered them into the hands of the nations;
41b. And those who hated them ruled over them.

42a. And their enemies oppressed them,
42b. And they were humbled under their hands.

The first wordplay is between αἷμα ("blood") and ἐμιάνθη ("was defiled"). The sharing α, ι, and μ, in chiastic order, emphasizes the consequence of Israel's bloodshed: defilement. These are standard translation equivalents and no transformation was made, but the similarity in sound and use in conjunction with two other wordplays grant this wordplay a moderate amount of confidence (a rating of 2).

The second wordplay is another paronomastic play between ἔργοις ("practices") and ὠργίσθη ("was angered") due to their shared ρ, γ, ι, and σ, in that order. Similarly, this wordplay connects Israel's sin, the practice of idolatrous infant sacrifice, with its consequences, angering the Lord. While ἔργον is somewhat of a standard translational equivalent (36 of its

54 occurrences in LXX Psalms are used to render מַעֲשֶׂה), the translator certainly had other options that were equally typical, for example, the participial use of עשׂה (Ps. 107:23). The use of ὀργίζω to render חרה is neither a translational norm nor a deviation from the norm. It is only used three times to render חרה, but the translator exhibits flexibility, using it also to translate several other terms, including אנף (four times in LXX Psalms).

The third component of this complex wordplay is the two-fold reference to χεῖρας ("hands") forming an *inclusio* around ἐκυρίευσαν ("they ruled"). These words share a κ/χ (with nearly identical phonetic value here), ρ, and σ, in the same order. The additional use of ἐχθροὶ ("enemies") contributes another χ and ρ to the paronomasia. This wordplay draws a connection between the hands, or authority, of Israel's enemies, and their ruling over Israel, co-referential means of describing Israel's subjection under enemy lordship. Κυριεύω is a *hapax* in the LXX Psalms; the translator uses δεσπόζω exclusively for the ruling sense of משׁל, so his choice of κυριεύω in this context is suggestive of intentional wordplay representation.

Wordplays Not Represented in the LXX

Of the 74 wordplays in the Hebrew text of Psalms 90–106, 51, or 67.1 percent, were not replicated in the LXX translation. The vast majority of these are cases wherein the translator rendered the sense of the wordplay, but either did not recognize or could not replicate the poetic device of wordplay. Forty-six, or 90.2 percent, of unreplicated wordplays fall into this category. However, five cases, or 9.8 percent, of unreplicated wordplays involve textual variations that impede or conceal the original Hebrew wordplay, naturally making it impossible for the translator to represent.

LXX Renders the Sense of the Wordplay
The primary function of a translation is to make the source text understandable in the target language. The LXX translators were able to do this with over 93.4 percent of the passages involving Hebrew wordplays, 71 in total. In over half of those, the poetic style of the wordplay was not represented. Most of these unrepresented wordplays are scattered throughout Book IV and involve various types of wordplay subcategories in the Hebrew. Most examples in this category are clear and uncomplicated renderings of the Hebrew sense of the text. The following examples will demonstrate how the Greek translator represented the sense of the text without appropriating the rhetorical style of the wordplay.

All three wordplays in Psalm 103 lack replication in the Greek translation, but are rendered accurately according to their sense. Psalm 103:1b-2a is a case in point:

בָּרֲכִי נַפְשִׁי אֶת־יְהוָה	1a	Bless the Lord, O my soul!
וְכָל־קְרָבַי אֶת־שֵׁם קָדְשׁוֹ	1b	And all that is within me, [bless] his holy name!
בָּרֲכִי נַפְשִׁי אֶת־יְהוָה	2a	Bless the Lord, O my soul!

The translator did not represent the parasonancy, but nonetheless made the text understandable in his target language:

1b. εὐλόγει ἡ ψυχή μου τὸν κύριον
1c. καί πάντα τὰ ἐντός μου τὸ ὄνομα τὸ ἅγιον αὐτοῦ
2a. εὐλόγει ἡ ψυχή μου τὸν κύριον

1b. Bless the Lord, O my soul!
1c. And all that is within me, [bless] his holy name!
2a. Bless the Lord, O my soul!

The LXX follows the word order of the Hebrew, uses standard translation equivalents, and even elides the verb εὐλόγει ("bless") in v. 1c, following the syntax of the Hebrew exactly.

Another example of accurate sense translation of Hebrew wordplay is the LXX rendering of the parasonancy in Ps. 106:32:

וַיַּקְצִיפוּ עַל־מֵי מְרִיבָה	32a	And they provoked [him] to wrath by the waters of Meribah
וַיֵּרַע לְמֹשֶׁה בַּעֲבוּרָם	32b	And he brought punishment to Moses on their account.

Whereas most translators render מְרִיבָה as a proper noun ("Meribah"), the LXX translator renders the sense of the proper noun:

32a. καὶ παρώργισαν αὐτὸν ἐφ' ὕδατος ἀντιλογίας
32b. καὶ ἐκακώθη Μωυσῆς δι' αὐτούς
32a. And they provoked him by the water of strife,
32b. And Moses was punished on account of them.

This, too, is an example of translating the sense of the wordplay, to the extent of even translating what most interpreters retain as a proper noun.⁶²

Psalm 102 is particularly worthy of note, containing the highest number of unrepresented wordplays: all ten Hebrew wordplays in this psalm are rendered with Greek equivalents that do not simulate wordplay. One such example is the translation of Ps. 102:5-6, the Hebrew of which contains alliteration and parasonancy within a complex wordplay:

הוּכָּה־כָעֵשֶׂב וַיִּבַשׁ לִבִּי	5a	My heart was smitten like grass and dried up.
כִּי־שָׁכַחְתִּי מֵאֲכֹל לַחְמִי	5b	Indeed, I have forgotten to eat my bread.
מִקּוֹל אַנְחָתִי	6a	On account of the sound of my groaning,
דָּבְקָה עַצְמִי לִבְשָׂרִי	6b	My bone clings to my flesh.

The LXX translation does not represent these wordplays, but provides a clear translation of the sense of the Hebrew text:

5a. ἐπλήγη ὡσεὶ χόρτος καὶ ἐξηράνθη ἡ καρδία μου
5b. ὅτι ἐπελαθόμην τοῦ φαγεῖν τὸν ἄρτον μου

6a. ἀπὸ φωνῆς τοῦ στεναγμοῦ μου
6b. ἐκολλήθη τὸ ὀστοῦν μου τῇ σαρκί μου

5a. My heart has been smitten like grass and dried up,
5b. For I have forgotten to eat my food.

6a. Because of the sound of my groaning,
6b. My bone clings to my flesh.

In addition to these two, six other wordplays in Psalm 102—vv. 11b (×2); 16a and 17b; 17a and 18a; 20-23; and 29—are rendered in this way.

The remaining Hebrew wordplay in Psalm 102 is rendered according to its sense in the LXX translation, albeit with slight interpretive differences. The Hebrew poet was able to use punning repetition in Ps. 102:27c because the same word has different meanings in the different stems:

---

62. In the Old Testament, מְרִיבָה is used five times as a proper noun (and one additional time as a common noun). In each case, the LXX translates the sense (Num. 20:13, 24; Deut. 33:8; Pss. 81:8; 106:32). All of these cases use ἀντιλογίας, except for Num. 20:24, which uses another word for "strife," λοιδορίας.

כִּלְבוּשׁ תַּחֲלִיפֵם וְיַחֲלֹפוּ 27c You change them like clothing and they pass away.

However, it appears that the LXX translator read the unpointed וְיַחֲלֹפוּ as a Hiphil (or Hophal) instead of a Qal, following the same sense as תַּחֲלִיפֵם ("to change"). He uses the same word, and with the same sense, thus constituting key word repetition, but not wordplay:

27c. καὶ ὡσεὶ περιβόλαιον ἀλλάξεις αὐτούς καὶ ἀλλαγήσονται
27c. And like a cloak, you will change them and they will be changed.

Thus, the translation represents the sense of one interpretive option of the unpointed Hebrew text.[63]

This category also includes cases where the LXX renders the Hebrew wordplay with a Greek wordplay, but it does so by using standard translation equivalents (without any additional supporting evidence) and thus it cannot be determined from the evidence whether or not the translator was intentionally trying to render the wordplay. One example is Ps. 97:9bc. The psalmist uses alliteration in this tricolon by repeating the consonant cluster על four times:

כִּי־אַתָּה יְהוָה 9a For you are the Lord,
עֶלְיוֹן עַל־כָּל־הָאָרֶץ 9b Most High above all the earth,
מְאֹד נַעֲלֵיתָ עַל־כָּל־אֱלֹהִים 9c Exceedingly exalted above all gods!

The LXX also contains alliteration for most of the same words in Greek:

9a. ὅτι σὺ εἶ κύριος ὁ ὕψιστος ἐπὶ πᾶσαν τὴν γῆν
9b. σφόδρα ὑπερυψώθης ὑπὲρ πάντας τοὺς θεούς

9a. For you are the Lord Most High over all the earth!
9b. You are exceedingly exalted above all the gods!

---

63. A similar phenomenon occurs in the translator's rendering of Ps. 91:3b and 6a, wherein he does not represent the Hebrew wordplay between the homonyms (דֶּבֶר) in Ps. 91:3b and 6a. In v. 3b, the translator read the consonantal text as דָּבָר, thus rendering it with the genitive λόγου ("word, thing," BAGD, 600; Lust, 1:284). In v. 6a, he uses πράγματος ("matter, deed," BAGD, 858–9; Lust, 2:391), translating the secondary meaning of דָּבָר. This case, too, does not qualify as misunderstanding or textual variation because the translator represented the sense of the one interpretive option of the consonantal text.

The four-fold repetition of υψ/π, with the additional three-fold repetition of the π, might seem to mark this as wordplay, but these words are all natural translation equivalents and no transformations were necessary to create this wordplay. The ease of the wordplay does not necessarily preclude its authenticity, but because it cannot be determined from the evidence, it will not factor into our analysis of the LXX translation technique.[64]

Textual Variations in the LXX Translation of Wordplay
In five cases, only 6.6 percent of the total wordplays in Book IV, the LXX renders neither the sense nor style of the wordplay, but contains a variation within the text. Three of these cases involve the confusion of a word in the Hebrew text for another word that looks similar. One case involves haplography of a line containing half of the Hebrew wordplay, and another case involves a dubious semantic variation.

In the wordplay bracketing Psalm 90, between אֲדֹנָי מָעוֹן[65] in v. 1b and אֲדֹנָי נֹעַם in v. 17a, the LXX reads ἡ λαμπρότης ("the brightness") instead of the MT's נֹעַם ("[the] pleasantness/kindness") in v. 17. This is the only time that λαμπρότης is used to translate נֹעַם, which is usually rendered with καλός or with τερπνότης in collocation with "the Lord" (as in Ps. 27:4). This deviation from the translational tendencies of the LXX suggests that the translator either read a different Hebrew *Vorlage* or did not understood the text.

We noted that the Hebrew poet uses assonance in Ps. 93:3bc to emphasize the words קוֹלָם and דָּכְיָם:

---

64. This translation nearly qualifies as a weak (rating of 3) wordplay representation, but would need other evidence to strengthen the case (e.g., closer proximity, more shared phonemes, working in conjunction with other wordplays).

65. As noted above, some scholars believe that the translator read מָעוֹז ("refuge") instead of מָעוֹן ("dwelling place") in v. 1, which would account for the LXX's καταφυγή ("refuge"); see Lust, 247. However, Tate contends that מָעוֹן contains the sense of "refuge" in addition to the broader sense of "dwelling place," particularly because it is often used of animals' dwelling places, which function as refuges. Tate (*Psalms*, 432) explains, "LXX is often said to support מעוד [sic], but καταφυγή simply means 'refuge,' which can be the extended meaning of מעון in such contexts as Deut. 33:27; 71:3; 91:9. The change to מעוד [sic] is unnecessary, though there seems to be little difference in meaning between the two words"; cf. Hossfeld and Zenger, *Psalms*, 2:417. This interpretation is supported by the rendering of מְעֹנֶךָ with καταφυγήν σου again in Ps. 91:9, especially since it is less likely that the same mistake would be made in two adjacent psalms.

נָשְׂאוּ נְהָרוֹת יְהוָה	3a	The seas have lifted up, O Lord!
נָשְׂאוּ נְהָרוֹת קוֹלָם	3b	The seas have lifted their voice!
יִשְׂאוּ נְהָרוֹת דָּכְיָם	3c	The seas lift up their pounding [waves]!
מִקֹּלוֹת מַיִם רַבִּים	4a	More than the sounds of many waters,

The LXX omits v. 3c, and thus half of the MT's wordplay:

3a. ἐπῆραν οἱ ποταμοὶ κύριε
3b. ἐπῆραν οἱ ποταμοὶ φωνὰς αὐτῶν
3c. [omitted]
4a. ἀπὸ φωνῶν ὑδάτων πολλῶν

3a. The floods have lifted up, O Lord!
3b. The floods have lifted up their voices/sounds!
3c. [omitted]
4a. Because of (the) sounds of many waters,

This is most likely a case of haplography, due to the repetition of the nearly identical parallel lines in v. 3bc and also to the repetition of the two forms of קוֹל in vv. 3b and 4a, which frame the omitted line. These factors would have made it easy for the translator to skip directly from v. 3b to v. 4a.[66]

The LXX translator also seems to have misread the Hebrew wordplay in Ps. 95:6, which uses two, adjacent parasonantic words:

בֹּאוּ נִשְׁתַּחֲוֶה וְנִכְרָעָה	6a	Come, let us worship and bow down!
נִבְרְכָה לִפְנֵי־יְהוָה עֹשֵׂנוּ	6b	Let us kneel before the Lord who made us!

By rendering נִבְרְכָה ("let us kneel") with κλαύσωμεν ("let us weep"), the translator changes the entire thrust of the psalm:

6a. δεῦτε προσκυνήσωμεν καὶ προσπέσωμεν αὐτῷ
6b. καὶ κλαύσωμεν ἐναντίον κυρίου τοῦ ποιήσαντος ἡμᾶς

6a. Come, let us worship and bow down to him!
6b. And let us weep before the Lord who made us!

---

66. The MT repeats the noun קוֹל in vv. 3b and 4a, which the LXX in turn renders with the repetition of forms of φωνή. While the repetition of קוֹל might help to reinforce the wordplay in the MT, the repetition in the LXX serves no such function.

According to Hossfeld, the LXX rendering is an "interpretation" and the MT should be favored.[67] He adds, "The LXX interprets the psalm as a whole as a penitential liturgy, a collective lamentation over the endangered covenant relationship between the people and YHWH."[68] By misreading נבכה ("let us weep") for נברכה,[69] the translator also misread the wordplay.

In Ps. 105:22a, the Hebrew poet uses alliteration in the phrase לֶאְסֹר שָׂרָיו ("to bind his princes"). The following colon is a purpose clause, explaining that Pharaoh raised Joseph to power and bound his princes in order that Pharaoh's elders might be made wise:

    לֶאְסֹר שָׂרָיו בְּנַפְשׁוֹ   22a   To bind his princes in his soul,

    וּזְקֵנָיו יְחַכֵּם   22b   So that he could make his elders wise.

The exact meaning of these lines is problematic, as discussed in the previous chapter. The LXX either misread the wordplay in v. 22a and changed it to conform to the sense in v. 22b, reading ליסר ("to instruct" or "to discipline") instead of לאסר ("to bind"), or he accurately read ליסר and the MT is in error. While such a reading would not have diminished the Hebrew wordplay, it directly affects the LXX and our evaluation of its wordplay translation technique, which is why it is categorized in this section:

22a. τοῦ παιδεῦσαι τοὺς ἄρχοντας αὐτοῦ ὡς ἑαυτὸν

22a. In order to instruct/discipline his rulers as himself

The Peshitta and Vulgate follow suit, and some scholars argue that this is the better reading.[70] However, the Peshitta and Vulgate do not support emendation because they were probably influenced by the LXX, or could have made the same mistake independently. Internal evidence is therefore the determining factor, and it too is inconclusive.

---

67. Hossfeld, *Psalms*, 2:458.
68. Ibid., 2:462.
69. Wolfgang Kraus, "Septuaginta Deutsch (LXXD)—Issues and Challenges: Ps 95 MT / 94 LXX as a Test Case," in Ausloos et al., eds., *Translating a Translation*, 125.
70. See, e.g., Kraus, *Psalms*, 2:307; Allen, *Psalms*, 38; Dahood, *Psalms III*, 58. Goldingay (*Psalms*, 3:211), however, disagrees and believes that the MT has the better reading because it maintains the link between Joseph (passively) being constrained or bound (Gen. 39:20; 40:3, 5) and then Joseph (actively) binding his adversaries. Likewise, Hossfeld (*Psalms*, 3:78) considers the LXX's reading "a deliberate variation on the MT."

3. LXX Translation of Wordplay in Book IV of the Psalms 151

We noted in the previous chapter how the LXX misread the rare word used in the MT's *double entendre* רָזוֹן ("wasting [disease]") in Ps. 106:15b as רָצוֹן ("goodwill, favor"):

וַיִּתֵּן לָהֶם שֶׁאֱלָתָם   15a   And he gave to them their request,

וַיְשַׁלַּח רָזוֹן בְּנַפְשָׁם   15b   And he sent a wasting (disease) among their souls.

15a.   καὶ ἔδωκεν αὐτοῖς τὸ αἴτημα αὐτῶν
15b.   καὶ ἐξαπέστειλεν πλησμονὴν εἰς τὰς ψυχὰς αὐτῶν

15a.   And he gave to them their request
15b.   And he sent satisfaction to their souls.

The translator's rendering πλησμονὴν ("satisfaction, abundance")[71] should therefore be understood as a misreading rather than a purposeful translation of the equivoque alluded to by the Hebrew poet.

Conclusions

According to Ausloos, "It is one of the most difficult problems for a translator to adequately render wordplay from a source language into a target language."[72] Representing wordplay in translation involves multiple obstacles. First, wordplay often employs obscure words or secondary meanings of words in order to achieve its phonetic or semantic effect. This poses a difficulty for wordplay recognition. Second, the representation of wordplay in a target text is limited by the phonetic and semantic resources of the target language. This poses a difficulty for wordplay representation.

From this analysis, it should be clear that the Greek translators often went to great lengths to translate and replicate Hebrew wordplays, showing skill, dexterity, and appreciation for the trope. It also shows that the translation technique employed was far from simplistic or mechanical.

A synthesis of the data will help us to draw concrete conclusions: (1) regarding the general translation tendency of wordplay in the LXX for Psalms 90–106; (2) regarding the transformations involved in these

---

71. Lust, 2:381.
72. Hans Ausloos, "Judges 3:12-30: An Analysis of the Greek Rendering of Hebrew Wordplay," in *Text-Critical and Hermeneutical Studies in the Septuagint*, ed. Johann Cook and Hermann-Josef Stipp, VTSup 157 (Boston: Brill, 2012), 53.

translations; and (3) regarding the strength of each wordplay identification. The following table summarizes the general tendencies of the LXX in dealing with wordplay:

Table 8. Translation Tendencies in Individual Psalms[73]

Psalm	Unrepresented Wordplay		Represented Wordplay		Total Wordplays in the MT	% of Wordplays Represented in the LXX
	LXX Contains a Textual Variation	LXX Renders the Sense	LXX Creates a Similar Wordplay	LXX Replicates the Same Wordplay		
90	1	7	6		14	42.9
91		6	2		8	25.0
92			2	1	3[74]	100.0
93	1	1			2	0
94		3	1		4	25.0
95	1	1		1	3	33.3
96		2	1		3	33.3
97		2	2		4	66.7
98						
99						
100						
101				1	1	100.0
102		10			10	0
103		3			3	0
104		3	1	1	5	40.0
105	1	3			4	0
106	1	5	6		12[75]	50.0
Total	5	46	21	4	76	32.9

The above table shows the distribution of individual wordplays. Although there were 74 total Hebrew wordplays, there are 76 represented and non-represented wordplays here. This is because, in two cases, the LXX translator used more wordplays in the Greek than were extant in

---

73. An earlier version of these data was published in my "Transformations in Translation: An Examination of the Septuagint Rendering of Hebrew Wordplay in the Fourth Book of the Psalter," *JBL* 137 (2018): 76.

74. There are only two wordplays in the Hebrew. In Ps. 92:7 the LXX translator uses a complex wordplay composed of two overlapping wordplays in order to render the one Hebrew wordplay.

75. Again, in Psalm 106, the LXX uses more wordplays that the MT; see Ps. 106:38-42.

the original Hebrew. So, in Ps. 92:7, the translator rendered a single Hebrew wordplay by using a complex Greek wordplay comprised of two, overlapping wordplays. Likewise, in Ps. 106:38-42, the translator rendered a Hebrew complex wordplay with three wordplays, whereas the Hebrew poet used two interlocking wordplays.

Because it is impossible to determine how many wordplays in the category "LXX Renders the Sense" were recognized by the translator but unreproducible (versus those that he overlooked), and because this category is so large, it is difficult to draw too many conclusions regarding patterns of translation technique. Of course, one could speculate, based on Greek translation options and how the translator could have conceivably rendered a wordplay, but this type of speculation is difficult and inconclusive. The remaining categories, however, are very significant.

Since, as a corpus, the LXX was able to render 25, or 32.9 percent, of the Hebrew wordplays, it is telling to evaluate the performance of each individual psalm, given that 32.9 percent is the average percentage of rendered wordplays per psalm. The translators of Psalms 90, 92, 97, 101, 104, and 106 were able to render an above-average number of wordplays, at least 35 percent. Of these psalms, Psalms 90 and 106 are most prominent because each contains at least twelve wordplays, offering a greater data pool from which to draw solid conclusions. Psalms 90 and 106 frame Book IV, suggesting that the translators might have recognized the structural connectedness of these psalms. It is surprising, therefore, that Psalm 102, which also has close affinities to Psalms 90 and 106, did not render any of the psalm's ten wordplays (although Ps. 102:4 renders the light alliteration of the Hebrew with clear wordplay).

The following table summarizes these findings according to the categories of wordplay and the broad categories of LXX translation technique: unrepresented and represented wordplays.

Table 9. Summary of LXX Translation of Hebrew Wordplay
According to Category

	Paronomasia	Polysemy	Total
Number of wordplays in the Hebrew Text	59	15	74
Wordplay is Not Represented in the LXX	40	11	51
Percentage Not Represented	67.8	73.3	68.9
Wordplay is Represented in the LXX	19	4	23
Percentage Represented	32.2	26.7	31.1

The total number of wordplays in this table is 74, and not 76, because this table is looking at the data from the perspective of the wordplay original to the MT (74), whereas the previous chart included the cases where the LXX used multiple wordplays for single Hebrew wordplays and the four categories are combined with others.

Of the 74 wordplays in Psalms 90–106, the LXX did not represent wordplay in 51 of those cases. The categories of polysemy and paronomasia are equally represented, showing that the LXX translator was capable of recognizing and rendering both types of wordplay.

It is remarkable that the translators were able to represent 23 of the 74 Hebrew wordplays, a total of 31.1 percent. Only four of these cases could be reproduced using the same words and the same categories of wordplay, which is not surprising given the difficulties of translating poetic features into another language. All four instances are types of paronomasia: three using alliteration, and one using root play. In 19 cases, the translator was able to represent the Hebrew wordplay in near proximity to the MT's wordplay, or by using a different type of wordplay. Of these, only four are polysemantic plays in the Hebrew, and the rest are various types of paronomasia, including root play, alliteration, parasonancy, and rhyme.

What was not found in the LXX translator's attempt at rendering Hebrew wordplay is also illumining. Several studies have been written on homophony between the Hebrew and Greek texts, or bilingual wordplay, wherein the translator attempted to translate a Hebrew word with a similar-sounding Greek word.[76] However, none of the Hebrew wordplays in Psalms 90–106 were rendered with homophonous words. In Ps. 102:6b, the translator renders לִבְשָׂרִי with τῇ σαρκί μου, which are phonetically very similar, but also standard equivalents and not an example of homophony between languages. Bilingual wordplay, therefore, does not appear to be a means of translating Hebrew for the LXX translators of Book IV.

Van der Louw's categories of translation transformation are helpful in discerning patterns in the translator's means of attempting to render wordplay, and evaluating the strength of each wordplay identification. The following table illustrates the types and quantities of transformations in the translations involving represented wordplays. This analysis is limited to those transformations relevant to the wordplays themselves, and not issues in the immediate context that are peripheral to the tropes under

---

76. G. B. Caird, "Homophony in the Septuagint," in *Jews, Greeks and Christians: Cultures in Late Antiquity. Essays in Honor of William David Davies*, ed. Robert Hamerton-Kelly (Leiden: Brill, 1976), 74–88; de Waard, "'Homophony' in the Septuagint."

scrutiny. This selectively is necessary in order to focus specifically on the technique of wordplay translation technique. The following table includes only the nine categories of transformations used in wordplay representation of these 17 psalms.

Table 10. Types of Transformations in the LXX Made in Order to Render Hebrew Wordplay

Transformation Category	Number of Transformations	Percentage of Transformations
Stylistic Translation and Compensation	13	54.2
Addition	3	12.5
Syntactic Function	1	4.2
Accidence	2	8.3
Word Class	1	4.2
Explication	2	8.3
Modification	1	4.2
Anaphoric Translation	1	4.2
Total	24	(100%)

It is not surprising that the majority of transformations, 54.2 percent, involve stylistic translation and compensation. Van der Louw defines stylistic translation saying

> A stylistic translation is a transformation whereby the correspondence between source text and target text is determined (mainly) by stylistic factors. As a result, semantic correspondence becomes secondary, especially in texts of which the form is very important, like in poetry.[77]

Compensation is a subcategory of stylistic translation which involves the addition of an element in the target language to compensate for the inability to translate another stylistic feature in the source text. It differs from the category of addition because its function is stylistic (whereas addition could use compensation for semantic purposes, for example) and because it is often added at a syntactical point that does not reflect the element in the source language for which it compensates.[78]

Several transformations involve grammatical changes. A transformation of syntactic function changes the way words or whole phrases function in a clause, such as a change from active to passive or direct

---

77. Van der Louw, *Transformations in the Septuagint*, 84.
78. Ibid., 74, 84.

object to subject. A transformation of accidence involves changes in the outward appearance of a word for the sake of grammatical clarity or precision in the target language. Transformations in word class involves such changes as verbs to nouns or participles to adjectives.

The translator uses explication when he needs to make something that is implicit in the source text explicit for his readers. Modification occurs when the translator chooses a term in the target language whose sense differs from that in the source language, but with the same level of specificity and often within the same semantic field as that which is in the source text (such as rendering עֳפָאיִם, "foliage," with πετρῶν, "rocks," in Ps. 104:12). Anaphoric translation occurs when elements in a similar passage influence another passage; van der Louw also refers to this transformation as "intertextual translation."[79]

The following table presents the distribution of transformations in Book IV of the Psalter, both in the paronomastic and polysemantic wordplays that the translator was able to represent. Whereas the concern in Table 10 above is with the types of transformations being made, Table 11 shows the distribution of transformations and the percentage of rendered wordplays employing them. Again, unrepresented wordplays are irrelevant here:

Table 11. Distribution of LXX Transformations in Individual Psalms[80]

Psalm	Wordplay is Represented in the LXX	Wordplays Involving Transformations	Percentage of Wordplays Using Transformations
90	6	3	50.0
91	2	2	100.0
92	3	1	33.3
94	1	1	100.0
95	1	0	0
96	1	0	0
97	2	1	50.0
101	1	1	100.0
102	0	0	0
104	2	1	50.0
106	6	2	33.3
Total	25	12	48.0

79. Ibid., 68–83.

80. An earlier version of these data was published in my "Transformations in Translation," 79.

The most important figure in this table is the overall total percentage of transformations used in rendering wordplay. In nearly half of the renderings, 48 percent, the translator used some sort of transformation, some sort of alteration to the source text in order to render the wordplay effectively in his target text. No doubt these variations are often or could often be construed as evidence of a different *Vorlage* or scribal error. However, the high percentage of both the translator's attempt at rendering wordplay and the use of transformations to do so should give pause to such accusations.

One final table (below) shows the lexemes used in the cases wherein the LXX translator was able to represent the Hebrew wordplay, the rating of confidence in each case, and some data that helped to determine that rating. As with the Hebrew wordplay, this rating does not describe the strength or quality of the wordplay or translation itself, but rather the strength of our confidence in its identity. A rating of 1 denotes a sure or very strong case for wordplay representation. A rating of 2 denotes a moderate degree of confidence that the LXX translator was trying to represent the wordplay. A rating of 3 is reserved for weak cases of wordplay translation, where the criteria set out in the introduction were met, but little evidence exists to suggest that the translator had to deviate from his translational norms in order to render the wordplay. Of course, some of these might very well be genuine attempts at rendering the wordplay, but without objective evidence (or a footnote from the translator!) these cases need to be considered with an open mind and caution.

The data in Table 12 show an average rating for all LXX wordplay translations is 1.79, between a moderate and strong strength of confidence. Of the 24 represented wordplays in the LXX, nine received a rating of 1, which is to say that they are certain or very strong. Eleven wordplays can be identified with moderate confidence (a rating of 2). Only four cases of weak examples of wordplay representation (ratings of 3). The strong and moderate groups together constitute 83.3 percent of the 24 LXX attempts at rendering Hebrew wordplay. Again, these statistics reflect the methodology set out in the Introduction: our criteria and guidelines maintained a relatively high rating of confidence in what was allowed into our data, while maintaining an openness towards potential wordplay translations that are outside the capacity of our testing made for a number of weak examples in keeping with that methodology.

Table 12. Rating of Confidence in the LXX Wordplay Translation

Reference	Hebrew *Vorlage* and the Number of Times It is Used in MT Pss	Greek Translation and the Number of Times It is Used in the LXX Pss	Number of Times the Hebrew Lexeme is Rendered with this Greek Word in Pss	Is this a Deviation from the Standard Translation Equivalent?	Are there Additional Transformations?	Rating
92:9a; 11a	מָרוֹם 13	ὕψιστος 25	1	Yes	Yes	1
	רוּם 52	ὑψόω 53	42	No		
95:1-2	רנן 25	ἀγαλλιάω 50	22	No	No	3
	רוּעַ 12	ἀλαλάζω 8	8	No		
101:3	שִׁית 34	προτίθημι 3	1	Yes	Yes	1
	לְנֶגֶד 5	πρό 15	1	Yes		
	דָּבָר 135	πρᾶγμα 3	3	Yes and no		
	בְּלִיַּעַל 3	παράνομος 8	2	Yes and no		
	עָשָׂה 110	ποιέω 114	109	No		
	סֵט 1	παράβασις 1	1	--		
104:12	עוֹף 8	πετεινός 6	4	No	Yes	1
	עֳפִי 1	πετρος 13	1	Yes		

3. LXX Translation of Wordplay in Book IV of the Psalms 159

90:3	שׁוּב 74	ἀποστρέφω 37	21	No	No	3
	שׁוּב 74	ἐπιστρέφω 40	38	No		
90:6	חלף 4	παρέρχομαι 7	2	Yes	Yes	1
	מלל 4	ἀποπίπτω 4	1	Yes		
	יבשׁ 6	ξηραίνω 7	6	No	Yes	1
	[Plus in LXX]	σκληρύνω 2		--		
90:10abc	עָמָל 14	κόπος 12	10	No	No	2
	אָוֶן 31	πόνος 12	4	Yes		
90:10cd	חִישׁ 1	πραΰτης 3	0	Yes	Yes	2
	עוּף 8	παιδεύω 12	0	Yes		
91:7	צַד 1	κλίτος 2	1	Yes	Yes	1
	אֶלֶף 10	χίλιοι 3	3	No		
91:12	פֶּן 9	μήποτε 12	9	No	Yes	2
	בְּ 1266	πρός 92		No		
	נגף 2	προσκόπτω 1	1	No		
	רֶגֶל 33	ποδός 35	34	No		
92:7	אִישׁ 45	ἀνήρ 21	11	Yes and no	No	2
	בַּעַר 11	ἄφρων 8	2 (cf., 94:8)	Yes		
	כְּסִיל 3	ἀσύνετος 2	2	No	No	2
	בין 29	συνίημι 27	17	No		

94:8	בער 11	ἄφρων 8	2 (cf., 92:7)	Yes and No	Yes	2
	שׂכל 12	φρονέω 1	1	Yes		
96:2-3	ברך 76	εὐλογέω 58	53	No	No	2
	בַּשְּׂרוּ 19	εὐαγγελίζω 3	3	No		
	סַפְּרוּ 40	ἀναγγέλλω 20	6	Yes and No		
97:2	עָנָן 4	νεφέλη 15	4	No	No	3
	עֲרָפֶל 2	γνόφος 2	2	No		
97:7	בוש 34	αἰσχύνω 18	18	No	Yes	1
	עבד 65	προσκυνέω 18	1	Yes		
	הלל 94	ἐγκαυχάομαι 4	2	No		
	חוה 18	προσκυνέω 18	1	Yes		
104:1	גדל 19	μεγαλύνω 17	14	No	No	3
	הוד 8	ἐξομολόγησις 9	4	Yes and no		
106:7	מרה 10	παραπικραίνω 12	10	No	Yes or No[81]	2[82]
	עָלֵי־יָם 38	ἀναβαίνω 13	0 (MT)/11 (emended)	Yes or No		
	בְּ 1266	ἐν 1017		No		

81. If the MT is retained, then the LXX contains a transformation. If the MT is emended (and if the *Vorlage* of the LXX is presumed to have the verbal form עלים instead of the prepositional phrase עֲלֵי־יָם) then there is no transformation.

82. Again, this rating is dependent on whether or not the *Vorlage* of the LXX is best understood as עלים or עֲלֵי־יָם. If the MT is retained (and the LXX made a transformation in order to create a wordplay) then the rating is 1. If the *Vorlage* is עלים, then it is uncertain whether or not the translator created a wordplay or it was incidental and the rating should be a 3. Since both options seem equally viable, I have split the difference and granted this case a 2.

106:23	שמד 6	ἐξολεθρεύω 22	6	Yes and No	Yes	1
	פֶּרֶץ 6	θραῦσις 2	1	Yes		
	שוב 143	ἀποστρέφω 37	21	No		
	שחת 18	ἐξολεθρεύω 22	1	Yes		
106:27	זרה 3	διασκορπίζω 10	1	Yes	No	2
	אֶרֶץ 190	χώρα 4	4	Yes		
106:38-42	דָּם 21	αἷμα 21	21	No	No	2
	טמא 2	μιαίνω 2	2	No		
	מַעֲשֶׂה 39	ἔργον 54	36	Yes and no	No	2
	חרה 6	ὀργίζω 13	3	Yes		
	יָד 94	χείρ 117	97	No		
	משל 13	κυριεύω 1	1	Yes	No	1
	אֹיֵב 74	ἐχθρός 104	69	Yes and No		
	יָד 94	χείρ 117	97	No		

This study shows that the difficulties of translating wordplay into a very different target language accounts for transformations in the LXX translation. However, these transformations, and their motives, are too often overlooked, resulting in at least two problems: (1) the inclination to overlook true and nuanced motives of transformations (such as those used to render style) and instead identify them as variants attributable to a different *Vorlage* or to scribal error or to theological or ideological agendas; and (2) the failure to appreciate the skill and dexterity involved in the translators' efforts to render such poetic features. The translator is thus criticized for being too literal (which we have already seen is not always a defect of translation), or too free, or just in error, resulting in an overall negative view of his skills as a translator.

Chapter 4

Conclusion

Julio Cortázar captures the wonder of wordplay when he states "Wordplay hides a key to reality that the dictionary tries in vain to lock inside every free word."[1] It is truly fitting that God would inspire poetry not only to convey information, and not only to do so beautifully, but to do it a way that would maximize, intensify, and showcase the complexity of his message. This final chapter will review the empirical findings of the study, looking at its methodology, the analysis of wordplay in Book IV of the Psalter, the LXX renderings of those wordplays, and then synthesizing those findings. The specific contributions that this study offers to various academic fields will then be explored, followed by recommendations for further work.

Empirical Findings

Several research questions drove this study: (1) What methodology will enable careful and consistent identification and classification of wordplays within the Hebrew psalms of Book IV, as well as the LXX translator's identification of those wordplays and attempt at rendering them? (2) What is the nature of the wordplay use in Psalms 90–106? Are there discernable patterns of usage? (3) How do the LXX translators treat these wordplays, or how do they balance their duty to render the sense of the text with their desire to render the style of the text, and are the two connected?

It was imperative to first define the constituents of wordplay for this study. The definition used for wordplay was "a literary device based on the exploitation of phonetic similarity and/or semantic ambiguity that has a structural or rhetorical function." It was important that this definition

---

1. Julio Cortázar, *Around the Day in Eighty Worlds*, trans. Thomas Christensen (San Francisco: North Point, 1986), 208.

included instances of either phonetic similarity or semantic exploitation because to limit wordplay to semantic play proved too subjective since some cases of paronomasia play on meaning as well, though that function is often inconclusive. Unless one is willing to limit wordplay exclusively to polysemantic plays of *double entendre* and punning repetition, such a defining characteristic is impossible. Several exclusions, however, were helpful in order to distinguish wordplay from other poetic devices that play exclusively on sound in "lighter" ways, such as alliteration and assonance that repeat only one phoneme, and end rhyme that is only incidental and a result of grammatical necessity. Words repeated with the same meanings were also excluded from this definition of wordplay because although they are important means of emphasizing key words and ideas, they are not playing with the words. Thus, the definition used in this study proved to be consistent and clear, providing guidelines for including true wordplay cases and for excluding other poetic devices.

Second, a typology of wordplay was necessary in order to consistently classify each wordplay. With the category of homophony unrepresented in Psalms 90–106, two primary types remained: paronomasia and polysemy. Also helpful were the subcategories of paronomasia, including alliteration, assonance, rhyme, metaphony, parasonancy, and root play; and those of polysemy, including *double entendre* and punning repetition. Such a detailed and consistent classification system helped to produce objective and specific conclusions.

In order to avoid giving the impression that all wordplay identifications and representations are equally certain, we ranked the strength of both Hebrew and Greek wordplays. These ratings reflected our confidence in the identification of each wordplay and not in the strength or quality of the wordplay or translation style. Tabulating these data showed exactly how many of the proposed original and represented wordplays are certain and how many are less certain, thus providing an honest representation of the data.

This study showed the use of wordplay in Book IV to be both profuse and variegated. Of the 74 wordplays, encompassing a vast 25.4 percent of the total corpus, the poets used paronomasia 80.8 percent of the time and polysemy 19.2 percent of the time. They also used a variety of combinations of wordplay, or complex wordplays, in both micro and macro structures. The wisdom psalm (Ps. 91) and laments (Pss. 90, 94, 102) displayed higher than average use of wordplay, and the distribution of higher wordplay within the "Mosaic Frame" of Psalms 90–91, 102, and 106 seems to support the editorial shaping of Book IV as proposed by Gerald Wilson.

The various functions of wordplay, though speculative in some cases and inconclusive in others, exhibit the power of the literary device. Wordplay was no mere side-thought, used solely to decorate the poet's message, but rather it enabled the poet to emphasize, draw structural connections, make semantic comparisons and contrasts, highlight irony or cause and effect, and paint a more nuanced picture of a key idea. It is also important to note that although aesthetics are not the sole function of wordplay, even of paronomasia, neither are aesthetics unimportant. P. P. Saydon argues this point with respect to assonance, but his words could apply to paronomastic wordplay in toto:

> Considered from a psychological point of view assonance may be defined as an endeavor to reproduce by means of close connexion or juxtaposition of like-sounding words that internal sensation of the Beautiful which is intended to affect the ear. The effect of assonance is, therefore, chiefly aesthetical.[2]

After eloquently describing one effect of assonance (or paronomasia, for our purposes), Saydon continues to say that the aesthetic purpose of wordplay is often combined with emphasis. This study has shown that other functions may be at work too.

Regarding the translation technique of the LXX, this study has shown that it is far from simplistic, inflexible, or inept. Every translator faces the challenge of best rendering the original words in the original style; indeed, one could argue that full understanding of the "meaning" of an illocution is possible only when both aspects are realized. Stefan Schorch explains, "A Hebrew text, when translated, has less effect on the reader than the original. The reason is that the ideal union between form and content which characterizes the original has been destroyed."[3] Wordplays are exemplars of texts whose form is as important as their content, and when the two are (often invariably) severed through translation, the perlocution is challenged.

Schorch attributes the attitude of ben Sirach's grandson, who famously apologized for the inherent inadequacy of translation, to the same debate between Hermogenes and Cratylus regarding the relationship between

---

2. Saydon, "Assonance in Hebrew as a Means of Expressing Emphasis," 37.

3. Stefan Schorch, "The Pre-Eminence of the Hebrew Language and the Emerging Concept of the 'Ideal Text' in Late Second Temple Judaism," in *Studies in the Book of Ben Sira: Papers of the Third International Conference on the Deuterocanonical Books, Shime'on Centre, Pápa, Hungary, 18-20 May, 2006*, ed. Géza G. Xeravits and József Zsengellér (Leiden: Brill, 2008), 54.

words and meaning. The naturalists, who believed that words were inherently tied to their referents, would have been reticent to translate sacred texts into other languages, since different words would not possibly point to the same referents. Schroch argues that this school of thought was in mind when ben Sirach's grandson explained the limitations of his translational work. Thus, the same ancient debate that informs one's view of the inner workings of wordplay also informs one's view of the feasibility of translation. Those who would be skeptical of wordplay because it breaks down the connection between a word and its natural referent would also be skeptical of its translation.

However, despite the challenges of rendering Hebrew wordplay into Greek verse, the translators of the LXX did not find the task insurmountable. In fact, they were able to represent 23 of the 74 wordplays, 31.1 percent, into their target language. Forty of the Hebrew wordplays (62.2 percent) were not replicated, but their sense was accurately translated, and five wordplays (6.8 percent) were not represented due to a textual variation. While 31.9 percent is not a majority, consider for the sake of perspective that even the most dynamic English translations and paraphrases of the Bible do not represent the Hebrew wordplays this well. Therefore, when characterizing the technique of the LXX translators, their ability to both recognize and represent wordplay should be considered as important criteria.

This ability, however, was not without cost. Of the 23 represented wordplays, the translators used transformations in twelve of them. Therefore, 52.2 percent of these commendable renderings involve some kind of change to the sense, grammar, or syntax of the text for the sake of rendering its style. Not surprisingly, the vast majority of transformations (54.2 percent) involved stylistic translation and compensation, or changes and additions made for the sake of rendering the style of the text. The identification of transformations made for the sake of representing wordplay also sheds light on many so-called variants which, rather than indications of a different *Vorlage* or scribal error, are in many cases better understood as transformations made for a purpose, in the instances outlined here, representing the poetic device of wordplay.

Contributions of this Study

It is clear from the above summary and conclusions that this study has filled a lacuna in its methodology, its identification of Hebrew wordplay, and its analysis of LXX translation technique of wordplay. It differs from other studies in its exhaustive analysis of the entire corpus of Book IV of the Psalter. It has also sought to advance the study of Hebrew wordplay by establishing a more objective and careful methodology, by virtue of a careful definition and typology, identification criteria, and thorough analysis. Other studies may now build on the findings of this study or use them for parallel work. In addition to these empirical findings, however, this study has contributed several theoretical insights and advancements in the fields of literary analysis, Hebrew exegesis, LXX studies, translation studies, and biblical theology.

Contribution to Wordplay Studies
Within the field of literary analysis, this study offers a better understanding of wordplay as a compositional strategy. Wordplay is used by different authors in different texts for different purposes. The poets who authored Psalms 90–106 used various types of wordplay extensively and purposefully. Their extensive use is evinced by the sheer number of wordplays used in the corpus, and in the percentage of that corpus employing the trope. However, their use was also selective. Not every type of wordplay is exhibited in Book IV; indeed, an entire category of wordplay, namely homophony, is completely absent, which probably is more attributable to the nature of the Hebrew language than to authorial preferences. Moreover, entire psalms are devoid of wordplay (Pss. 98–100) while others use it extensively (Pss. 90–91, 102, 106), just as certain genres of psalms (such as wisdom and laments) tend to use it far more than others (such as Enthronement/Royal). Finally, it is clear that the poets had motives for using each wordplay, be they structural, semantic, or stylistic. They did not employ wordplay simply because they could, but because the trope served to enhance or clarify their messages in some way.

Contribution to Hebrew Exegesis
Within the field of Hebrew exegesis, this study has provided better controls and greater objectivity in interpreting Hebrew wordplays. This was achieved in several ways: (1) by providing a clear definition of wordplay, (2) by providing a thorough taxonomy of wordplay typology, and (3) by providing clear criteria for what constitutes wordplay and for what distinguishes it from other phonetic and semantic poetic devices. These controls and methodological tools for maintaining consistency have now been tested throughout this extensive study and, though open to revision and improvement, promise a fruitful and solid way forward into further research on exegeting Hebrew wordplay.

One important contribution of methodology that deserves further mention is the criteria for defining and identifying wordplay in this study. We noted that Ausloos and Kabergs maintained that plays with both sound and meaning were essential for their identification of wordplay. This study, however, has shown that playing on meaning is not always an objective, clear function of the wordplay. Certainly, polysemantic wordplays are by definition plays with meaning, but many paronomastic wordplays also play with meaning, as a function of the wordplay. Many examples could be cited, but the very first instance of wordplay in Book IV is an excellent case in point. In Ps. 90:1 and 17, the poet uses a chiastic, paronomastic *inclusio* to play with the phrases אֲדֹנָי מָעוֹן and נֹעַם אֲדֹנָי. One function is clearly structural—to frame the entire psalm—but another possible function is to make a connection between the psalmist's assertion that the Lord is his dwelling place (v. 1) and his plea for the Lord to grant his favor or pleasantness (v. 17), thus showing that those who make the Lord their dwelling place may seek the blessing of his favor. This connection is one of meaning, connecting two ideas that otherwise might remain disengaged due to the distance between them. This example, and many like it, illustrates the uncertainty of many wordplay functions, including plays on meaning, and thus the subjectivity required in defining wordplay based on its function.

Contribution to Septuagint Studies
Within the field of LXX studies, this research project offers an increased understanding of LXX translation technique in the poetry of the Psalms, and it also provides a workable methodology for analysis. The translator's ability to both recognize the Hebrew wordplays and represent so many of them into Greek exhibits his aptitude as a linguist. Eberhard Bons asserts, "the Greek translator was much more creative than is usually supposed."[4] The translators considered poetic style to be an integral part of the poet's message, giving us a better understanding of their translational technique and also a reminder of the importance of the trope when interpreting the Hebrew text. If the translations of Psalms 90–106 are classified toward the literal end of the translation spectrum, then the freedom and skill in rendering the poetic style contributes to our methodological construal of translation technique. In other words, this study supports the trends in LXX studies to both widen the criteria for characterizing translation technique and use a descriptive approach when analyzing that technique.

---

4. Bons, "Rhetorical Devices in the Septuagint Psalter," 69.

By finding such nuance and concern for style within a more literal translation, this study complements that of James Aitken, who argues that the LXX translation of Ecclesiastes, though literal to the point of being classified as a product of Aquila's school, nonetheless exhibits many efforts toward translating various poetic devices, including alliteration, assonance, and end-rhyme. While Aitken notes that the translator was unable to render any of the Hebrew wordplays, various other poetic devices, such as alliteration, seem to have been used to acknowledge and compensate for the trope.[5] Studies such as this one and Aitken's show that translation technique can be more complex and variegated than sometimes caricatured and that translators who created more literal, formal translations did not do so slavishly or out of ignorance of either the Hebrew or Greek rhetorical style, but often sought to strike a very careful balance between rendering the original author's words and style faithfully. Striking such a balance often required transformations from the Hebrew to the Greek, the prevalence of which also contributes to translational studies in general. The translator's task was complex and required sacrifices and choices. Translating not only the words but also the style of those words and the effect they are intended to illicit was a difficult task, sure to require nuance and balance.

Contribution to the Theological Interpretation of Psalms
Within the field of biblical theology, this study offers a richer insight into the theological purpose of the psalmists and how that purpose was enriched by the use of wordplay. The Hebrew poets were able to use wordplay for many theological purposes to:

- heighten the contrast between God's ability to both end and restore life (Ps 90:3);
- show causal relationships only implicit in the surface level of the text (Ps. 90:8-9);
- use sarcasm in contrasting a fool's lack of understanding with elucidation (Pss. 91:6-7; 94:8);
- compare and contrast the nations and the faithful, both of whom receive the Lord's discipline (Ps. 94:10-12);
- paint more vividly the word picture of the burning fire of God's wrath (Ps. 97:3);
- connect theological dots between God's provenance, response to the needy, and their response of praise (Ps. 102:20-22);

---

5. Aitken, "Rhetoric and Poetry in Greek Ecclesiastes," 59.

- offer hope within contexts of despair (Ps. 102:11);
- to emphasize the Lord's creating work (Ps. 104:2);
- draw a connection between creation's hope and subsequent satisfaction in the Lord (Ps. 104:27-28);
- draw the causal relationship between giving thanks to the Lord and then proclaiming the reason for such gratitude to those who do not know him (Ps. 105:1);
- emphasize the blessedness of those who keep God's judgments (Ps. 106:3).[6]

Of course, the other functions of wordplay most often work in tandem with the author's theological purposes. For example, the poets often used wordplay to maintain the reader's interest (such as in Ps. 97:4), which has direct bearing on the readers' reception of the author's theological message. Wordplay is used extensively to reinforce other poetic devices, such as parallelism (Pss. 90:6; 96:2; 102:29; 104:2; 105:1, 15, 20; 106:10) and simile (Ps. 102:4). When used for structural purposes, to bind together strophes, stanzas, or create *inclusios* in the psalms, or to create chiastic structures in the poems, the author often had theological motives. It has been noted, for example, that the paronomasia creating an *inclusio* around all of Psalm 90 in vv. 1 and 17 also serves to connect the Lord's dwelling place with pleasantness. Likewise, the chiastic, complex wordplay in Ps. 104:27-28 emphasizes God's provision of goodness to his creation. The paronomasia employed in Ps. 106:38 and 42 serves structural purposes, but also connects Israel's child sacrifice with the judgment of their own spilled blood by the hand of their enemies, highlighting justice and casting the Israelites as enemies of their own children. These select examples illustrate the multifaceted functionality of wordplay and encourage careful reading of the text in order to uncover its theological richness.

Contribution to Communication Theory

Speech-act theory has helped biblical scholars to better understand how authorial intent, meaning, and reader responsibility relate in hermeneutics. Communication happens when ideal readers understand the authorial

---

6. Notice how many of the theological functions of wordplay draw connections (or contrasts) between two ideas that may not be so easily connected in the surface structure of the text. In this way, wordplay functions much like metaphor, using creative and accessible means to lead readers to similarities between key theological words and ideas.

intent and the meaning communicated through a text. Brilliant wordplays and theological truths, therefore, are not fully communicated until they are received by the reader. Ausloos confirms the importance of understanding wordplay, arguing:

> If one would like to understand the full meaning of a biblical text, it is not sufficient to have a good knowledge of Hebrew grammar and syntax. From the first chapters of the Old Testament on, it becomes clear that wordplay—whatever this may be—seems to be constitutive for biblical literature. If the reader does not succeed in tracing present forms of wordplay within a pericope, its full meaning undoubtably gets lost.[7]

Because wordplay is part of both the means and the message of that communicative act, ideal readers—not least of all biblical critics and theologians—must seek to identify and rightly interpret all of a text's poetic devices, including wordplay. Wordplay is based on similarity and ambiguity, attributes that can be exploited and used for rhetorical purposes by the author, but also cause confusion and error for the reader. The tools and model provided in this study can be used to equip others to rightly interpret wordplay and thus receive the author's intended and inspired message.

Recommendations for Further Study

The significance of this study and the niche it has filled is clear; however, it has also uncovered the need for further research. Certainly, more parallel work can be done on the study of Hebrew wordplay and LXX translation of wordplay in other biblical corpora. While function was an important facet of this study, our primary concern was the identification of wordplay for the purpose of then analyzing the LXX translator's methodology; the field is ripe for further exploration of wordplay function. Comparative studies between the use of wordplay in the Psalter, or a given corpus, and the use of wordplay in other poetic corpora would also help to distinguish the patterns and tendencies discussed in the psalmists' use of the trope in Psalms 90–106 with the style of other authors. Finally, translation theory would benefit from further study of the complexities and issues involved in faithfully rendering specific poetic features such as wordplay, and such contributions would in turn assist efforts toward translating modern, vernacular versions of Scripture.

---

7. Ausloos, "Judges 3:12-30," 53.

4. Conclusion

In conclusion, the Hebrew poets used wordplay to enhance their messages for various purposes, encouraging readers to slow down and soak in every aspect of the poetry. The LXX translators were often able to render the style of the original Hebrew poetry without sacrificing its divinely inspired message, which is an attestation to their divine guidance and, ultimately, the power and grace of God to both create and preserve, for the glory of his name and the blessing of his people.

Bibliography

Aejmelaeus, Anneli. "Characterizing Criteria for the Characterization of the Septuagint Translators: Experimenting on the Greek Psalter." In *The Old Greek Psalter: Studies in Honour of Albert Pietersma*. Edited by Robert J. V. Hiebert, Claude E. Cox, and Peter J. Gentry, 54–73. Journal for the Study of the Old Testament Supplement Series 332. Sheffield: Sheffield Academic, 2001.

———. "Faith, Hope and Interpretation: A Lexical and Syntactical Study of the Semantic Field of Hope in the Greek Psalter." In *Studies in the Hebrew Bible, Qumran and the Septuagint Presented to Eugene Ulrich*. Edited by Peter W. Flint, Emanuel Tov, and James C. VanderKam, 360–76. Supplements to Vetus Testamentum 101. Leiden: Brill, 2006.

———, ed. *On the Trail of the Septuagint Translators: Collected Essays*. Kampen, The Netherlands: Kok Pharos, 1993.

Ahl, Frederick. *Metaformations: Soundplay and Wordplay in Ovid and Other Classical Poets*. Ithaca: Cornell University Press, 1885.

Aitken, James K. "Jewish Worship Amid Greeks: The Lexical Context of the Old Greek Psalter." In *The Temple in Text and Tradition: A Festschrift in Honour of Robert Hayward*. Edited by R. Timothy McLay, 48–70. Library of Second Temple Studies. London: Bloomsbury, 2015.

———. "The Language of the Septuagint." In *The Jewish-Greek Tradition in Antiquity and the Byzantine Empire*. Edited by James Aitken and James Carleton Paget, 120–34. Cambridge: Cambridge University Press, 2014.

———. "Psalms." In *The T&T Clark Companion to the Septuagint*. Edited by James K. Aitken, 320–34. London: Bloomsbury T&T Clark, 2015.

———. "Phonological Phenomena in Greek Papyri and Inscriptions and Their Significance for the Septuagint." In *Studies in the Greek Bible: Essays in Honor of Francis T. Gignac, S.J.* Edited by Jeremy Corley and Vincent Skemp, 256–77. The Catholic Biblical Quarterly Monograph Series 44. Washington, D.C.: The Catholic Biblical Association of America, 2008.

——— "Rhetoric and Poetry in Greek Ecclesiastes." *Bulletin of the International Organization for Septuagint and Cognate Studies* 38 (2005): 55–77.

———. "The Septuagint and Egyptian Translation Methods." In *XV Congress of the IOSCS, Munich 2013*. Edited by Wolfgang Kraus, Michaël N. van der Meer, and Martin Meiser, 269–94. Septuagint and Cognate Studies. Atlanta: SBL, 2016.

Allen, Leslie C. *Psalms 101–150*. Word Biblical Commentary 21. Waco, TX: Word, 1983.

Alter, Robert. *The Art of Biblical Poetry*. New York: Basic Books, 1985.

Aristotle. *On Sophistical Refutations*. Translated by E. S. Forster. Edited by G. P. Goold. Loeb Classical Library. Cambridge, MA: Harvard University Press, 1955.

Arndt, William, Frederick W. Danker, and Walter Bauer. *A Greek-English Lexicon of the New Testament and Other Early Christian Literature*. Chicago: University of Chicago Press, 2000.

Attridge, Derek. "Unpacking the Portmanteau, or Who's Afraid of *Finnegans Wake*?" In *On Puns: The Foundation of Letters*. Edited by Jonathan Culler, 140–55. Oxford: Blackwell, 1988.

Ausloos, Hans. "Judges 3:12–30: An Analysis of the Greek Rendering of Hebrew Wordplay." In *Text-Critical and Hermeneutical Studies in the Septuagint*. Edited by Johann Cook and Hermann-Josef Stipp, 53–68. Supplements to Vetus Testamentum 157. Boston: Brill, 2012.

Ausloos, Hans, Bénédicte Lemmelijn, and Valérie Kabergs. "The Study of Aetiological Wordplay as a Content-Related Criterion in the Characterization of LXX Translation Technique." In *Die Septuaginta: Entstehung, Sprache, Geschichte*. Edited by Kreuzer, Siegfried Meiser, Martin Meiser, and Marcus Sigismund, 273–94. Wissenschaftliche Untersuchungen zum Neuen Testament 286. Tübingen: Mohr Siebeck, 2012.

Austerman, Frank. *Von der Tora zum Nomos: Untersuchungen zur Übersetzungsweise und Interpretation im Septuaginta-Psalter*. Göttingen: Vandenhoeck & Ruprecht, 2003.

Backfish, Elizabeth H. P. "Transformations in Translation: An Examination of the Septuagint Rendering of Hebrew Wordplay in the Fourth Book of the Psalter." *Journal of Biblical Literature* 137 (2018): 71–86.

Barr, James. *The Semantics of Biblical Language*. London: Oxford University Press, 1961.

———. *The Typology of Literalism in Ancient Biblical Tradition*. Göttingen: Vandenhoeck & Ruprecht, 1979.

Bates, Catherine. "The Point of Puns." *Modern Philology* 96, no. 4 (1999): 421–38.

Ben Zvi, Ehud. *A Historical-Critical Study of the Book of Obadiah*. Beihefte zur Zeitschrift fur die alttestamentliche Wissenschaft 242. Berlin: de Gruyter, 1996.

Berlin, Adele. *The Dynamics of Biblical Parallelism*. Bloomington: Indiana University Press, 1985.

Bons, Eberhard. "Die Rede von Gott in den Psalmen^{LXX}." In *Im Brennpunkt: Die Septuaginta. Band 3: Studien zur Theologie, Anthropologie, Ekklesiolgoie, Eschatologie, und Liturgie der Griechischen Bibel*. Edited by H. H. Fabry and D. Böhler, 182–202. Beiträge zur Wissenschaft vom Alten (und Neuen) Testament 174. Stuttgart: Kohlhammer, 2007.

———. "Rhetorical Devices in the Greek Psalter." In *Et Sapienter et Eloquenter: Studies on Rhetorical and Stylistic Features of the Septuagint*. Edited by Eberhard Bons and Thomas J. Kraus, 69–79. Göttingen: Vandenhoeck & Ruprecht, 2011.

Boyd-Taylor, Cameron, ed. *A Question of Methodology: Albert Pietersma Collected Essays on the Septuagint*. Biblical Tools and Studies 14. Leuven: Peeters, 2013.

Brown, James. "Eight Types of Puns." *Publications of the Modern Language Association of America* 71 (1956): 14–26.

Caird, G. B. "Homoeophony in the Septuagint." In *Jews, Greeks and Christians: Cultures in Late Antiquity. Essays in Honor of William David Davies*. Edited by Robert Hamerton-Kelly, 74–88. Studies in Judaism in Late Antiquity 21. Leiden: Brill, 1976.

Calvin, John. *Commentary on the Book of Psalms*. Translated by James Anderson. 22 vols. Grand Rapids: Baker, 2005.

Carroll, John B., ed. *Language, Thought, and Reality: Selected Writings of Benjamin Lee Whorf*. Cambridge, MA: MIT, 1956.

Casanowicz, Immanuel Moses. *Paronomasia in the Old Testament*. Boston: Norwood, 1984.

Chesterton, G. K. *The Well and the Shallows*. London: Sheed & Ward, 1935.
Chisholm, Robert B., Jr. "Wordplay in the Eighth-Century Prophets." *Bibliotheca Sacra* 144 (1987): 44–52.
Clifford, Robert J. "What Does the Psalmist Ask for in Psalms 39:5 and 90:12?" *Journal of Biblical Literature* 119 (2000): 59–66.
Collins, Terence. *Line-Forms in Hebrew Poetry: A Grammatical Approach to the Stylistic Study of the Hebrew Prophets*. Rome: Biblical Institute, 1978.
Conybeare, F. C., and St. George Stock. *Grammar of Septuagint Greek, With Selected Readings, Vocabularies, and Updated Indexes*. Boston: Hendrickson, 1995.
Cook, Johann. "The Translation of a Translation: Some Methodological Considerations on the Translation of the Septuagint." In *Translating a Translation: The LXX and Its Modern Translations in the Context of Early Judaism*. Edited by H. Ausloos, J. Cook, F. García Martínez, B. Lemmelijn, and M. Vervenne, 9–33. Leuven: Uitgeverij Peters, 2008.
Cortázar, Julio. *Around the Day in Eighty Worlds*. Translated by Thomas Christensen. San Francisco: North Point, 1986.
Culler, Jonathan. "The Call of the Phoneme: Introduction." In *On Puns: The Foundation of Letters*. Edited by Jonathan Culler, 1–16. Oxford: Blackwell, 1988.
———, ed. *On Puns: The Foundation of Letters*. Oxford: Blackwell, 1988.
Dahood, Mitchell. *Psalms I: 1–50, Introduction, Translation, and Notes*. The Anchor Bible 16. Garden City, NY: Doubleday, 1996.
———. *Psalms II: 51–100, Introduction, Translation, and Notes*. The Anchor Bible 17. Garden City, NY: Doubleday, 1968.
———. *Psalms III: 101–150, Introduction, Translation, and Notes*. The Anchor Bible 17A. Garden City, NY: Doubleday, 1970.
Danker, Frederick William, ed. *A Greek-English Lexicon of the New Testament and Other Early Christian Literature*. 3rd ed. Chicago: The University of Chicago Press, 2000.
deClaissé-Walford, Nancy, Rolf A. Jacobson, and Beth LaNeel Tanner. *The Book of Psalms*. New International Commentary on the Old Testament. Grand Rapids, MI: Eerdmans, 2014.
Dines, Jennifer M. *The Septuagint*. Edited by Michael A. Knibb. London/New York: T&T Clark, 2004.
Driver, G. R. "Playing on Words." In *Proceedings of the 4th World Congress of Jewish Studies*, 1:121–29. Jerusalem: World Union of Jewish Studies, 1967.
Empson, William. *Seven Types of Ambiguity*. Rev. ed. Edinburgh: T. & A. Constable, 1947.
Flint, Peter W. "The Book of Psalms in Light of the Dead Sea Scrolls." *Vetus Testamentum* 48 (1998): 453–72.
———. *The Dead Sea Psalms Scrolls and the Book of Psalms*. Studies on the Texts of the Desert of Judah 17. Leiden: Brill, 1997.
Frank, Roberta. "Some Uses of Paronomasia in Old English Scriptural Verse." *Speculum* 47 (1972): 207–26.
Gauthier, Randall X. "Examining the 'Pluses' in the Greek Psalter: A Study of the Septuagint Translation Qua Communication." In *Septuagint and Reception: Essays Prepared for the Association for the Study of the Septuagint in South Africa*. Edited by Johann Cook, 45–76. Leiden: Brill, 2009.
Geller, Stephen. *Parallelism in Early Biblical Poetry*. Missoula, MT: Scholars Press, 1979.
Glück, J. J. "Paronomasia in Biblical Literature." *Semitics* 1 (1970): 50–78.
Goitein, S. D. "Ma'on'—A Reminder of Sin." *Journal of Semitic Studies* 10 (1965): 52–3.

Goldingay, John. *Psalms, Vol. 3, 90–150*. Baker Commentary on the Old Testament: Wisdom and Psalms. Grand Rapids: Baker, 2008

Greaves, Sheldon W. "Ominous Homophony and Portentous Puns in Akkadian Omens." In *Puns and Pundits: Word Play in the Hebrew Bible and Ancient Near Eastern Literature*. Edited by Scott B. Noegel, 103–15. Bethesda, MD: CDL, 2000.

Greenstein, E. L. "Wordplay, Hebrew." In *Anchor Bible Dictionary*. Edited by David N. Freedman, 6:968–71. 6 vols. New York: Doubleday, 1992.

Guillaume, A. "Paronomasia in the Old Testament." *Journal of Semitic Studies* (1964): 282–90.

Gunkel, Hermann. *An Introduction to the Psalms: The Genres of the Religious Lyric of Israel*. Completed by Joachim Begrich. Translated by James D. Nogalski. Macon, GA: Mercer University Press. 1998.

———. *The Psalms: A Form-Critical Introduction*. Translated by T. M. Horner. Philadelphia: Fortress, 1967.

Halpern, Baruch, and Richard Elliott Friedman. "Composition and Paronomasia in the Book of Jonah." *Harvard Annual Review* 4 (1980): 79–92.

Hammond, Paul, and Patrick Hughes. *Upon the Pun: Dual Meanings in Words and Pictures*. London: W. H. Allen, 1978.

Handy, Lowell K. "Sounds, Words and Meanings in Psalm 82." *Journal for the Study of the Old Testament* 47 (1990): 51–66.

Hartman, Geoffrey. "The Voice of the Shuttle: Language from the Point of View of Literature." In *Beyond Formalism: Literary Essays, 1958–1970*. New Haven: Yale University Press, 1970.

Hatch, Edwin, and Henry A. Redpath. *A Concordance to the Septuagint: On the Greek Versions of the Old Testament (Including the Apocryphal Books)*. 2 vols. Grand Rapids: Baker, 1987.

Heim, Knut. "Wordplay." Pages 925–9 in *Dictionary of the Old Testament: Wisdom, Poetry and Writings*. Edited by Tremper Longman III and Peter Enns. Downers Grove: InterVarsity, 2008.

Heller, L. G. "Toward a General Typology of the Pun." In *Linguistic Perspectives on Literature*. Edited by Marvin K. L. Ching, Michael C. Haley, and Ronald F. Lunsford, 305–18. London: Routledge & Kegan Paul, 1980.

Holladay, William L. "Form and Word-Play in David's Lament over Saul and Jonathan." *Vetus Testamentum* (1970): 153–89.

Hossfeld, Frank-Lothar. "Akzentsetzungen der Septuagint aim vierten Psalmenbuch: Ps 90–106 (Ps 89–105 btz. 106 LXX)." In *Der Septuaginta-Psalter: Sprachliche und Theologische Aspekte*. Edited by Erich Zenger, 163–9. Herders Biblische Studien 3. Freiburg: Herder, 2001.

Hossfeld, Frank-Lothar, and Erich Zenger. *Psalms 2: A Commentary on Psalms 51–100*. Edited by Klaus Baltzer. Translated by Linda M. Maloney. Hermeneia. Minneapolis: Fortress, 2005.

———. *Psalms 3: A Commentary on Psalms 101–150*. Edited by Klaus Baltzer. Translated by Linda M. Maloney. Hermeneia. Minneapolis: Fortress, 2011.

Howard, David M. *The Structure of Psalms 93–100*. Biblical and Judaic Studies 5. Winona Lake, IN: Eisenbrauns, 1997.

Hurowitz, Victor Avigdor. "Alliterative Allusions, Rebus Writing, and Paronomastic Punishment: Some Aspects of Word Play in Akkadian Literature." In *Puns and Pundits: Word Play in the Hebrew Bible and Ancient Near Eastern Literature*. Edited by Scott B. Noegel, 63–88. Bethesda, MD: CDL, 2000.

Instone Brewer, David. *Techniques and Assumptions in Jewish Exegesis before 70 CE.* Texte und Studien zum antiken Judentum. Tübingen: Mohr, 1992.
Jobes, Karen H. "Relevance Theory and the Translation of Scripture." *Journal of the Evangelical Theological Society* 50, no. 4 (2007): 773–98.
Joosten, Jan. *Collected Studies on the Septuagint: From Language to Interpretation and Beyond.* Forschungen zum Alten Testament 83. Tübingen: Mohr Siebeck, 2012.
———. "Rhetorical Ornamentation in the Septuagint: The Case of Grammatical Variation." In *Et Sapienter et Eloquenter: Studies on Rhetorical and Stylistic Features of the Septuagint.* Edited by Eberhard Bons and Thomas J. Kraus, 11–22. Göttingen: Vandenhoeck & Ruprecht, 2011.
———. "Translating the Untranslatable: Septuagint Renderings of Hebrew Idioms." In *"Translation is Required": The Septuagint in Retrospect and Prospect.* Edited by Robert J. V. Hiebert, 59–70. Septuagint and Cognate Studies 56. Atlanta: Society of Biblical Literature, 2010.
Joüon, Paul, and T. Muraoka. *A Grammar of Biblical Hebrew.* 2 vols. Rome: Editrice Pontificio Istituto Biblico. 2005.
Kabergs, Valérie. "Lovely Wordplay in Canticles 8,6a." *Zeitschrift für die alttestamentliche Wissenschaft* 126, no. 2 (2014): 261–4.
Kabergs, Valérie, and Hans Ausloos. "Paronomasia or Wordplay? A Babel-like Confusion Towards a Definition of Hebrew Wordplay." *Biblica* 93 (2012): 1–20.
Kalimi, Isaac. "Paronomasia in the Book of Chronicles," *Journal for the Study of the Old Testament* 67 (1995): 27–41.
Khan, Geoffrey. "Biblical Hebrew, Linguistic Background of the Masoretic Text." In *Encyclopedia of Hebrew Language and Linguistics.* Edited by Geoffrey Khan. Leiden, Boston: Brill, 2013.
Kilmer, Anne Draffkorn. "More Word Play in Akkadian Poetic Texts." In *Puns and Pundits: Word Play in the Hebrew Bible and Ancient Near Eastern Literature.* Edited by Scott B. Noegel, 89–101. Bethesda, MD: CDL, 2000.
Kjerkegaard, Stefan. "Seven Days without a Pun Makes One Weak: Two Functions of Wordplay in Literature and Literary Theory." *Journal of Literature, Language and Linguistics* 3 (2011): 1–9.
Klein, Jacob, and Yitschak Sefati. "Word Play in Sumerian Literature." In *Puns and Pundits: Word Play in the Hebrew Bible and Ancient Near Eastern Literature.* Edited by Scott B. Noegel, 23–61. Bethesda, MD: CDL, 2000.
Koehler, Ludwig, and Walter Baumgartner. *The Hebrew and Aramaic Lexicon of the Old Testament.* Study ed. Rev. Walter Baumgartner and Johann Jakob Stamm. 2 vols. Leiden: Brill, 2001.
Kraus, Hans-Joachim. *Psalms 60–150: A Commentary*, Vol. 2. Translated by Hilton C. Oswald. Minneapolis: Augsburg, 1989.
Kraus, Thomas J. "Translating the Septuagint Psalms—Some 'Lesefrüchte' and Their Value for an Analysis of the Rhetoric (and Style) of the Septuagint (Psalms)." In *Et Sapienter et Eloquenter: Studies on Rhetorical and Stylistic Features of the Septuagint.* Edited by Eberhard Bons and Thomas J. Kraus, 49–68. Göttingen: Vandenhoeck & Ruprecht, 2011.
Kraus, Wolfgang. "Septuaginta Deutsch (LXXD)—Issues and Challenges: Ps 95 MT / 94 LXX as a Test Case." In *Translating a Translation: The LXX and Its Modern Translations in the Context of Early Judaism.* Edited by H. Ausloos, J. Cook, F. García Martínez, B. Lemmelijn, and M. Vervenne, 119–32. Leuven: Uitgeverij Peters, 2008.

Kselman, John S. "Double Entendre in Psalm 59." In *Book of Psalms: Composition and Reception*. Edited by Peter W. Flint and Patrick D. Miller, Jr., 184–9. Leiden: Brill, 2005.

———. "Janus Parallelism in Psalm 75:2." *Journal of Biblical Literature* 121 (2002): 531–2.

Kugel, James L. *The Idea of Biblical Poetry: Parallelism and Its History*. Baltimore: Johns Hopkins University Press, 1998.

Lee, John A. L. "Translations of the Old Testament: Greek." In *Handbook of Classical Rhetoric in the Hellenistic Period: 330 B.C.–A.D. 400*. Edited by Stanley E. Porter, 775–83. Boston: Brill, 2001.

Lemmelign, Bénédicte. "Two Methodological Trails in Recent Studies on the Translation Technique of the Septuagint." In *Helsinki Perspectives on the Translation Technique of the Septuagint: Proceedings of the IOSCS Congress in Helsinki 1999*. Edited by Raija Sollamo and Seppo Sipilä, 43–63. Publications of the Finnish Exegetical Society 82. Gottingen: Vandenhoeck and Ruprecht, 2001.

Lemmelijn, Bénédicte, Marieke Dhont, and Valérie Kabergs. "'The Medium is the Message': On the 'Meaningfulness' of Stylistic Features in Psalm 145." *Indian Theological Studies* 50 (2013): 133–52.

Lim, Guek-Eng Violet Lee. "Cognitive Process and Linguistic Forms in Old Testament Hebrew and Chinese Cultures: Implications for Translation (Oriental, Occidental Language)." PhD diss., Fuller Theological Seminary, 1986.

Lopriendo, Antonio. "Puns and Word Play in Ancient Egypt." In *Puns and Pundits: Word Play in the Hebrew Bible and Ancient Near Eastern Literature*. Edited by Scott B. Noegel, 3–20. Bethesda, MD: CDL, 2000.

van der Louw, Theo A. W. *Transformations in the Septuagint: Towards an Interaction of Septuagint Studies and Translation Studies*. Contributions to Biblical Exegesis and Theology 47. Leuven: Peeters, 2007.

Lust, J., E. Eynikel, and K. Hauspie. *A Greek-English Lexicon of the Septuagint*. 2 vols. Stuttgart: Deutsche Bibelgesellschaft, 1992.

Macintosh, A. A. "Psalm XCI 4 and the Root *sḥr*." *Vetus Testamentum* 23 (1973): 52–62.

Mahood, M. M. *Shakespeare's Wordplay*. London: Methuen. 1957.

van der Merwe, Christo H. J., Jackie A. Naudé, and Jan H. Kroeze. *A Biblical Hebrew Reference Grammar*. London: Sheffield Academic/Continuum, 2002.

Moshavi, Adina Mosak. *Word Order in the Biblical Hebrew Finite Clause: A Syntactic and Pragmatic Analysis of Preposing*. Linguistic Studies in Ancient West Semitic 4. Winona Lake, IN: Eisenbrauns, 2010.

Mozley, Francis Woodgate. *The Psalter of the Church: The Septuagint Psalms Compared with the Hebrew, with Various Notes*. Cambridge: Cambridge University Press, 1905.

Muraoka, Takamitsu. *A Greek-English Lexicon of the Septuagint*. Louvain: Peeters, 2009.

———. "Pairs of Synonyms in the Septuagint Psalms." In *The Old Greek Psalter: Studies in Honour of Albert Pietersma*. Edited by Robert J. V. Hiebert, Claude E. Cox, and Peter J. Gentry, 36–43. Journal for the Study of the Old Testament Supplement Series 332. Sheffield: Sheffield Academic, 2001.

Naudé, Jacobus A. "It's All Greek: The Septuagint and Recent Developments in Translation Studies." In *Translating a Translation: The LXX and Its Modern Translations in the Context of Early Judaism*. Edited by H. Ausloos, J. Cook, F. García Martínez, B. Lemmelijn, and M. Vervenne, 229–50. Leuven: Uitgeverij Peters, 2008.

Noegel, Scott B. ed. *Puns and Pundits: Word Play in the Hebrew Bible and Ancient Near Eastern Literature*. Bethesda, MD: CDL, 2000.

Olofsson, Staffan. *God Is My Rock: A Study of Translation Technique and Theological Exegesis in the Septuagint*. ConBOT 31. Stockholm: Almqvist & Wiksell International, 1990.

———. "Law and Lawbreaking in the LXX Psalms." In *Der Septuagint-Psalter: Sprachliche und Theologische Aspekte*. Edited by Erich Zenger, 291–30. Herders Biblische Studien. Freiburg: Herder, 2001.

———. *The LXX Version: A Guide to the Translation Technique of the Septuagint*. ConBOT 30. Stockholm: Almqvist & Wiksell International. 1990.

Petrotta, Anthony J. *Lexis Ludens: Wordplay and the Book of Micah*. New York: Peter Lang, 1991.

Pietersma, Albert. "Exegesis in the Septuagint: Possibilities and Limits (The Psalter as a Case in Point)." In *Septuagint Research: Issues and Challenges in the Study of the Greek Jewish Scriptures*. Edited by Wolfgang Kraus and R. Glenn Wooden, 33–45. SBL Septuagint and Cognate Studies 53. Leiden: Brill, 2006.

———. "The Greek Psalter: A Question of Methodology and Syntax." *Vetus Testamentum* 26 (1976): 60–9.

———. "On the Place of Origin of the Old Greek Psalter." In *The World of the Aramaeans*: I. Biblical Studies in Honour of Paul-Eugene Dion. Edited by P. M. M. Daviau, 252–74. Journal for the Study of the Old Testament: Supplement Series 324. Sheffield: Sheffield Academic, 2001.

———. "Septuagint Research: A Plea for a Return to Basic Issues." *Vetus Testamentum* 35 (1985): 296–311.

Pollack, John. *The Pun Also Rises: How the Humble Pun Revolutionized Language, Changed History, and Made Wordplay More Than Some Antics*. New York: Gotham, 2011.

Quilligan, Maureen. *The Language of Allegory: Defining the Genre*. Ithaca, NY: Cornell University Press. 1979.

Quintilian. *The Orator's Education: Books 9–10*. Loeb Classical Library. Edited and Translated by Donald A. Russell. Cambridge, MA: Harvard University Press, 2001.

Raabe, Paul R. "Deliberate Ambiguity in the Psalter." *Journal of Biblical Literature* 110 (1991): 213–27.

Rajak, Tessa. *Translation and Survival: The Greek Bible of the Ancient Jewish Diaspora*. Oxford: Oxford University Press, 2009.

Rankin, Oliver Shaw. "Alliteration in Hebrew Poetry." *Journal of Theological Studies* 31 (1930): 285–91.

Redfern, Walter. *Puns*. Oxford: Blackwell, 1984.

Rendsburg, Gary A. "Bilingual Wordplay in the Bible." *Vetus Testamentum* 38 (1988): 354–7.

Roberts, J. J. M. "Double Entendre in First Isaiah," *Catholic Biblical Quarterly* 54 (1992): 39–48.

Sailhamer, John H. *The Translational Technique of the Greek Septuagint for the Hebrew Verbs and Participles in Psalms 3–41*. Studies in Biblical Greek 2. New York: Peter Lang, 1991.

Sanders, S. *The Dead Sea Psalms Scroll*. Ithaca, NY: Cornell University Press, 1967.

Sartre, Jean-Paul. *L'Idiot de la Famille*. Vol. 2. Paris: Gallimard, 1971.

Sasson, Jack M. "Word-Play in Gen 6:8–9." *Catholic Biblical Quarterly* 37 (1975): 165–6.

———. "Word Play in the O.T." In *Interpreter's Dictionary of the Bible: Supplementary Volume*. Edited by Keith Crim, 968–70. Nashville: Abingdon, 1976.

de Saussure, Ferdinand de. *Course in General Linguistics*. Translated by Roy Harris. LaSalle, IL: Open Court, 1986.

Saydon, Paul P. "Assonance in Hebrew as a Means of Expressing Emphasis." *Biblica* 36 (1955): 36–50.

Schökel, Luis Alonso. *A Manual of Hebrew Poetics*. Subsidia Biblica 11. Rome: Editrice Pontificio Istituto Biblico, 1988.

Schorch, Stefan. "The Pre-Eminence of the Hebrew Language and the Emerging Concept of the 'Ideal Text' in Late Second Temple Judaism." In *Studies in the Book of Ben Sira: Papers of the Third International Conference on the Deuterocanonical Books, Shime'on Centre, Pápa, Hungary, 18–20 May, 2006*. Edited by Géza G. Xeravits and József Zsengellér, 43–54. Leiden: Brill, 2008.

Sedley, David. "Plato's *Cratylus*." In *The Stanford Encyclopedia of Philosophy*. Edited by Edward N. Zalta. Stanford: Stanford University. Online: http://plato.stanford.edu/archives/fall2008/entries/plato-cratylus (accessed August 3, 2011).

Segal, David S. "Pun and Structure in Medieval Hebrew Poetry: The Case of Shmuel Hanagid." In *Puns and Pundits: Word Play in the Hebrew Bible and Ancient Near Eastern Literature*. Edited by Scott B. Noegel, 307–24. Bethesda, MD: CDL, 2000.

Seiler, Stefan. "Theologische Konzepte in der Septuaginta." In *Der Septuagint-Psalter: Sprachliche und Theologische Aspekte*. Edited by Erich Zenger, 197–225. Herders Biblische Studien. Freiburg: Herder, 2001.

Smith, Jannes. "Meaning and Function of αλληλουια ('Hallelujah') in the Old Greek Psalter." In *XII Congress of the International Organization for Septuagint and Cognate Studies, Leiden, 2004*. Edited by Melvin K. H. Peters, 141–51. Atlanta: Society of Biblical Literature, 2006.

———. *Translated Hallelujahs: A Linguistic and Exegetical Commentary on Select Septuagint Psalms*. Leuven: Peeters, 2011.

Sollamo, Raija. *Renderings of Hebrew Semiprepositions in the Septuagint*. Helsinki, Finland: Suomalainen Tiedeakatemia, 1979.

Spero, Shubert. "Multiplicity of Meaning as a Device in Biblical Narrative." *Judaism* 34, no. 4 (1985): 462–73.

Swanson, Dwight D. "Qumran and the Psalms." In *Interpreting the Psalms: Issues and Approaches*. Edited by David Firth and Philip S. Johnston, 247–62. Downers Grove, IL: IVP Academic, 2005.

Tate, Marvin E. *Psalms 51–100*. Word Biblical Commentary 20. Nashville: Thomas Nelson, 1990.

Thackeray, Henry John. *A Grammar of the Old Testament in Greek According to the Septuagint*. Cambridge: Cambridge University Press, 1909.

Tov, Emanuel. "Loan-Words, Homophony, and Transliteration in the Septuagint." *Bib* 60 (1979): 216–36.

Ullmann, Stephen. *Semantics: An Introduction to the Science of Meaning*. New York: Harper & Row, 1979.

Ulmer, Gregory. "The Puncept in Grammatology." In *On Puns: The Foundation of Letters*. Edited by Jonathan Culler, 164–90. Oxford: Blackwell, 1988.

VanGemeren, Willem, ed. *The New International Dictionary of Old Testament Theology and Exegesis*. 5 vols. Grand Rapids, MI: Zondervan, 1997.

———. *Psalms*. The Expositor's Bible Commentary 5. Grand Rapids: Zondervan, 2008.

Vorm-Croughs, Miriam. *The Old Greek of Isaiah: An Analysis of Its Pluses and Minuses*. Society of Biblical Literature Septuagint and Cognate Studies 61. Atlanta: SBL, 2014.

de Waard, Jan. "'Homophony' in the Septuagint." *Biblica* 62 (1981): 551–61.

Wallace, Daniel B. *Greek Grammar: Beyond the Basics: An Exegetical Syntax of the New Testament*. Grand Rapids: Zondervan, 1996.

Waltke, Bruce K., and M. O'Connor. *An Introduction to Biblical Hebrew Syntax*. Winona Lake, IN: Eisenbrauns, 1990.

Watson, Wilfred G. E. *Classical Hebrew Poetry: A Guide to its Techniques*. Sheffield: JSOT Press, 1984.

———. *Traditional Techniques in Classical Hebrew Verse*. Journal for the Study of the Old Testament Supplement Series 170. Sheffield: Sheffield Academic, 1994.

Weinstock, Leo I. "Sound and Meaning in Biblical Hebrew." *Journal of Semitic Studies* 28 (1983): 49–62.

Westermann, Claus. *The Living Psalms*. Edinburgh: T. & T. Clark: 1989.

Wieder, Arnold A. "Ugaritic-Hebrew Lexicographical Notes." *Journal of Biblical Literature* 84, no. 2 (1965): 160–4.

Williams, Ronald J. *Hebrew Syntax: An Outline*. 2nd ed. Toronto: University of Toronto Press, 1976.

Williams Tyler F. "Toward a Date for the Old Greek Psalter." In *The Old Greek Psalter: Studies in Honour of Albert Pietersma*. Edited by Robert J. V. Hiebert, Claude E. Cox, and Peter J. Gentry, 248–76. Journal for the Study of the Old Testament Supplement Series 332. Sheffield: Sheffield Academic, 2001.

Wilson, Gerald H. *The Editing of the Hebrew Psalter*. Society of Biblical Literature Dissertation Series 76. Chico, CA: Scholars Press, 1985.

———. "Shaping the Psalter: A Consideration of Editorial Linkage in the Book of Psalms." In *Shape and Shaping of the Psalter*. Edited by J. Clinton McCann, Jr., 72–82. Journal for the Study of the Old Testament Supplement Series 159. Sheffield: JSOT, 1993.

Wolters, Al. "*Ṣôpiyyâ* (Prov 31:27) as Hymnic Participle and Play on *Sophia*." *Journal of Biblical Literature* 104 (1985): 577–87.

Index of References

Old Testament/
Hebrew Bible

Genesis
39:20	150
40:3	150
40:5	150

Exodus
10:19	139
13:18	139
15:4	139
23:31	139
32:1-14	100

Numbers
11	98
11:33	98, 99
16	100
20:2-13	102
20:13	146
20:24	146

Deuteronomy
1:40	139
26:15	50
33:8	146
33:27	148
71:3	148
91:9	148

Joshua
2:10	139
4:23	139

Ruth
1:13	92

1 Samuel
4:20	16

2 Samuel
1:18-27	4, 113

1 Chronicles
16:27	77, 137, 138
16:31	77
29:25	138

Esther
9:1	92

Job
19:20	84
37:22	138
39:20	138

Psalms
1:1-2	81
1:1	72
5:10	112
7:16	112
9:14	62
9:28	128
10	106
10:7	128
10:12	106
10:15	106
10:16	106
21:6	77, 137, 138
27:2	83
27:4	148
33:2	72
35:2	62
39:12	71
40:5	72
44:19	112
47:3	75
54:5	121
56:9	112
60:5	112
68:6	51
69:30	112
69:31-36	87
71:19	118
73:22	132
74:19	112
75:6	67
78:17	139
78:24	83
78:38-39	123
80:10	112
81:2	74, 120
81:8	146
85:4-5	123
86:1	112
86:14	121
88:10	112
88:16	112
88:18	112
89:15	135
90–106	37, 41, 50, 118, 144, 151, 154, 162, 163, 166, 167, 170
90–92	65
90–91	65, 82, 163, 166
90	47, 50, 58, 60, 82, 87, 96, 109–12, 114, 123, 139, 148, 152, 153, 156, 163, 169
90:1-5	53
90:1	43, 50, 51, 54, 55, 106, 119, 148, 167, 169

Psalms (cont.)

Ref	Pages
90:2	58, 123
90:3-6	53
90:3	51–3, 59, 106, 113, 123, 159, 168
90:4-6	52, 58, 125
90:4	52–4, 106, 125
90:5-6	59
90:5	52–4, 125
90:6-12	53
90:6	52–4, 85, 106, 125, 126, 159, 169
90:7-10	55
90:7	55
90:8-9	55, 168
90:8	55, 106
90:9-11	56
90:9-10	56
90:9	55, 56, 59, 106
90:10	36, 54, 56–8, 123, 127–9, 159
90:11	56
90:12	58
90:13-16	59
90:13-15	59, 60
90:13	59
90:14-16	59
90:14	59
90:15	59
90:16	59
90:17	44, 50, 106, 148, 167, 169
91	47, 51, 60, 61, 63–5, 109–12, 129, 152, 156, 163
91:1-6	60, 61, 65
91:1	60, 61, 63, 64, 106
91:2	61
91:3-13	64
91:3	61, 62, 106, 147
91:4	61, 62, 106
91:5	61, 62, 106
91:6-7	63, 129, 168
91:6	61–3, 106, 129, 147
91:7	63, 106, 129, 159
91:9	63, 64, 106
91:10-13	64
91:11-13	60, 130
91:11	106, 130
91:12	64, 65, 106, 123, 130, 159
91:13	64, 65, 106, 130
91:14-16	113
92	47, 65, 67, 108–12, 131, 152, 153, 156
92:2	65
92:4	65
92:5-10	65
92:6-7	65, 70, 131
92:6	65, 66, 106, 131, 132
92:7	65, 66, 106, 127, 131–3, 152, 153, 159
92:8	65, 133
92:9	67, 106, 118, 158
92:10	67
92:11	67, 106, 118, 158
92:13-14	65
93	47, 67, 69, 108–10, 112, 122, 132, 152, 156
93:1-2	67, 68
93:1	68, 106
93:2	68, 106
93:3-4	149
93:3	68, 69, 74, 91, 106, 148, 149
93:4	69, 149
94	47, 69, 71, 109–12, 132, 152, 156, 163
94:1-15	69
94:1-7	70
94:8-11	72
94:8	70, 106, 126, 132, 160, 168
94:10-12	71, 168
94:10-11	71
94:10	71, 72
94:11	71, 72
94:12-15	72
94:12	71, 72, 106
94:16-21	69
94:17-19	73
94:17	73
94:18	73
94:19	73, 106
94:22-23	69
95-101	112
95	47, 74, 109, 110, 133, 152, 156
95:1-2	74, 75, 119, 120, 158
95:1	74, 106, 119
95:2	74, 106, 119
95:3	74, 75, 81, 91, 105, 106
95:4-5	75
95:6	74, 75, 106, 149
95:8-11	113

96	47, 76, 77, 109, 110, 133, 152, 156	99:3	80	102:29	87, 88, 107, 146, 169
		100	47, 110, 152	103-104	112
		101	47, 81, 108, 110, 136, 152, 153, 156	103	47, 89, 110, 122, 137, 145, 152
96:1-3	133, 134				
96:1-2	76, 94, 106, 133				
		101:3-4	81	103:1-20	87
96:1	76, 133, 134	101:3	81, 106, 120, 123, 158	103:1-2	89, 145
96:2-3	134, 160			103:1	89, 90, 107, 145
96:2	76, 133, 134, 169	102	47, 82, 88, 89, 108, 110–12, 114, 122, 136, 146, 152, 156, 163, 166		
				103:2	90, 107, 145
96:3	133, 134			103:10-14	90
96:4	81			103:10	90
96:5	79			103:11	90, 107
96:6	76, 77, 91, 106, 120, 128, 137, 138			103:12-13	90
		102:2	86	103:12	107
		102:4	82, 122, 136, 137, 153, 169	103:13	107
96:11	77, 106			104	47, 91, 108, 110, 137, 152, 153, 156
97	47, 77–9, 109–11, 134, 135, 152, 153, 156	102:5-6	82–4, 146		
		102:5	83, 84, 107, 146		
				104:1	77, 91, 107, 120, 128, 137, 138, 160
		102:6-12	83		
97:2-3	135	102:6	83, 84, 107, 146, 154		
97:2	78, 134, 135, 160			104:2	91, 105, 107, 169
97:3-4	78	102:11	84, 85, 107, 146, 169		
97:3	78, 106, 134, 135, 168			104:3	91
		102:13-18	85	104:4	91
97:4	78, 106, 135, 169	102:15-18	85	104:12-13	122
		102:16-18	82	104:12	92, 107, 121–3, 156, 158
97:7-9	80	102:16	85, 86, 107, 146		
97:7	79, 80, 106, 135, 136, 160			104:16-17	122
		102:17	43, 85, 86, 107, 146	104:18	122
97:9	79, 81, 105, 106, 147			104:27-28	92, 169
		102:18	43, 85, 107, 146	104:27	92, 93, 107
98–101	82	102:20-23	86, 146	104:28	92, 93, 107
98–100	80, 136, 166	102:20-22	87, 168	104:29	123
98	47, 110, 152, 156	102:20	87, 107	104:34	92
		102:21	86, 87, 107	105–106	112
98:4	74, 120	102:22	86, 87, 100, 107	105	47, 48, 94, 96, 110, 111, 122, 138, 152
99	47, 110, 152				
99:1-2	80	102:27	87, 107, 146, 147		
99:1	80				
99:2	80	102:28	87, 88		

Psalms (cont.)

105:1	76, 94, 107, 169	106:38-42	127, 142, 143, 152, 153, 161		
105:11	113	106:38	102–4, 107, 142, 143, 169		
105:15	94, 107, 113, 169				
105:20	169	106:39	142, 143		
105:21	95	106:40	142, 143		
105:22	43, 95, 107, 150	106:41	142, 143		
		106:42	102–4, 107, 142, 143, 169		
105:30	96, 107				
105:44	142				
106	47, 96, 97, 100, 102, 103, 110, 111, 114, 138, 139, 152, 153, 156, 163, 166	106:43	97, 103		
		106:44-46	103		
		106:47	101		
		107:3	142		
		107:23	144		
		111:3	77, 137, 138		
		119:166	92		
		127:5	72		
106:3	96, 107, 169	137:5	112		
106:4	98, 99	137:8-9	72		
106:7	97, 139, 160	144:15	72		
106:10	97, 98, 107, 169	145:15	92		
		148:13	137		
106:13-15	98	149:1	118		
106:13	97				
106:14	99	*Proverbs*			
106:15	98, 99, 101, 104, 107, 151	3:1-7	81		
		25:27	83		
		31:27	23		
106:17-18	100				
106:17	100, 107	*Ecclesiastes*			
106:18	100, 107	1:4	51, 52		
106:19-23	100				
106:23-24	100	*Isaiah*			
106:23	100, 101, 107, 139, 140, 161	12:4	94		
		24:5	55		
		30:30	138		
		38:18	92		
106:24	101, 107				
106:27	101, 107, 141, 142, 161	*Jeremiah*			
		13:14	141		
		25:30	51		
106:32	102, 107, 145, 146				
106:33	97, 102	*Lamentations*			
		2:8	141		

Ezekiel

20:30-31	103
22:30	141

Hosea

5:2	81
13:14	62

NEW TESTAMENT

Matthew

4:6	130
16:18	23

Luke

4:11	130

APOCRYPHA

Wisdom of Solomon

14:31	121

Ecclesiasticus

32:20	130

2 Maccabees

15:10	121

CLASSICAL AND ANCIENT CHRISTIAN LITERATURE

Augustine

City of God

6:2	22

Quintilian

The Orator's Education

9:3:31	124
9:3:45	124
9:3:70	23, 35
9:3:86	23
9:73	23
9:76	23

ANCIENT NEAR EASTERN SOURCES

Ugaritic Textbook

49:5:1-3	69

Index of Authors

Aejmelaeus, A. 12–14, 39, 123, 124
Ahl, F. 20, 22, 23
Aitken, J. K. 7–9, 19, 119, 123, 168
Allen, L. C. 83, 86, 87, 89, 91, 97, 98, 103, 104, 121, 139, 150
Alter, R. 4, 52
Attridge, D. 26–8, 32
Ausloos, H. 18, 19, 33, 34, 36, 39, 151, 170
Austerman, F. 115

Backfish, E. H. P. 152, 156
Barr, J. 11, 12
Bates, C. 24, 25, 27, 29, 48, 49
Baumgartner, W. 53
Ben Zvi, E. 2
Berlin, A. 4, 104, 105
Beyer, B. E. 66
Bons, E. 18, 116, 130–2, 167
Boyd-Taylor, C. 12
Brown, J. 3

Caird, G. B. 154
Calvin, J. 100
Carroll, J. B. 30
Casanowicz, I. M. 3, 5, 32, 44, 57, 74, 77, 127, 134
Chesterton, G. K. 25
Chisholm, R. B., Jr. 5, 103
Clifford, R. J. 59
Collins, T. 4
Conybeare, F. C. 118
Cook, J. 7
Cortázar, J. 162
Culler, J. D. 3, 28, 29

Dahood, M. 6, 51, 62, 64, 67–9, 75, 79, 80, 85, 86, 91–3, 99, 103, 104, 112, 123, 150
Danker, F. W. 124, 125
deClaisse-Walford, N. 59, 81, 95
Dhont, M. 6
Dines, J. M. 7, 10
Driver, G. R. 3

Empson, W. 3
Eynikel, E. 121

Flint, P. W. 7
Frank, R. 2
Friedman, R. E. 5

Gauthier, R. X. 12, 14, 116
Geller, S. 4
Glück, J. J. 2, 4, 37
Goitein, S. D. 51, 54
Goldingay, J. 51, 53, 54, 61, 68, 76, 78, 86, 90, 99, 121, 122, 150
Greaves, S. W. 21
Greenstein, E. L. 5, 43
Guillaume, A. 3
Gunkel, H. 111

Halpern, B. M. 5
Hammond, P. 35, 36
Handy, L. K. 6
Harrison, R. K. 62
Hartman, G. 33
Hauspie, K. 121
Heim, K. 6, 32, 38, 39, 43, 44
Heller, L. G. 27, 31, 37
Holladay, W. L. 4, 113
Hossfeld, F.-L. 52, 62, 69, 89, 91, 92, 103, 122, 129, 137, 140, 150
Howard, D. M. 72
Hughes, P. 35, 36
Hurowitz, V. A. 21

Instone Brewer, D. 2

Jacobson, R. A. 81, 95
Jobes, K. H. 30
Joosten, J. 16, 17, 46
Joüon, P. 53, 73

Kabergs, V. 6, 18, 19, 33, 34, 36, 39
Kalimi, I. 2, 5
Khan, G. 40
Kilmer, A. D. 21
Kjerkegaard, S. 31, 38

Klein, J. 21
Koehler, L. 53
Kraus, H.-J. 51, 54, 57, 62, 69, 70, 75, 89, 91, 97, 103, 139, 150
Kraus, T. J. 13, 18, 42, 116, 129
Kraus, W. 150
Kroeze, J. H. 58
Kselman, J. S. 6
Kugel, J. L. 51, 52

Lee, J. A. L. 9
Lemmelijn, B. 6, 18, 19
Lim, G.-E. V. L. 6
Lopriendo, A. 20
van der Louw, T. A. W. 9, 14–16, 155, 156
Lust, J. 121, 125, 126, 129, 136, 137, 140, 147, 151

Macintosh, A. A. 61
Mahood, M. M. 23
van der Merwe, C. H. J. 58
Moshavi, A. M. 58
Mozley, F. W. 8
Muraoka, T. 124–6, 130, 136

Naudé, J. A. 14, 58
Noegel, S. B. 5

O'Connor, M. 58
Olofsson, S. 9, 11–13, 40, 41, 45, 46, 119, 139

Pan, C.-W. 70
Petrotta, A. J. 2, 3, 33, 37
Pietersma, A. 8, 11, 45
Pollack, J. 20, 21, 24, 29, 37, 38, 49

Quilligan, M. 24, 30, 31, 38

Raabe, P. R. 6, 43, 44
Rajak, T. 9, 10
Rankin, O. S. 6
Redfern, W. 3, 10, 22, 24–6, 31, 32, 115
Rendsburg, G. A. 37
Roberts, J. J. M. 49

Sailhamer, J. H. 13, 40
Sanders, S. 7
Sartre, J.-P. 115

Saussure, F. de 28
Sasson, J. M. 5, 6, 113
Saydon, P. P. 38, 164
Schökel, L. A. 32, 33, 44
Schorch, S. 164
Schoville, K. N. 61
Sedley, D. 21
Sefati, Y. 21
Segal, D. S. 23
Seiler, S. 137
Smith, J. 7, 8
Sollamo, R. 41
Sperber, D. 30
Spero, S. 2
Stallman, R. C. 65
Stock, St. G. 118
Swanson, D. D. 7

Tanner, B. L. 81, 95
Tate, M. E. 51, 55, 57, 62, 64, 68, 69, 72, 81, 136, 148
Thackeray, H. J. 13
Tov, E. 19

Ullmann, S. 3, 25–8, 35, 44
Ulmer, G. 30

VanGemeren, W. 50, 53, 58, 59, 62, 68–71, 80–2, 95, 121, 141
Vorm-Croughs, M. 17, 18

Waard, J. de 16, 154
Wallace, D. B. 118
Waltke, B. K. 58
Watson, W. G. E. 5, 32, 39, 53, 72, 86, 101
Weinstock, L. I. 22
Westermann, C. 52
Wieder, A. A. 66
Williams, R. J. 53, 83
Williams, T. F. 7
Wilson, G. H. 30, 110
Wolters, A. 6, 23, 37

Younger, K. L. 62

Zenger, E. 51, 52, 62, 67, 77–81, 123, 148

www.ingramcontent.com/pod-product-compliance
Lightning Source LLC
Chambersburg PA
CBHW052044300426
44117CB00012B/1975